FOREX OPTIONS TODAY

By
James Dicks

A comprehensive book covering the strategic and hedging uses of currency options, in addition to basic currency option pricing and risk management principles.

Introduction

I wanted to take a brief moment of your time while you begin to further your education in the forex. I have now been writing on and trading in the forex market for nearly 15 years. I have long been a proponent of forex options and have followed the progress here in the United States that this financial tool is making.

Forex options are becoming more popular today than ever. I have been using option strategies in the equities markets since the early 90's — and in contrast to most people — I find that options are not as risky as one might think. In fact, options were created as an insurance strategy to actually help mitigate the risk on positions you might already have in your portfolio.

My first exposure to forex options was in 2002 when some brokers here in the United States were experimenting with offering exotic forex options, which included one touch, no touch and double touch trigger options. Although they had previously been offered in the over the counter forex market for the previous decade, these types of options did not seem that well received by retail traders initially.

One of the primary reasons that these brokers lacked market depth was that there were simply not enough people interested in trading them to make these markets liquid.

Thanks to a growing awareness of how to use these products appropriately, that is changing today and — although traders in the United States

still seem a bit behind other parts of the world —exotic forex options like binary options are getting much more popular.

Throughout the book, I write about forex options and the different types of forex option strategies. In general, currency options are similar in nature no matter whether you are trading forex stocks or futures. If you already have a favorite option strategy that you use in the stock or commodity market, you will most likely be able to adapt that to trading forex options.

This book has been many years in the making and, prior to my most recent book "The Forex Edge", I was also working on this topic. Now it is ready, and I hope you enjoy it.

Dedication

This book and project is dedicated to a team of professionals that I have had the honor of working with for nearly ten years. Without them, I would not have been able to complete my projects on time, and you would not have been able to get the support you may have been seeking. These team members are more than employees, contractors etc…, they are family. Thanks to Larry, Rocky, Terrance, Mike and Michael. My thanks and appreciation would not be complete without mentioning a few of the other members of our team. I certainly cannot thank everyone, but these few were instrumental in the total team's synergy and success. Thanks to Ian, Tyler and Nagender's team.

Table of Contents

Chapter 1: An Introduction to Forex Options

Introduction to the Forex and Forex Options Market

The foreign exchange or forex market is the largest international financial marketplace in the world. In it, national currencies are exchanged for other national currencies between market participants largely operating in an over the counter market connected by telephone, brokers and electronic dealing systems. In addition, currency futures contracts trade on major exchanges like the CME Group's International Monetary Market or IMM based in Chicago.

Most forex dealers and market makers are situated in the major financial trading hubs of New York, USA, London, England and Tokyo, Japan, and the three main forex trading sessions are named accordingly. After the New York session's close, some forex trading also takes place in Wellington, New Zealand and then Sydney, Australia before the Tokyo session opens. Due to its international nature, the forex market operates on a round the clock basis from Sunday afternoon to Friday afternoon New York time.

In the forex market, the trading of currencies takes place at rates of exchange or exchange rates that fluctuate continuously while the market is open. Most of the transaction volume in this huge marketplace takes place among professional traders and market makers working at major international banks. Market makers operating at such banks also quote exchange rates to their bank's clients that typically include corporations, hedge funds, and high net worth individuals. Central banks are also sometimes active in the forex market, and they can intervene in the market to defend or devalue their national currency.

Smaller currency speculators and hedgers have traditionally accessed the forex market by trading currency futures contracts on exchanges. Nevertheless, in recent years, it has become increasingly popular to trade currencies electronically using an online forex broker's trading platform accessed via the Internet.

The primary financial derivatives whose values depend on exchange rates quoted in the vast forex market include exchange traded currency futures, as well as the foreign exchange related options contracts that will be the main topic discussed in this book. Such forex or currency options trade actively in the over the counter forex market, as well as on several U.S. based exchanges, such as those run by the CME Group in Chicago and the Philadelphia Stock Exchange.

These days, the forex options market even has its own specialized brokers who facilitate transactions between professional market makers looking to offset option related risk. In addition, many major banks actively involved in the foreign exchange market employ currency option specialists to advise clients and assist with client transactions, as well as forex option risk managers to manage their currency option portfolios and quote prices to customers.

Forex Option Basics

In essence, forex or currency options are financial derivatives whose values depend upon the exchange rate of one or more underlying currency pairs. Such currency pairs consist of a base currency and a counter currency, since all national currencies are quoted in the foreign exchange market in terms of another currency.

Furthermore, at their most basic level, forex options are agreements or contracts that give their holder or buyer the right — but not the obligation — to exchange a given amount of one currency for another currency at a particular exchange rate either within or at the end of a specified time frame.

A forex option holder's right to exchange currencies at the option's contractually specified exchange rate expires at the conclusion of this time frame on a date known as the option's expiration or expiry date. The exchange rate at which the currencies can be exchanged under the option contract is known as the option's strike price.

The lack of an obligation for the option holder to perform on this forex option contract in case of an adverse market move is compensated for by having the holder pay the seller or writer of the option an amount of money typically known as the option's premium. This terminology arose because buying an option is analogous to a person buying an insurance policy by paying an upfront premium to an insurance company.

As with an insurance policy, this option premium is paid upfront by the option buyer to its seller in order for the buyer to purchase the option. In the forex options market, an option's premium is computed from a price expressed as either a percentage of one of the currency amounts or in currency or counter currency pips.

When the life of a forex option reaches its expiration date and is nearing its time of expiration, its holder needs to compare the strike price of the option with the prevailing spot exchange rate for the underlying currency pair.

If it would be advantageous for the holder to exercise the option at its strike price and then close out the resulting position in the spot market, they will typically contact the seller to exercise their option.

If this transaction would not be advantageous, they will typically allow the option to expire worthless. In the situation where the option's strike price is close to the prevailing spot rate, they might choose to sell the option back to the writer if it still has some residual value.

The next chapter will cover the essential and specialized terminology widely used in the currency option market among option market makers, traders and hedgers.

An Introduction to Key Forex Option Terminology

As in many other businesses, the forex option market has its own specialized terminology or jargon that allows professional option traders operating within that market to communicate specific concepts to each other efficiently, and usually with a minimum of time and words spoken.

Furthermore, transaction mistakes and wasted time can have very costly consequences in the fast moving foreign exchange market. For this reason alone, traders or hedgers considering using forex options would be well advised to learn this specialized market terminology thoroughly in order to avoid any confusion, uncertainty or misunderstandings that can arise when transacting forex options with professional currency option dealers and market makers who use this jargon on a regular basis.

To assist with this process of becoming familiar with the extensive jargon used in the forex options market, the reader is referred to the glossary at the rear of this book for definitions and examples of the terms that will be used throughout this book that they may not already be familiar with. This summary of key forex option terminology can also be used as a reference by anyone interested in learning about currency options. This glossary can also be a helpful terminology review that should assist the reader in better understanding the forex option market and its jargon that will be employed in the balance of this book.

Some of the important forex option related terms defined in the glossary have already been defined and used in the previous chapter when introducing this topic, while other terms will be covered in greater detail in later chapters. In addition, the reader may note that some glossary terms are common to all other option markets, while others may pertain to the underlying over the counter foreign exchange market or to the exchange traded currency futures markets.

Chapter 2: Vanilla Forex Options

Vanilla Forex Options

When applied to currency options, the descriptive term "vanilla' refers to a plain or normal type of forex option. This usage is analogous to vanilla flavored ice cream being commonly seen a plain or normal flavor of ice cream.

The term "vanilla" is often used in the forex options market to distinguish the most common and traditional types of currency options from the newer and more exotic forex option varieties that have been defined above and will be described in greater detail in a later chapter dedicated to the subject.

Virtually all exchange traded currency options are vanilla forex options, as are almost all forex options traded in the over the counter market.

Vanilla Calls and Puts

In general, a vanilla call option gives the holder the right to buy the underlying asset at its strike price, while a vanilla put option gives the holder the right to sell the underlying asset.

Since the two currencies that make up a currency pair are exchanged for one another in any foreign exchange transaction involving that pair, forex options are somewhat unusual in that they are both put and call options. For example, an option to buy Euros in exchange for selling the U.S. Dollar would be both a Euro Call and a U.S. Dollar Put. The common market shorthand used to denote such an option would be a EUR Call/USD Put.

A currency option trader therefore needs to be very careful to specify exactly which currency is the call currency and which currency is the put currency when transacting forex options. This normal precaution helps to avoid any misunderstanding that could end up being costly if discovered only after the underlying currency market has moved or a hedge for the option has already been executed.

European Style versus American Style

Plain vanilla forex options come in two basic types: American Style options and European Style options. The primary difference between these two primary vanilla option types is that European style options can only be exercised on their expiry dates up until a pre-specified cutoff time, while American style options can be exercised at any time prior to their expiration date and cutoff time.

Both American and European style options can only be exercised economically if they are in the money relative to the underlying exchange rate. A currency option is considered in the money only if the spot or futures position resulting from that option's exercise can be immediately closed out in the appropriate underlying market for a profit.

The vast majority of the vanilla forex options traded in the over the counter market are European style options, although American Style options are usually available from banks upon the request of a client that strongly desires their early exercise feature, usually for some practical business reason.

Since European style forex options can only be exercised on their expiration dates, they are usually considered options on the forward rate prevailing for the option's ultimate settlement date. In the over the counter market, this settlement date is typically the spot settlement date for the underlying currency pair if it were traded on the option's expiration date. For most currency pairs, the settlement of the currencies exchanged when an over the counter currency option contract is exercised occurs two business days after its exercise. The sole exception to this rule is for forex options on the USD/CAD currency pair, which typically settle in just one business day after exercise.

In contrast to European Style options, in the money American Style options can be exercised at any time to result in a spot position in the underlying currency pair at the strike price. For this reason, American Style forex options are often considered options on the spot rate, rather than options on the forward rate.

With respect to their relative fair values, American style options typically have a higher theoretical option price than their European style counterparts due to the potential advantages to their early exercise feature. The price difference between European and American style options with otherwise identical parameters is sometimes known as the "Ameriplus".

Although American Style options do seem to offer holders more flexibility in determining when to take delivery of the underlying currency, most purchased American style forex options that become in the money relative to the underlying exchange rate should actually be sold back to a market maker rather than exercised prior to expiration.

This is so that the holder of the American Style option can capture any remaining time value the option may have over and above what the buyer would otherwise obtain from exercising the option and then closing out the resulting foreign exchange position in the prevailing underlying spot or futures market.

An exception to this general rule of avoiding early exercise for American Style options occurs when the option is deep in the money — so it has almost exclusively intrinsic value and little to no time value — and it gives the holder the right to call or buy the higher interest rate currency and put or sell the lower interest rate currency. To economically exercise an American Style option early, the positive carry obtained from investing the higher interest rate currency for the remainder of the option's lifetime, and simultaneously borrowing the lower interest rate currency for the same period, should be greater than any remaining time value left in the option.

The CME Group's IMM Currency Options

The Chicago-based Chicago Mercantile Exchange or CME Group lists a variety of currency option contracts on its International Monetary Market or IMM exchange. Most of the exchange traded currency options listed on the CME Group's IMM exchange are American Style options on currency futures contracts, which are also listed on that exchange. Furthermore, while the IMM exchange lists some European Style currency options based on futures contracts for the major currency pairs, the trading volume in these contracts is dwarfed by the volume seen in the corresponding American style options.

The IMM listed currency options are all options on a physical delivery currency futures contract, so they are all settled by exchanging the applicable underlying currency futures contract between the holder and the writer of the option. Upon exercise, the holder of a currency call option receives a long position in the call currency via the underlying futures contract, while the writer receives a short futures position in the call currency. If the holder owns a put on a currency, they receive a short position in the futures contract in that currency, while the writer receives a long position. The ultimate settlement dates for these IMM listed forex options are the relevant currency futures' settlement dates they are based upon.

The IMM currently offers standardized option contracts for the major currencies of the Euro, Japanese Yen, British Pound, Swiss Franc, Australian Dollar, Canadian Dollar and New Zealand Dollar versus the U.S. Dollar. For these currency pairs, the IMM currently lists options with standardized expiration dates four months apart in a quarterly cycle that includes March, June, September and December expiration dates. In addition, the IMM offers two serial month expiration dates, and four weekly expiration dates. Cross rate options for the British Pound, Japanese Yen and Swiss Franc versus the Euro are also currently listed on the IMM.

In addition, the IMM lists forex options on various emerging market currencies, which presently include: the Mexican Peso, the Russian Ruble, the Hungarian Forint, the Chinese Renminbi, the Korean Won, the Polish Zloty, the Brazilian Real, the Israeli Shekel, the South African Rand and the Czech Koruna. While most of these emerging market currencies are quoted versus the U.S. Dollar, some are also quoted versus the Euro or Japanese Yen. In addition, the listed expiration series for options on some of these minor currencies are on a monthly and weekly basis, while others are on the standardized quarterly basis.

For the Euro, the IMM lists currency option contracts in the size of 125,000 Euros. This moderate size tends to appeal to medium size speculative traders or smaller corporate hedgers.

NASDAQ's Philadelphia Stock Exchange Currency Options

As of this writing, The NASDAQ-owned Philadelphia Stock Exchange or PHLX quotes European Style currency options for the following currencies versus the U.S. Dollar: the Euro, the Japanese Yen, the British Pound, the Swiss Franc, the Australian Dollar, the Canadian Dollar, the New Zealand Dollar, the Mexican Peso, the Norwegian Krone, the Swedish Krona and the South African Rand.

All of the Philadelphia Stock Exchange's currency option contracts expire on the Saturday immediately following the third Friday of the expiration month. This third Friday is also the last trading day for these options. A unique feature of these PHLX exchange traded options is that they are not settled by performing an underlying foreign exchange or futures transaction. Instead, expiring PHLX contracts are cash settled in U.S. Dollars relative to the spot price observed at 12:00 p.m. Eastern Time on the Friday before expiration.

For the Euro, the PHLX lists currency option contracts in the size of 10,000 Euros each. This modest size tends to appeal to smaller size speculative traders or those hedging personal currency exposures.

Forex Option Expiration Cut off Times

European style forex options traded in the over the counter currency option market generally expire at a standardized 10:00 a.m. New York cutoff time. This is usually the same as 3:00 p.m. London time, unless a one-hour daylight savings time difference occurs. Some over the counter forex options do trade for a Tokyo cutoff expiration time of 3:00 p.m., especially among Japanese and other Far Eastern counterparties.

Furthermore, options on various emerging markets currencies can have special cutoffs and settlement conventions. For Turkish Lira options, the cutoff time is 12:00 p.m. London time, while for Polish Zloty it is 11:00 a.m. Warsaw time, which is usually 10:00 a.m. London time. Hungarian Forint options have a 12:00 p.m. Budapest time cutoff, which is usually 11:00 a.m. London time. Forex options involving the Norwegian Krone, Swedish Krona, Czech Republic Koruna, and South African Rand typically use the standard New York cut-off. Options on the Russian Ruble, Chinese Renminbi and Brazilian Real tend to be cash settled against a specific forex market fix for those currencies.

Exchange traded options on futures contracts traded at the Chicago Mercantile Exchange or CME have different expiration cutoff times depending on their style. CME traded European style options on futures expire at 10:00 a.m. New York time, while CME traded American style options on futures expire at 3:00 p.m. New York time. Both option styles expire on Fridays. Some option traders aim to exploit this expiration time difference by buying the American style and selling the European style CME options that expire on the same Friday in order to briefly end up with a cheap or even free option.

The CME currently automatically exercises currency options on the six major currencies by comparing their strike prices with a daily fixing calculated by taking a volume weighted average of currency futures price trades observed over the thirty second period immediately preceding the options' expiry time. Auto exercise will occur if an option is one pip or more in the money relative to that calculated fixing price.

Forex Option Pricing, Models and Parameters

The process of estimating theoretical forex option prices has benefitted greatly from the use of computers and calculation devices in recent years, which substantially improve the speed at which option fair value prices can be calculated and quoted. The pricing of forex options is typically performed using rather complex mathematical models coded into computer programs.

The currency option market's standard model for the calculation of forex option prices is known as the Garman Kohlhagen model. This mathematical model modifies the very well known Black Scholes option pricing model in ways that better apply to the continuous interest rate returns observed for currencies traded in the foreign exchange market.

The option pricing results obtained from these mathematical models generally depend on the degree of movement expected in a particular currency pair by currency option market makers over a particular time frame known as the implied volatility. This movement-related parameter is related to the standard deviation of the currency pair's exchange rate, and it represents the forex option market's current best estimate of the volatility in the underlying exchange rate that will be observed during the option's lifetime.

Once an option market maker provides an implied volatility quote for a particular maturity and strike price, that key parameter is then entered into a standardized currency option pricing model along with other essential contract and observable market parameters in order to obtain the desired option's fair value price.

This fair value price can be expressed in four different ways: as a percent of the base currency, as a percent of the counter currency, in base currency pips or in counter currency pips. The most common quotation used in the over the counter market is as a percent of the base currency — especially if the base currency is U.S. Dollars. In contrast, exchange traded options, such as those traded on the Chicago CME, typically have their prices expressed in U.S. Dollar pips and their principal amounts expressed in foreign currencies.

Inputs into typical forex option pricing models include the following contract parameters:

- The currency to be sold or the “put” currency
- The currency to be bought or the “call” currency
- The amount of one of the currencies
- The forex option’s strike price
- Whether the option is European style or American style
- The option’s expiration date
- The option’s delivery date (which can be different from the usual spot delivery date)

In addition, various parameters determined by prevailing conditions in the forex, options, deposit rate, forward or futures markets also need to be entered into the typical forex options pricing model. These markets determined pricing model inputs include:

- The implied volatility, which is determined by market expectations of future fluctuations in a currency pair
- The spot exchange rate for the currency pair
- The prevailing forward exchange rate at the option’s expiration date or the underlying futures contract price
- The prevailing market interest rates for both currencies
- The implied volatility for the currency pair that pertains to the option’s expiration date.

The complex subject of theoretical currency option pricing will be revisited in greater detail later in this book when the Garman Kohlhagen pricing model is discussed.

Implied Volatility

As mentioned briefly in the previous section, implied volatility is a key market-determined element in the pricing of currency options. Implied volatility can also be seen as the forex option market's estimated measure of the risk involved in holding a spot position in that currency pair over the lifetime of the option. Since implied volatility is based on what the option market expects will happen in the future, it cannot be known in advance and can only be estimated by option market makers.

Furthermore, implied volatility quotes can vary significantly for different expiry dates quoted, and implied volatility can even be different for each option strike price quoted on a particular expiration date. When plotted over time and by strike price, the three dimensional implied volatility surface tends to be relatively smooth, although it is not usually flat and is instead somewhat curved.

In fact, one notable feature of implied volatility is that it tends to be higher for out of the money options than for at the money options to reflect greater market demand for cheaper out of the money options relative to that for the more costly at the money options. This situation typically results in a smile shaped implied volatility curve for options with different strike prices quoted on any particular expiration date.

Nevertheless, if the market in an underlying currency pair is trending in a highly directional manner, an implied volatility skew might result where out of the money options that will benefit from the direction of that trend tend to trade at higher implied volatilities than those that will not benefit. Thus, out of the money calls tend to trade at higher implied volatilities in a rising market, and out of the money puts tend to trade at higher implied volatilities in a falling market.

In part because of the importance of implied volatility to forex option pricing, most professional currency option traders operating in the over the counter forex options market make quotations to one another in terms of implied volatility. Once the implied volatility of an option contract of a particular maturity and strike price is agreed upon, that parameter is then entered into a computer program of a standardized currency option pricing model along with the other essential contract details and market observables to compute the desired option's fair value price.

Vanilla Forex Options in Practice

Now that the basics of forex options and their key market terminology have been introduced, it is time to discuss how they work in practice in both the over the counter and exchange traded currency options markets.

In terms of their practical applications, vanilla forex options can be used by hedgers as a form of insurance policy to protect an underlying currency exposure that may arise in the course of their normal business or investment activities. Such a hedger can purchase a vanilla forex option to protect their exposure at a particular exchange rate in exchange for the premium they will need to pay up front for the option.

Buying an option as a protective hedge for an anticipated forex risk allows profits to continue to accrue on the underlying exposure if the market moves favorably, while at the same time providing the hedger with the peace of mind in knowing that their downside risk is limited.

Hedgers can also use vanilla currency options to modify the risk profile of an underlying currency exposure. One popular way to do this is to limit the risk on the currency exposure by buying a protective forex option with a strike price set at a less favorable exchange rate, while financing that option's purchase by selling an option to limit their upside potential beyond a certain more favorable exchange rate.

In addition to hedging applications, vanilla currency options can be used by speculative traders to take a position reflecting a specific directional view on a currency pair traded in the forex market. Such traders often use fundamental and technical analysis to develop such a market view, and they can then use forex options to implement it in a very specific manner with the goal of profiting from their view, if it turns out to be correct.

Forex options are especially useful when taking longer term positions on an overnight basis since a trader typically does not have to worry so much about intervening market moves or managing stop loss orders that can be triggered by sharp and usually unanticipated market swings.

Speculative currency traders can even obtain additional income from writing forex options that they see as unlikely to be worth more when they expire than the initial premium received when they were sold. They can also sell options against an underlying trading position to improve their breakeven rate on the initial transaction, while at the same time limiting its upside potential during the option's lifetime.

A Vanilla Forex Option Example

For illustration purposes, first consider the example of a European style forex option representative of those commonly traded in the over the counter market: a EUR call and USD put with an At the Money Spot strike price expiring in three months' time in an amount of 10 million Euros.

Given that three month implied volatility for EUR/USD is 11 percent, the spot rate is trading at 1.3900, the three month Euro deposit rate is 0.10 percent and the three month U.S. Dollar deposit rate is 0.105, then the option's fair value price would be computed as 3.06 percent of the Euro amount by an option trader using the industry standard Garman Kohlhagen currency option pricing model.

For the option's principal or face amount of 10 million Euros, the total premium cost of this forex option would therefore be 306,000 Euros, which is readily obtained by multiplying the face amount by the price expressed as a percent of the Euro amount. This option's premium in U.S. Dollars would be obtained by multiplying the Euro premium amount by the prevailing 1.3900 spot rate to result in an equivalent cost of 425,340 U.S Dollars.

Delta Hedging the Option in This Example

Professional option traders transacting an option like the Euro call/U.S. Dollar put described in the previous example with other professionals will almost always exchange a spot hedge at the market spot rate used to compute the currency option's fair value.

Nevertheless, most customers contacting their banks to obtain a live price on, and ultimately transact such a forex option would not wish to exchange a spot hedge for the option, so they would ask for a live price. When dealing with such customers on a live quotation basis, the professional option trader will usually want to hedge the spot risk associated with this option as soon as possible to prevent unwanted forex market losses.

The trader will therefore obtain a live spot quote first in order to then quote a live option price to their client. Once they transact the option with their client, they then immediately hedge the option by making a transaction in the spot market.

In order for an option trader to most accurately hedge the spot market risk associated with this particular EUR/USD option, they would also calculate an important option risk management parameter known as its Delta. Delta is the sensitivity of the option's price with respect to a one percent change in the spot rate, and it will be discussed in greater detail in the chapter of this book devoted to forex options risk management.

In this example, the option's Delta is computed as 51.08 percent, so the equivalent spot position to use as a hedge for this option would be 5,108,000 Euros. If the client wished to buy the EUR Call/USD Put option on 10 million Euros from an option market maker, the market maker would then need to buy 5,108,000 Euros in the spot market to hedge the option transaction against movements in the underlying spot market.

This initial hedging process is typically known as delta hedging, as is the ongoing risk management process of rebalancing the option's delta hedge while the underlying market fluctuates.

Chapter 3: Exotic Forex Options

Introduction to Exotic Forex Options

As the sophistication level of currency traders and hedgers has expanded to encompass and demand new risk profiles and option types, the professional currency option market has in turn evolved to meet this growing client demand.

In response to this trend, several different non-vanilla option types have been developed and widely marketed by financial institutions to suit a number of varied hedging and trading needs.

These so-called "exotic" option types differ from plain vanilla European and American style options in a variety of ways. Some exotic options have a trigger rate incorporated into them that has consequences for the derivative if it ever trades, while other forex exotic options have an underlying that is not a simple exchange rate.

In addition to having their own unique risk profiles, many exotic options can be combined with each other or with vanilla options to establish a particular risk profile desired by a forex trader to conform to their market view. Exotic currency options can also act as a hedge for an underlying foreign exchange exposure with unusual risk characteristics that they can help a more sophisticated currency hedger offset.

In general, an exotic forex option can perhaps best be described as a derivative contract granting the buyer the right to exchange one currency for another within a specified period of time that is not a plain vanilla European or American style option. Furthermore, exotic forex options are usually traded in the OTC currency option market among financial institutions and their customers, so they usually have a European style rather than American style type of exercise policy.

Exotic options and structured options are often used to satisfy particular hedging needs under certain circumstances or to establish a specific trading position given a detailed market view, often at a reduced premium cost.

The more common types of exotic options that are readily available in the forex market include binary options, knock out and knock in options (also known as trigger or barrier options), average rate and average strike options, binary options and basket options. Most of these standard exotic option types can now be obtained from major financial institutions operating actively in the over the counter forex options market, and standardized pricing models already exist to provide approximate theoretical valuations for them.

Nevertheless, depending on the sophistication of the financial institution and its client's needs, an exotic option can often be further customized as a structured product. This might mean including an additional risk component, such as a variable expiration date or some other special feature that can be theoretically evaluated using more sophisticated option pricing models designed with greater product flexibility in mind. The added risk component can involve the use of other currency derivatives or even derivatives dependent on other financial markets, all in the interest of tailoring a financial product to the specific needs of businesses or traders involved in making foreign exchange transactions or strategically taking currency market risks.

While two way prices for vanilla forex options are generally quoted among professional counterparties based on the bid and offer implied volatility corresponding to their expiration date and strike price, exotic options are instead usually quoted as bid and offer prices based on a particular exchange rate. This is generally done because the exotic option product may not have the same implied volatility sensitivity as a similar vanilla option, and so the implied volatility spread may differ substantially from what would be observed for a similar vanilla forex option.

Some exotic options even have a negative volatility sensitivity or Vega, so this situation would result in an inverted price if a standard volatility spread were used in pricing such an option. In addition, the pricing models developed in-house by quantitative analysts working for different financial institutions may provide different theoretical valuations for exotic options, even given the same implied volatility, exchange rate and other forex market and option parameters.

When transacting an exotic forex option, most clients will generally request a live price on the option, since they have no intention of exchanging a delta hedge with the financial institution providing such a price. In contrast, most exotic options dealt among professional counterparties are quoted with an agreed upon spot reference exchange rate and the transaction typically involves the exchange of a delta hedge. This reference exchange rate is used as the basis for calculating and pricing the exotic option that allows a trader to more accurately compare quotes coming from different financial institutions. The reference spot rate is usually also used as the basis for computing the size of the corresponding delta hedge to be exchanged between the professional counterparties in order to neutralize the exchange rate risk of the option when the transaction is initiated.

Binary Options

An especially popular component of the exotic forex option market in recent years is the binary or digital currency option. The appeal of binary options has even been expanded and actively marketed to retail forex traders. Such retail traders typically operate via online binary option brokers that provide binary option prices for a number of underlying markets besides various foreign exchange currency pairs.

The basic concept behind a binary option is relatively simple: the holder of the binary option initially pays a fixed up front premium and is then paid a fixed sum of money called the "payout" if the strike price of the option is in the money with respect to the price of its underlying asset at its expiration. If the strike price of the binary option is out of the money in relation to the underlying asset at expiration, the payout of the binary option is typically zero, although some binaries are structured to provide a smaller token payout as a consolation to the buyer.

Furthermore, two distinct types of binary options currently exist in the forex options market. The first type is the "at expiration" binary option, which has its payout amount determined by where the underlying spot rate lies relative to its strike price at expiration. The second type is the "one touch" binary option, which has a payout that can be disbursed before expiration if the option's strike or trigger price is ever touched.

Perhaps due to the simplicity of the forex market bet being placed, binary options have become one of the most common exotic derivative trading vehicles for many smaller forex speculators. The basic idea is that the long binary option transaction involves paying a limited and known amount of premium up front in return for the possibility of obtaining a known limited reward or payout if the option holder's view turns out to be correct.

This simplicity — in addition to the relative cheapness of binary options relative to the more complex and costly bet of buying a plain vanilla option with limited risk but unlimited upside potential — has also contributed to the widespread and growing attraction of binary options for speculative purposes among currency traders.

Because binary options generally involve a cash payout when they are in the money — not the actual exchange of currencies — they are generally subject to being automatically exercised at their expiration date and time if they are in the money relative to a pre-specified reference exchange rate. Also, since a binary option's payout is typically cash settled for value spot, a binary option's holder generally does not have the right to purchase or sell the underlying currency pair at expiration, as with most vanilla currency options. This cash settled feature of binaries may suit a speculative currency trader very well, but a hedger that desires the underlying forex transaction may need to take additional steps to it when their binary option hedge expires.

Binary options can also be combined with other exotic option types, such as the knock out options described in the following section, to create specific option bets.

Knockout Options

The next most popular form of exotic forex options are commonly known as "knockout" or trigger options because they incorporate the risk of being cancelled or knocked out before expiration and are therefore path dependent options. Knockout options are similar to vanilla options with the main difference being that if a pre-determined price target is achieved during the life of the option, the option expires worthless.

The term knockout describes the payout mechanism, which makes the contract valid as long as a certain price level in the underlying asset, called a barrier or trigger is not touched.

If the barrier or trigger is touched, then the option is knocked out, or rendered worthless. As long as the barrier remains untouched by the time the option expires, the option typically becomes a European style vanilla option and pays out accordingly. In the event the barrier is breached before the expiration date, the option immediately ceases to exist and the option holder receives no payout.

Due to the risk of early cancellation, the knockout component will generally make knockout options more affordable than the corresponding European style vanilla option, and this can increase their attractiveness to traders and hedgers that desire a reduced cost option product. The price of a knockout forex option will reflect an increasing discount relative to the vanilla price the closer the option's trigger level is to the prevailing market exchange rate in the underlying currency pair.

Most regular knockout options have their barrier levels set at an exchange rate that would cause the option to be cancelled when it is out of the money, and this is the most popular form of these exotic options. This means that for a regular knock out base currency call option, the knock out barrier would be below the spot rate, while for a regular knock out base currency put, the barrier would be set above the spot rate.

Nevertheless, a reverse knockout option has its knockout barrier level set at a level which would cause the option to be cancelled when it is in the money. Hence, for a base currency reverse knockout call option, the knockout barrier would be above the spot rate, while for a base currency reverse knockout put, the barrier would be set below the spot rate. If the knockout barrier is not triggered to cancel the option prior to expiration, the reverse knockout's payout is then identical to the corresponding vanilla style option of the same strike price and expiration, although its initial premium cost will be significantly reduced.

Reverse knockout options are rather unusual in that they typically have a negative Vega or volatility sensitivity since a rise in volatility can make their knockout level more likely to be triggered to result in the complete loss of their accumulated intrinsic value.

Knock In Options

Knock In options are complimentary to knock out options. While knock out options get cancelled when their trigger or barrier level is reached, knock in options do not even exist until their trigger price in the underlying asset or exchange rate is touched.

For forex knock in options, their exchange rate trigger level is typically known as the "knock in rate". Once the knock in option's barrier rate trades in the forex market, the knock in option then assumes all the characteristics of a corresponding European style vanilla forex option.

Because of the risk that the knock in level may never be attained during the life of the option, knock in options tend to trade at a considerable discount to their corresponding European style option. This discount depends on how close the knock in barrier lies to the prevailing underlying spot rate. The knock in option's discount relative to the corresponding vanilla option diminishes as the underlying asset or exchange rate in the prevailing market approaches the knock in option's trigger level.

Most regular knock in options have their barrier levels set at an exchange rate that would cause the exotic option to come into existence when it is further out of the money than when the transaction was initiated, and this is the most popular form of these exotic options seen in the forex market. This means that for a regular knock in base currency call option, the knock in barrier would be below the spot rate, while for a regular knock in base currency put, the barrier would be set above the spot rate.

Nevertheless, a so-called reverse knock in option has its knock in barrier level set at a rate which would cause the option to start to exist when it is further in the money (or closer to being in the money) than when it was initially purchased. This means that for a reverse knock in base currency call option, the knock in barrier would be above the spot rate, while for a reverse knock in base currency put, the barrier would be set below the spot rate. If the knock in barrier is not triggered to bring the option into existence prior to its expiration, the reverse knock in option has no value at expiration and the holder's only loss on the transaction is the reduced initial premium they paid for the exotic option relative to a similar vanilla option.

Another interesting fact is that the combination of a long knock out option and a long knock in option with the same strike price and trigger price is virtually equivalent to a long vanilla style option position with that same strike price. This not only presents arbitrage traders with an possible opportunity, but it also gives traders and hedgers the ability to convert a long knock in option position to a long vanilla option by purchasing a knock out option, or to convert a knock out option to a vanilla option by buying a knock in option.

Average Rate Options

An Average Rate Option or ARO consists of an option contract that has its value at expiration calculated by comparing a fixed strike price with the average value of the underlying asset observed at specific dates and times during the life of the option. These averaging dates are typically known as "fixing dates", and they are generally observed periodically throughout the life of the option, such as daily, weekly or monthly, although the observations do not have to be periodic and can instead be made on specified dates. Along with the Average Strike options discussed in the following section, these options are sometimes also called Asian Options.

Exercise for Average Rate Options is typically only on the expiration date like European style options, although it is possible to specify an American style early exercise provision in the contract based on the average rate observed to date.

An Average Rate Option is considered to be in the money at expiration if the option's strike price is below the average of the observed fixings for a call option or if the strike is above the average of the observed fixings for a put option. If it expires in the money, an Average Rate Option will generally pay out a cash settlement to the holder at expiration based on the difference between its strike price and the computed average rate. If an Average Rate Option expires out of the money relative to the computed average rate, it is worthless and pays out nothing to its holder.

For most Average Rate Options, the fixings used to compute their underlying average rate are given equal weightings in the averaging process. Underlying average rates can be computed arithmetically or geometrically, and they can also be arithmetically or geometrically weighted in a pre-specified manner.

Furthermore, alternative weightings for the fixings can be structured to specifically fit a particular hedging requirement. For example, a weighted Average Rate Option may suit a hedger who has a series of future cash flows of varying amounts over a period of time and wants to obtain a single option hedge to protect them all. Purchasing a custom weighted Average Rate Option to protect these cash flows typically offers the hedger both simplicity and a considerable discount versus purchasing a series of options expiring on each of the fixing dates to cover each of the various cash flow amounts anticipated.

The discount in the price of an Average Rate option arises because the volatility observed in the average value of an underlying asset tends to be less than the volatility of the value of that asset or exchange rate. Also, if the underlying asset or currency pair is illiquid or highly manipulated, an option with an averaging component offers extra protection for a hedger because it is harder to manipulate the average value of an asset over an extended time frame than to influence it just at an option's expiration.

Average Strike Rate Options

An Average Strike Option, Average Strike Rate Option or ASRO consists of a forex option contract that has its value at expiration calculated by comparing the spot rate for the underlying currency pair to a strike price determined by performing a pre-specified type of averaging process over a given period of time.

The strike price of Average Strike Rate Options, also sometimes known simply as Average Strike Options, is typically calculated according to a specific degree of moneyness relative to the specified currency pair's fixing rate, which is generally a spot rate. For example, an Average Strike Option might be struck at the money spot or two percent out of the money spot. The strike price of the Average Strike Option is then computed by taking an average according to a pre-determined averaging process initially agreed upon and the final averaged strike price is determined at any point between the final fixing date and expiration.

An Average Strike Option on a currency pair is considered in the money at expiration if the prevailing exchange rate for the currency pair is less advantageous to exchange the currencies at than the computed average strike price. Hence, in order for the option to pay off, a positive difference must exist between the averaged underlying value observed and the final averaged strike price of the Average Strike Option. In the case of a base currency call/counter currency put, the spot rate would have to be higher than the computed average strike. In the case of an Average Strike base currency put, the spot rate at expiration for the currency pair would have to be lower than the averaged strike price.

Unlike Average Rate Options, Average Strike Options on a currency pair can be settled normally by exchanging the underlying currency pair at the averaged strike price, although they can usually also be cash settled like Average Rate Options. Exercise is typically only on the expiration date like European style options, although it is possible to specify an early exercise provision in the contract based on the average strike observed to date. Average strikes can be computed arithmetically or geometrically and they can also be weighted in a pre-specified manner.

Basket Options

Basket currency options traded in the over the counter forex option market have all the usual features of vanilla currency options, with the primary exceptions being that the underlying asset is a portfolio or basket of currencies and the strike price is based on the weighted value of that portfolio's component counter currencies, as long as the weighting is positive.

A forex basket option confers to the holder the right to buy, if a call, or sell, if a put, a portfolio consisting of a selection of various underlying counter currencies at a specified net total value expressed in the base currency, which acts as the option's effective strike price.

A basket option cannot simply be split into a set of options on its individual currency pair components because the volatility of a basket of currencies is generally lower than the weighted average of its components due to the existence of cross correlations between the currency components.

Basket options are usually priced by considering the basket's base currency value as a single underlying asset and using standard option pricing formulas. A minor error arises in doing so because a weighted sum of log-normally distributed random variables in not itself lognormal, but this is typically overlooked in practice.

In order to transact a basket option, the basket option's base currency principal amount must be first calculated and the foreign currency amounts that make up the basket must be specified. In addition, the maturity of the option, the strike price expressed in units of the base currency and whether the option is a call or a put on the base currency must be specified.

Forex basket options are a popular exotic option for hedging foreign exchange risk when multiple currency exposures are involved. A corporation or fund manager looking to hedge a portfolio of currency exposures can protect the combined portfolio more simply and at a discount by buying a basket option versus buying individual forex options on each currency pair.

Contingent Premium Options

Contingent premium options are the same as European style options with the exception that their premium payment is deferred until the option's expiration date and is due only when the option expires in the money. If the Contingent Premium Option expires worthless, no premium is due from the holder.

The expiration value of a contingent premium option equals its payoff, and the option holder will take a loss if it expires just slightly in the money. Hence, the holder of a contingent premium option either wants the option to expire worthless or sufficiently well into the money to cover the premium then due at expiration.

Another interesting fact is that a Contingent Premium option can be synthesized from the combination of a sold at expiration binary option with a premium equal to the amount necessary to purchase the desired European style option. According, a contingent premium option can be readily priced by evaluating each constituent part.

Compound Options

Simply put, any option on an option is a Compound Option. Compound options can either be calls on calls or on puts, or puts on calls or puts.

To transact a compound option, the client needs to specify two strike prices and two expiration dates: one strike and date for the compound option and one strike and date for the underlying option.

Furthermore, two types of premium payments are involved in Compound Options. The first is the premium paid initially for the compound option, and the second is the premium to be paid for the underlying option, but only if the compound option is in the money at expiration and gets exercised. Although Compound Option premium amounts are usually quite low, the underlying option will cost that amount more to purchase than it would have if only the underlying option were initially purchased. Compound option premiums are sensitive to the volatility of volatility.

One interesting application of Compound Options is to combine them with vanilla options to allow the expiration of the original option to be extended further at either the holder's or the writer's option. With either form of extendable option, the second option may have different parameters, including a different strike price. The holder extended version grants the holder the right to pay an additional premium at the original expiration date to extend its expiration date. The writer extended version can extend the option automatically at the original expiration date upon some condition being met, such as the option expiring out of the money. In general, no further premium would be required upon extension.

In practice, Compound Options can suit corporations hedging contingent currency exposures that will only materialize if another condition is met sometime in the future, such as a takeover attempt still in progress. If the second condition is not met for some reason, like the takeover falling through perhaps, then the corporation does not need to purchase the underlying option and has only paid the considerably lower premium for the Compound Option.

Chapter 4: Forex Options Analysis and Pricing

One of the keys to successful options trading in the foreign exchange or any other financial market is the accurate and dependable pricing and analysis of the options in relation to the underlying currency pair or asset.

This chapter will discuss the importance of the mathematical pricing models used to evaluate forex options and how currency option traders and hedgers can employ profit and loss diagrams to quickly assess the risk profiles for different option positions they are considering entering into.

In addition, this chapter will go into detail about the importance of volatility, its effect on options pricing, and the differences between implied and historical volatilities.

Forex Option Profit and Loss Diagrams

Profit and loss or P&L diagrams are two-dimensional graphs that allow currency option traders to visually and quickly assess how a particular forex option strategy performs at a variety of different exchange rates, given a particular point in time and with all other parameters remaining equal.

Interestingly, option profit and loss diagrams have also aided in the naming of more complex strategies. One example is the butterfly spread that typically involves spreading a straddle against a strangle. This classic option strategy took its name from the shape of the profit and loss diagram for the strategy that looks somewhat like a stick drawing of a butterfly with spread wings. Another example is the condor option strategy, which involves spreading a closer to the money strangle against a further from the money strangle, and which has an option profit and loss diagram that looks a bit like a bird in flight.

In plotting a profit and loss diagram for a currency option position, the first step is to draw a simple vertical line known as the Y axis. The vertical Y axis line represents the profit and loss of the option position with the profitability of the option position usually drawn increasing from bottom to top. The next step is to draw a horizontal line known as the X axis perpendicular to the Y axis line. The horizontal X line typically divides the Y axis at its zero point and represents the spot exchange rate of the underlying currency pair, with the exchange rate generally drawn gradually increasing from left to right in equal increments.

When interpreting the profit and loss diagram for an option position, a reading of the curve depicted above the X line axis would represent a profit of the option position at a particular exchange rate, with a loss on the position shown as a reading on the curve situated below the X axis.

Most option profit and loss diagrams depict the profit and loss curve of the option position at expiration, and each sharp angle observed in the curve represents an option's strike price. Nevertheless, it is entirely possible to show the profit and loss curve at other times prior to expiration. An option analyst can even create a three dimensional surface with an extra Z axis of time to expiration that shows how the option position's profit and loss varies as its expiration time approaches, as well as over different exchange rates. The sharp angles observed in the at expiration profit and loss diagram at strike prices are more smoothly curved when depicted prior to expiration.

Perhaps the simplest example of a forex profit and loss diagram is that of a spot position in a particular currency pair. Shown below in Figure #1 is a profit and loss diagram for a long EUR 10,000,000 EUR/USD spot position, where the holder would be long 10,000,000 European Union Euros and short the equivalent amount of United States Dollars given the varying exchange rate.

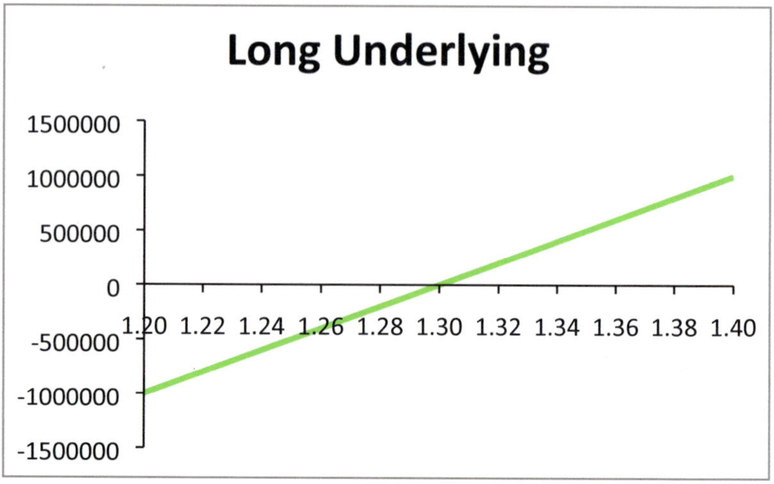

Figure #1: Graph of a profit and loss diagram on an X/Y axis with profit and loss on the vertical Y axis and the EUR/USD exchange rate plotted on the horizontal X axis. The long underlying position in EUR/USD was initiated starting at an exchange rate of 1.3000 and the profit or loss of the position is computed at +/- 10 intervals of 0.0100 or 100 pips from the trade initiation rate.

As you will note from Figure #1, the Y axis of the graph shows a value of 0 at the X line and goes to maximum shown value of +/- $1,000,000 on either side of the X line that represent the accumulated profit and loss on the position at the corresponding exchange rates on the X line, although it could extend further in either direction. Amounts on the Y axis above the X line are positive, or profits, while amounts shown below the X line are negative, or losses.

A diagonal arrow with two tips is typically drawn from the lower left side of the profit and loss diagram to the upper right side of the graph. This straight line shows an unlimited loss running to the left side of lower exchange rates and an unlimited increasing profit as the exchange rate increases to right, which is typical of this sort of long position in a currency pair. In contrast, a short position established at the same exchange rate in the same amount and currency pair would be depicted by a straight line running from the upper left side to the lower right side.

As the graph in Figure #1 immediately illustrates to an experienced analyst, the potential profits and losses are unlimited on a long outright position taken in a currency pair. Basically, while a currency trader can attain large gains if the spot market moves in their currency position's favor, their losses can add up considerably with no downside protection if the forex market moves in an adverse direction. Among currency option traders, this sort of unhedged and open spot position would be said to have unlimited upside potential and unlimited downside potential.

The flip side of the diagram of the long underlying exposure shown in Figure #1 is a profit and loss diagram for a short EUR 10,000,000 EUR/USD spot position, where the holder would be short 10,000,000 European Union Euros and long the equivalent amount of United States Dollars given the varying exchange rate. The corresponding profit and loss profile of such a position is presented below in Figure #2 for comparison purposes. Note the unlimited losses as the spot rate increases, and the unlimited gains as the spot rate falls.

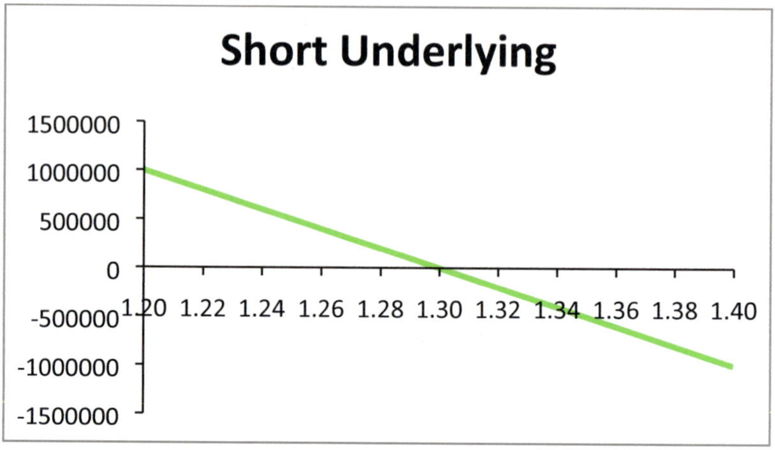

Figure #2: Graph of a profit and loss diagram on an X/Y axis with profit and loss on the vertical Y axis and the EUR/USD exchange rate plotted on the horizontal X axis. The short underlying position in EUR/USD was initiated starting at an exchange rate of 1.3000 and the profit or loss of the position is computed at +/- 10 intervals of 0.0100 or 100 pips from the trade initiation rate.

The next profit and loss diagram example to be considered is that of a long EUR call/USD put position with a strike price of 1.3000, a principal amount of EUR 10,000,000, an upfront cost of $144,320 and an expiration date in one month's time. The at expiration profit and loss diagram for this option is depicted in Figure #3 below.

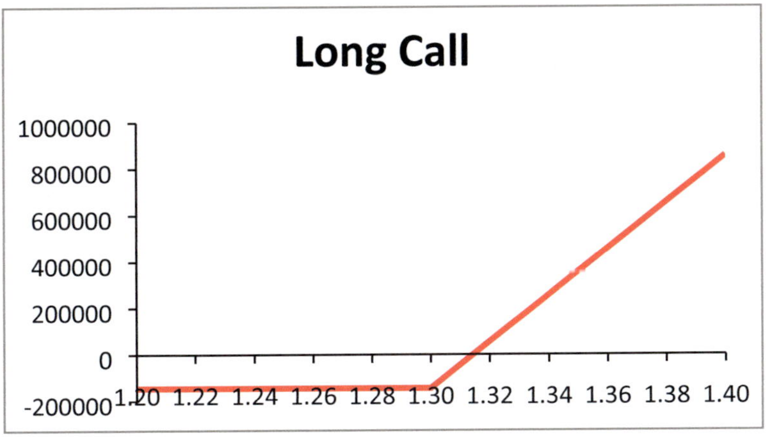

Figure #3: The at expiration profit and loss diagram for a long 1.3000 EUR call/USD put costing $144,320 for a EUR 10,000,000 face amount depicted over same range of possible spot outcomes as the previous graph in Figure #1.

Notice that the flat line on the left side of Figure #3 above demonstrates the limited downside risk of the option position if the EUR/USD exchange rate falls. Also, the level of this flat line is equal to the amount of premium a trader paid for the EUR call/USD put option.

Then, after a sharp angle at the spot rate corresponding to the EUR call/USD put's strike price, the graph continues to rise to the right showing an arrow to the upside as the exchange rate rises, which represents the long position's unlimited upside potential as the spot rate rises above the option's strike price.

Furthermore, the arrow on the downside seen in Figure #1 for an outright long spot position in

EUR/USD has now been replaced with a horizontal line situated below the zero point on the Y axis at a negative level of loss corresponding to the fixed amount of premium the trader paid for the long EUR call position, which is also equal to the total limited risk involved in holding that long EUR call position.

The next profit and loss diagram example to be considered is that of a short EUR call/USD put position with a strike price of 1.3000, a principal amount of EUR 10,000,000, an upfront premium yield of $144,320 and an expiration date in one month's time. The at expiration profit and loss diagram for this option is depicted in Figure #4 below.

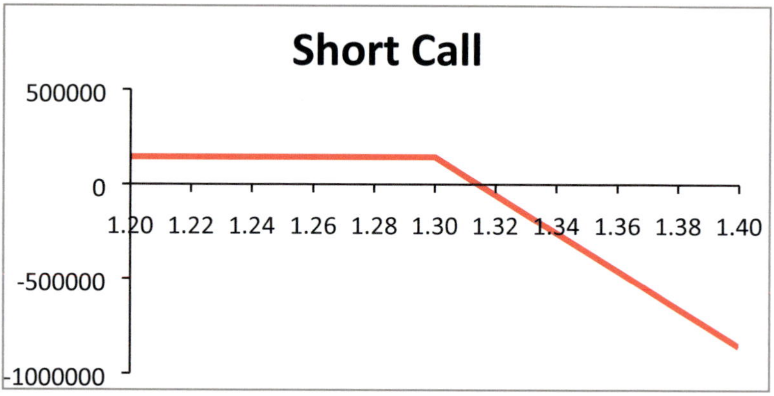

Figure #4: The at expiration profit and loss diagram for a short 1.3000 EUR call/USD put yielding $144,320 for a EUR 10,000,000 face amount depicted over same range of possible spot outcomes as the previous graphs in Figures #1, #2 and #3.

Note that the graph of a short EUR call/USD Put position's profit and loss diagram is essentially a mirror image of the graph for the long EUR call/USD put with the mirror situated parallel to the X-axis. The flat line on the left side of Figure #4 above demonstrates the limited upside potential of the short option position if the EUR/USD exchange rate falls. Also, the level of this flat line is equal to the amount of premium the trader received for selling the EUR call/USD put option.

Then, after a sharp angle at the spot rate corresponding to the EUR call/USD put's strike price, the graph continues to fall to the right showing an arrow to the downside as the exchange rate rises. This arrow represents the short option position's unlimited downside potential as the spot rate rises above the option's strike price. In this region, it shows a similar unlimited loss exposure as the short underlying spot position depicted in Figure #2 above.

This section has been a general introduction to the key concept of option profit and loss diagrams, and the characteristic profit and loss diagrams of each classic option strategy will be presented in the sections below dealing specifically with those strategies.

Forex Option Volatility

The simplest definition of volatility is the amount of fluctuation observed or expected in an underlying asset (a currency pair in the forex market) over a specific period of time. In practice, measures of volatility are generally annualized so that a volatility level for one time period can be readily compared to the volatility level for other time periods.

A relatively high volatility in a currency pair's exchange rate indicates that the level of its exchange rate fluctuates over a wider range of values than normal. In practice, this usually means that the probability of a significant move in either direction is more likely in a smaller space of time, than for a currency pair exhibiting a lower volatility in its exchange rate movements, and hence holding a position in that currency pair conveys more risk.

Conversely, a relatively low volatility in a currency pair's exchange rate implies that the level of its rate of exchange will probably move less dramatically and over a longer period of time than normal, and hence holding a position in that currency pair conveys less risk.

Volatility can be computed as an annualized standard deviation of percentage changes actually observed in an asset's price, in which case it is typically known as historical or statistical volatility since it applies to past data.

Volatility is also defined as a variable in the standardized mathematical option pricing models where it is termed implied volatility because its value is implied by the prevailing prices for options observed in the option market. Implied volatility reflects the anticipated level of future price changes for the underlying asset during the lifetime of the option, as determined by the relevant option market.

In summary, the two key measures of volatility are called “implied volatility”, when an option’s theoretical price implies what the market expects for the underlying currency pair’s future volatility, and “historical volatility” when derived from the annualized standard deviation of percentage exchange rate changes observed over a given period of time.

While both historical and implied volatility measures are relevant to the currency options market, it is very important to remember that the historical volatility of a currency pair is not the same as the implied volatility use to price options on that currency pair. In fact, the two measurements can differ substantially in value, especially if a major risk event — such as an election or a key economic data release — is included in one volatility measurement, but not in the other.

Nevertheless, some option traders do compare historical to implied volatility for similar time frames in order to assess the relative cheapness or richness of the current market prices for options as reflected in their implied volatilities compared to what might have been a fair price for them computed over some past time frame using historical volatility as an estimate.

Historical Volatility

As the name implies, historical volatility is a matter of historical fact and is generally expressed and computed as an annualized standard deviation of past percentage movements in an asset's price or exchange rate observed over a sampled period of time. Historical volatility is also sometimes known as statistical volatility since its value depends on known statistics of the actual price changes for the underlying asset that have been observed in past trading sessions.

Currency traders should be aware that the historical volatility of a currency pair only provides an assessment of past percentage movements in its exchange rate, not of directional trends. Furthermore, while some traders like to use historical volatility as an indication of the risk involved in holding an asset, the fact is that historical volatility may not accurately reflect the degree of future exchange rate movements since greater market risks may lie ahead.

In the forex market, the historical volatility for a currency pair is usually calculated by using a well established formula to obtain the standard deviation of past exchange rate movements over a chosen period and then multiplying the result by an appropriate factor in order to annualize it for ready comparison to the volatility observed for other time periods. In the modern era, this calculation can readily be done by using a computer program or spreadsheet.

For example, the following method would typically be used to compute the annualized 10 day historical volatility for closing exchange rates in the EUR/USD currency pair observed over a 30 day time frame using a spreadsheet:

Step #1: Observe the closing exchange rate for EUR/USD over the past 11 trading days or obtain past closing data. You should not use any data for weekends or market holidays. Enter the eleven observed closing exchange rate data points into Column A of a spreadsheet program like Microsoft's Excel.

Step #2: Now compute the daily close to close percentage exchange rate changes by subtracting the first day's closing rate from the next day's closing rate, dividing the result by the first day's rate, and then multiplying by 100 percent. Place the results in Column B starting with cell B2, and do this for each sequential pair in the first column to obtain a second column with ten results. For Excel, you would enter a formula like this:

Cell B2 = Percent Change #1 = (A2-A1)/A1
Cell B3 = Percent Change #2 = (A3-A2)/A2
Etc…
Cell B11 = Percent Change #10 = (A11-A10)/A10

Where A1 is the closing exchange rate observed on Day #1, and A2 is the closing exchange rate observed on Day #2, etc. You will now have a total of ten daily exchange rate percentage changes.

Step #3: To compute the standard deviation of the second column (Column B) of close to close percentage exchange rate changes, you can conveniently use Excel's built in standard deviation formula. For Excel, you would enter a formula like this into your spreadsheet:

Standard Deviation of Column B = STDEV(B2:B11)

where B2 is the location of your first percent change data point and B11 is the location of your last percent change data point.

Step #4: To annualize your standard deviation result to obtain the historical volatility for the series of 10 daily percentage exchange rate changes listed in Column B, you will need to multiply the standard deviation you previously obtained in Step #3 by the square root of the number of trading days in the 365 day year, which is typically around 254. For Excel, you would enter a formula like this into your spreadsheet:

Historical Volatility = SQRT(254)*STDEV(B2:B11)

The above computation process for historical volatility is based on changes in successive daily closes as a simplifying technique, and forex option traders typically compute historical volatility over periods like 10 days, 20 days and 30 days. Nevertheless, other historical volatility computational methods exist that can help traders take into account significant intra-day volatility. For example, some forex option analysts might use both the high and the low exchange rates, or they might take an average of high, low and closing exchange rates. This is typically done to help capture the intraday movement information lost when using only closing exchange rates to calculate historical volatility.

Implied Volatility in Practice

Unlike historical volatility that can be calculated from past data, implied volatility is a market determined — and hence tradable — quantity that suggests the option market's current best guess of probable future exchange rate volatility over that option's lifetime.

Implied volatility is both an input entered into a standardized mathematical option pricing model in order to obtain an option's theoretical price, and it is also a result that can be obtained from such a pricing model, if the option's market price is already known. In forex options trading, the implied volatility is the volatility measure most commonly used, not just because of its key role in pricing entire series of options using mathematical models, but also because of its future implications for volatility in the exchange rate.

In practice, the implied volatility of an option can also reflect supply and demand effects. An example of this might arise in a trending market, such as when out of the money low strike price put options for a particular expiration date trade at higher implied volatilities than correspondingly out of the money high strike call options in a notably declining market. This is due to the fact that bearish option traders are usually busy buying OTM puts and selling the OTM calls, thereby an implied volatility skew in favor of the OTM puts for the time frame in which such a down trend is expected to prevail in the underlying market.

Furthermore, a skew in implied volatilities across a particular maturity of option contracts can arise when a particular market direction generally suggests a riskier trading environment so that volatility levels tend to rise under such conditions. In practice, the implied volatility level of an option position is a very important component of its actual worth. Even a delta hedged portfolio of forex options that is fully protected from movements in the underlying exchange rate will still have a significant exposure to movements in implied volatility.

In the options market, many professional currency option traders go long volatility or “premium” in anticipation of periods of increased activity in the exchange rate or short volatility in anticipation of decreased exchange rate activity. Their resulting delta hedging activities can even cause or reduce observed forex market volatility accordingly.

For example, an option trader that expects the EUR/USD exchange rate to stay relatively non-directional within a certain trading range over a period of time can sell a straddle or strangle depending on the level of risk they are willing to take and the amount of capital they are willing and able to put up as margin.

If the option trader is ultimately correct in their view of a relatively stable future exchange rate market, then the time premium on the sale of these directionally neutral option strategies will not only decline naturally due to the passage of time, but will also fall due to a probable reduction in implied volatilities. This can allow the trader to take a profit before the options expire by buying them back at a price below what they were sold for.

Nevertheless, in the event that a large move in either direction takes place in the exchange rate after the naked sale of the straddle or strangle, then the option trader in this example stands to lose a considerable amount of money since both the short straddle and short strangle positions have an unlimited degree of downside risk if not hedged.

Conversely, if the options trader expects a big move in a currency pair in either direction, then the trader can go long a straddle or strangle. The trader will typically benefit from such a pronounced move once it occurs, as long as the market does so before the options' time values have declined too far, especially since premium deterioration due to time decay accelerates considerably as an option approaches its expiration date.

Forex Option Pricing Models

In 1976, Myron Scholes and Fisher Black published their paper entitled, *“The Pricing of Options and Corporate Liabilities”*, which contained and described one of the first option pricing models widely used in the financial markets and still applies to stock option pricing.

Nevertheless, it was not until 1983 that S. W. Garman and M. B. Kohlhagen published their paper entitled *"Foreign Currency Option Values"* in the Journal of International Money and Finance. This new forex option pricing model extended the earlier Black-Scholes formula to (1) include two different interest rates for both of the currencies involved in a currency pair, and (2) to account for the possible discount in the forward rate due to the interest rate differential between the two currencies.

The formula used in the Garman Kohlhagen currency option pricing model appears below and uses the following term definitions:

s = the current exchange rate (domestic currency per unit of foreign currency)

x = the strike price expressed as an exchange rate

r = the continuously compounded domestic risk free interest rate

q = the continuously compounded foreign risk free interest rate

t = the time in years until the expiration of the option

σ = the market determined implied volatility for the currency pair's exchange rate corresponding to the option's expiration date.

Φ = the standard normal cumulative distribution function.

Values for a call price *c* or put price *p* are computed as follows:

$$c = se^{-q\tau}\Phi(d_1) - xe^{-r\tau}\Phi(d_2)$$

$$p = xe^{-r\tau}\Phi(-d_2) - se^{-q\tau}\Phi(-d_1)$$

Where ϕ denotes the standard normal probability density function. The terms d_1 and d_2 are defined as follows:

$$d_1 = \frac{log(s/x) + (r - q + \sigma^2/2)t}{\sigma\sqrt{t}}$$

$$d_2 = d_1 - \sigma\sqrt{t}$$

Where "log(n)" denotes the natural logarithm of n.

In addition, values for the Greek risk management parameters Delta, Gamma, Vega, Theta, domestic Rho and the foreign Rho (or Phi) are computed as follows for a call option:

$$\text{delta} = e^{-qt}\Phi(d_1)$$

$$\text{gamma} = \frac{\phi(d_1)e^{-qt}}{s\sigma\sqrt{t}}$$

$$\text{vega} = se^{-qt}\phi(d_1)\sqrt{t}$$

$$\text{theta} = -\frac{se^{-qt}\phi(d_1)\sigma}{2\sqrt{t}} + qse^{-qt}\Phi(d_1) - rxe^{-rt}\Phi(d_2)$$

$$\text{domestic rho} = xte^{-rt}\Phi(d_2)$$

$$\text{foreign rho} = -ste^{-qt}\Phi(d_1)$$

For a put option, the Greek risk management parameters are computed as follows:

$$\text{delta} = e^{-qt}[\Phi(d_1)-1]$$

$$\text{gamma} = \frac{\phi(d_1)e^{-qt}}{s\sigma\sqrt{t}}$$

$$\text{vega} = se^{-qt}\phi(d_1)\sqrt{t}$$

$$\text{theta} = -\frac{se^{-qt}\phi(d_1)\sigma}{2\sqrt{t}} - qse^{-qt}\Phi(-d_1) + rxe^{-rt}\Phi(-d_2)$$

$$\text{domestic rho} = -xte^{-rt}\Phi(-d_2)$$

$$\text{foreign rho} = ste^{-qt}\Phi(-d_1)$$

These Greek risk management parameters are used by option portfolio managers to assess their exposure to various market related risks. Computing these Greeks allows them to determine what sensitivities their cumulative option positions have in terms of the underlying spot rate itself (Delta), changes in the underlying spot rate (Gamma), the implied volatility (Vega), the passing of time (Theta), the domestic currency interest rate (Domestic Rho or just Rho) and the foreign currency interest rate (Foreign Rho or Phi).

A significant modification made by Garman and Kohlhagen to the Black-Scholes model was necessitated by the fact that all forex option prices are affected by two risk free interest rates — one for the domestic or base currency and one for the foreign or counter currency. Hence, currency options have two Rho parameters, with the foreign currency Rho also often being referred to as Phi by many forex option risk managers and risk management programs.

Large option market makers managing an extensive portfolio of options, as well as many experienced options traders, typically manage their positions using sophisticated option trading and risk management computer programs. Such programs automatically price and evaluate every option in their portfolio using the above forex option pricing model, as well as any others that may apply for the more exotic option types discussed in the previous chapter.

Such risk management programs typically automatically net all option long and short positions, and they evaluate the portfolio's net risk position in term of all the Greek variables. Perhaps the most important Greek from a risk management perspective is the portfolio's delta equivalent spot position, which is usually actively rebalanced by the option risk manager in order to avoid unwanted spot risks from accumulating in the portfolio as the underlying exchange rate moves.

A typical computerized option risk management system is also capable of generating a series of graphical images of the entire overall option position showing every possible risk profile at all levels of the underlying exchange rate in the present, and at various future dates. This not only helps an option trader better manage the risks of their options portfolio, but it can also help their managers determine whether traders working under them are operating within their assigned risk limits.

In addition to helping traders manage their existing forex option and spot related risk, this important type of option computer software is especially useful in helping traders devise and develop new option positions before actually committing real funds. This is because an option trader can enter a new proposed transaction or set of transactions into the system before actually dealing them to determine the effects they may have on the trader's existing portfolio.

The trader can also use this technique to assess roughly how much of an initial transaction loss or gain they might incur relative to the position's mark to market value for the day. This helps give the trader a clearer picture of their position's risk profile and possible initial drawdowns the new proposed option position might result in once it is actually executed.

Chapter 5: Vanilla Forex Option Trading Strategies

Using Vanilla Forex Options to Trade Currencies

Trading in the foreign exchange market takes on a new dimension when vanilla options are included in a trading strategy. To start with, currency options offer a useful way to express just about any form of long or short foreign exchange trading view. Forex options also offer numerous ways for a trader to offset outright foreign exchange trading position risks strategically that can be especially helpful to longer term currency traders.

Forex options also offer a considerable degree of leverage, and when combined with the significant amount of leverage that can already be had in the forex market, the result can provide a savvy trader with extremely high returns and — if properly managed — a reduced degree of risk.

In addition, options can be combined with currency futures and forex forward contract positions to give the more sophisticated currency trader even more flexibility in establishing and managing their forex portfolio. Furthermore, once a forex trader becomes sufficiently familiar with the various classic option strategies that will be discussed in this section, trading the underlying currency pair could simply be a matter of adjusting their positions after expiration, with very little — if any — currency trading required between the option's initial execution and its final expiration.

Basically, the use of vanilla options in forex trading broadens a currency trader's arsenal to include virtually endless combinations that can express any number of directional, time and premium oriented trading positions. For example, a trader using forex options cannot only take advantage of moving markets in a currency pair, but they can also profit from a static market as well. Such option positions can either complement a larger trading portfolio, or they can be developed and established independently to take a particular forex market view over a given time frame. In addition, options positions in the foreign exchange market can also be incorporated into a corporation's or fund manager's regular futures or forward hedging book to protect against or strategically take currency exposures of a contingent or non-contingent nature.

The differences observed in trading in the foreign exchange market exclusively using spot, forward and futures contracts versus combining options with other forex trading positions is a bit like comparing a relatively simple game like checkers to a much more sophisticated and strategic game like chess. Trading and hedging take on a completely different dynamic when options are incorporated into an overall strategy, often allowing a trader to maximize returns when it comes to generating income, while at the same time managing their risk to a degree that no stop-loss order could ever achieve, especially in a fast market when order slippage is unfortunately quite common.

Puts and Calls

The basis for all long option strategies consists of directional trading using either a purchased call to take advantage of or protect against an upward move in an exchange rate, or a purchased put to profit from or defend against a decline in the spot rate. This very basic strategy of buying an option has a number of advantages for traders with limited equity and for those wishing to limit their losses when taking longer term strategic directional trades.

Buying a call or a put limits losses effectively to the strike price adjusted by the premium paid up front, while at the same time allowing the option trader to participate in a favorable move in the underlying exchange rate, but again less the up front premium paid for the option.

A purchased at the money call or put option should either have a strike price set at either the spot or the forward exchange rate, or at the nearest to the money available strike price if forex options on futures contracts are being used. Such an at the money forex option will usually have a delta near the 0.50 or 50 percent level, which indicates that the objective chances of the option ending up in the money are roughly 50-50. If a lower cost option is desired, a 25 or 30 percent delta option can be purchased instead, although the chances of it being exercised on its expiration date are understandably lower.

With respect to selecting the optimal expiration date for such a long option strategy, buying a near or medium term expiration put or call option with as little time premium — and hence time decay — as possible would probably be the optimum option purchase. All else being equal, near term options will generally have the lowest time premium, but also the highest probability of expiring worthless and the highest rate of time decay. In addition, a longer-term option may be required depending on the time frame of the trader's outlook and their trading objectives.

If the trader is uncertain as to the timing of the exchange rate move, then a medium term option could well make more sense. Not only will it have lower time decay, but it can also be sold back to the market once the anticipated movement has occurred. Another advantage of a put or call buying strategy is the amount of leverage the option would offer and the reduced risk versus taking an outright position in the spot market. Depending on the terms of the option purchased, the holder could leverage the transaction by as much as in the spot market.

Risk Profiles for Long and Short Call Trading Positions

This section will show the classic profit and loss diagrams for long and short call positions when used as a naked trading strategy. These diagrams graphically display the risk profiles for a particular trading strategy.

As illustrated in Figure #1 below, the naked long call position has a limited risk equal to the premium paid for it, while the long call position's profit potential is unlimited in the direction of rising exchange rates once the option's breakeven point has been attained. The kink in the curve is at the long call option's strike price.

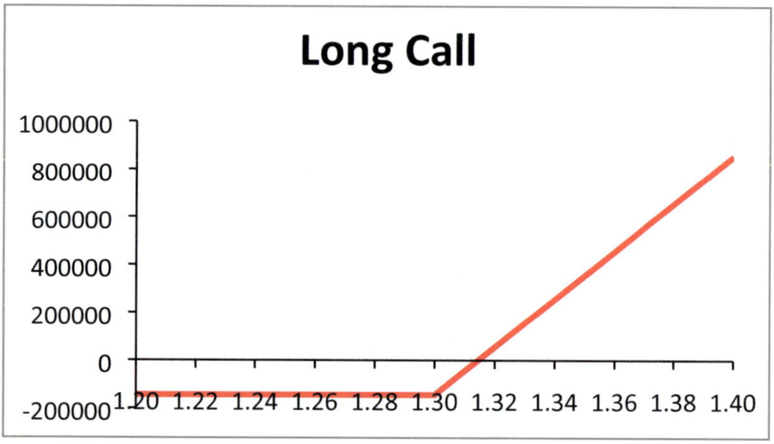

Figure #1: Profit and Loss diagram of a naked long call option used to take a long position in the underlying with limited risk.

A naked sold call's profit and loss diagram looks like the profile for the purchased call, but it is inverted around the horizontal X axis as illustrated in Figure #2 below. The naked short call strategy has a limited reward equal to the premium received for it if the call option expires worthless, but the strategy has unlimited losses should the currency pair fall below the strategy's breakeven point.

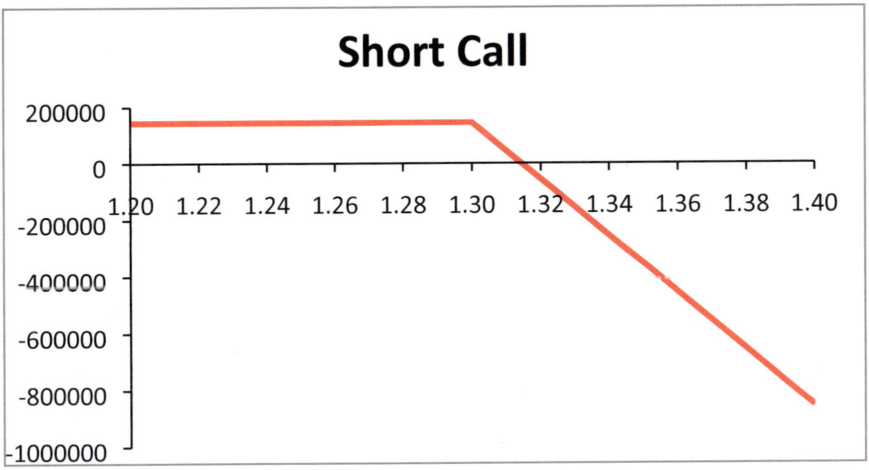

Figure #2: Profit and Loss diagram of a naked short call option used to take a short position in the underlying with limited reward but unlimited risk.

Risk Profiles for Long and Short Put Trading Positions

This section will show the classic profit and loss diagrams for long and short put positions when used as a naked trading strategy. As illustrated in Figure #3 below, the naked long put position has a limited risk equal to the premium paid for it, while the long put position's profit potential is unlimited in the direction of falling exchange rates once the option's breakeven point has been reached. The kink in the curve is at the long put option's strike price.

The profit and loss profile of a purchased base currency put looks exactly like the purchased call diagram, but it is inverted around the vertical Y axis, with the position's unlimited profit potential and upward pointing arrow drawn on the side of the graph corresponding to lower exchange rates.

Figure #3 below shows how this risk profile might look for a long put option position. As illustrated in the graph below, the long put position has a limited risk equal to the premium paid for it, while the long put position's profit potential is unlimited in the direction of falling exchange rates once the option's breakeven point has been reached. The kink in the curve is at the long put option's strike price.

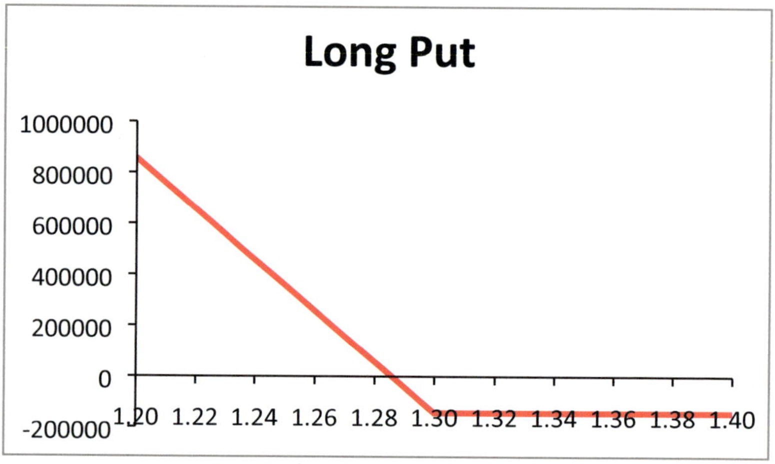

Figure #3: Profit and Loss diagram of a naked long put option used to take a long position in the underlying with limited risk and unlimited profit potential.

A naked sold put's profit and loss diagram looks like the profile for the purchased put, but it is inverted around the horizontal X axis as illustrated in Figure #4 below. The naked short put strategy has a limited reward equal to the premium received for it if the put option expires worthless, but the strategy has unlimited losses should the currency pair rise above the strategy's breakeven point.

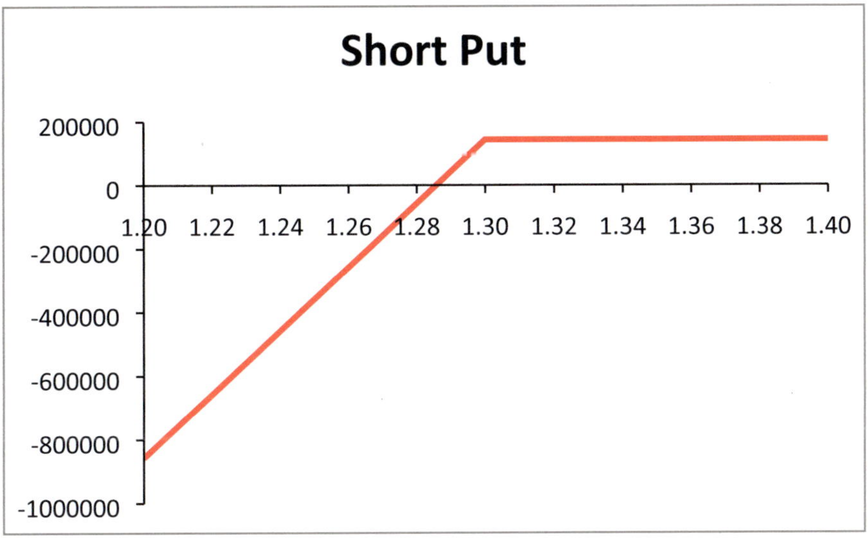

Figure #4: Profit and Loss diagram of a naked short put option used to take a long position in the underlying with limited reward but unlimited risk.

Call Option Buying for Bullish Directional Speculation

Buying a naked base currency call option can be a sound strategic trading decision if a trader anticipates an upward move in a currency pair. The factors for a trader to consider consist of the magnitude of the expected move, the time frame in which it is expected to occur and the amount of the particular option considered for purchase.

Furthermore, if the long base currency call option might be sold back prior to expiration, then the trader's view on implied volatility could also be relevant, since a rise in implied volatility could benefit the position.

Consider the example of a strategic trader who expects a sharp upward move in the EUR/USD currency pair's exchange rate within two months' time to take the rate well beyond the 1.3500 level when the exchange rate is currently at 1.3000.

The bullish trader desiring a limited risk position has the choice of purchasing a two month or longer term Euro call/U.S. Dollar put option, with a strike price of 1.3000, 1.3250 or 1.3500. In practice, few traders would every elect to purchase an in the money option due to the added expensive involved in doing so.

Also, while the client can request just about any custom strike price or maturity from a market maker in the over the counter market, exchange traded forex option markets generally have fixed strike prices and option maturities to select among.

Depending on the expected magnitude of the move in the exchange rate, the bullish trader may decide to purchase three 1.3500 Euro calls, or two 1.3250 Euro calls, instead of one 1.3000 Euro call. Although their chances of being exercised are lower, the price per option for the 1.3250 and 1.3500 out of the money strike call options would be lower than the 1.3000 strike at the money call option. Furthermore, the higher strike options would probably offer a higher potential return than the at the money option if the trader's expected exchange rate scenario played out as anticipated.

Naked Call Option Selling for Bearish Directional Speculation

Selling a naked base currency call option is a somewhat risky proposition due to its unlimited downside potential. Nevertheless, such naked option writes can be a sound strategic trading decision if a trader anticipates a downward move in a currency pair without much risk of a move higher beyond the call option's strike price. The factors for a trader to consider consist of the magnitude of the expected down move, the time frame in which it is expected to occur, and the amount of the particular option considered for sale.

Furthermore, if the short base currency call option might be repurchased prior to expiration, then the trader's view on implied volatility could also be relevant, since a decline in implied volatility could benefit the position.

Consider the example when the EUR/USD exchange rate is currently at 1.3000 of a bearish or neutral strategic trader. They expect either a stable market or an orderly downward move in the EUR/USD currency pair's exchange rate over the next two months, without seeing much risk of the market trading above the 1.3500 level.

In this case, the bearish trader desiring premium income could sell a two month Euro call/U.S. Dollar put option with a strike price of 1.3500. In practice, few retail traders would every elect to sell an in the money option due to the added risk and margin involved in doing so.

Just about any strike price or maturity call option can be sold to an over the counter market maker if sufficient credit lines exist, but exchange traded forex option markets will generally only have certain round number strike prices and maturities to choose from and a margin deposit will probably be required in case the position loses the trader money.

Depending on the expected magnitude of the down move in the exchange rate, the bearish trader may decide to sell three 1.3500 Euro calls, or two 1.3250 Euro calls, instead of one 1.3000 Euro call. Although their chances of being exercised are lower, the price per option received for the 1.3250 and 1.3500 out of the money strike call options would be lower than the 1.3000 strike at the money call option. Also, depending on implied volatility levels, a trader would have similar initial premium received when selling one 1.3000 call or two 1.3250 calls.

Put Option Buying for Bearish Directional Speculation

Buying a naked base currency put option can be a sound strategic trading decision if a forex trader anticipates a downward move in a currency pair. The factors for a trader to consider consist of the magnitude of the expected down move, the time frame in which it is expected to occur and the amount of the particular option considered for purchase. If the long base currency put option might be sold back prior to expiration, then the trader's view on implied volatility could also be relevant, since a rise in implied volatility could benefit the position.

Consider the example of a Euro put buyer in the EUR/USD currency pair who expects a sharp downward move in the exchange rate within two months' time. The exchange is currently at 1.3000. The trader has the choice of purchasing a two month or longer term Euro put/U.S. Dollar call option, with a strike price of 1.3000, 1.2750, 1.2500, 1.2250, 1.2200, etc. In practice, few traders would every elect to purchase an in the money put option due to the extra cost of doing so.

Depending on the expected magnitude of the move in the underlying exchange rate, the trader may decide to purchase three 1.2500 Euro puts, or two 1.2750 Euro puts, instead of one at the money spot 1.3000 Euro put.

The price per option for the out of the money Euro put options would be lower than that for the at the money Euro put option price, with the lower strike put options offering higher potential returns than the at the money option if the trader's bearish scenario played out. Also, depending on implied volatility levels, a trader would have similar initial position costs when buying one 1.3000 put or two 1.2750 puts.

Naked Put Option Selling for Bullish Directional Speculation

Selling a naked base currency put option is a rather risky strategy due to its unlimited downside potential. Nevertheless, such naked put option writes can be a sound strategic trading decision if a trader anticipates a upward move in a currency pair's exchange rate without much risk of a move lower than the base currency put option's strike price. The factors for a trader to consider consist of the magnitude of the expected up move, the time frame in which it is expected to occur, and the amount of the particular put option considered for sale.

Furthermore, if the short base currency put option might be repurchased prior to expiration, then the trader's view on implied volatility could also be relevant, since a decline in implied volatility could benefit the position.

Consider the example of a strategic trader who expects a neutral to orderly upward trending move in the EUR/USD currency pair's exchange rate over the coming two months. They also do not expect the rate will trade below support at the 1.2500 level when the exchange rate is currently at 1.3000.

The bullish trader who is willing to accept unlimited downside risk in return for an up front premium payment can elect to sell a two month Euro call/U.S. Dollar put option. They could choose from strike prices of 1.3000, 1.2750 or 1.2500.

In practice, few traders would elect to sell a naked in the money base currency put option with a strike price above 1.3000 due to the added margin and/or risk involved in doing so. Also, while the client can request just about any custom strike price or maturity from a market maker in the over the counter market, exchange traded forex option markets generally have fixed strike prices and option maturities to select among.

Depending on the expected magnitude of the move in the exchange rate, the bullish trader may decide to sell three 1.2500 Euro puts, or two 1.2750 Euro puts, instead of one 1.3000 Euro put. Although their chances of being assigned on the short put are lower than for the at the money 1.3000 put, the price per option for the 1.2750 and 1.2500 out of the money strike put options would be lower than the 1.3000 strike at the money put option.

Nevertheless, the higher strike put options would offer a higher potential return in the form of the greater premium received, if the trader's expected bullish to stable exchange rate scenario played out as anticipated.

The price per option received for the out of the money Euro put options would be lower than that received for the at the money Euro put option price. Also, depending on implied volatility levels, a trader would have similar initial premium received when selling one 1.3000 put or two 1.2750 puts.

Call and Put Spreads

The simultaneous buying and selling of two different options is known as a "spread" trade. In addition, spread option positions can be entered into at different times, and this is commonly known as "legging into" a spread, since each option component of the spread is considered an individual "leg" of the overall option position. Closing out one leg of a spread trade is sometimes called "lifting a leg".

Option spread strategies can be composed of either calls or puts, and the component options will generally have different strike prices. The component options in a spread may also have different expiration dates.

A put or call spread with the same strike price but with options of different expiration dates is called a "calendar", "horizontal" or "time" spread. When the spread involves options in the same expiration cycle, but with different strike prices, it is said to be a "vertical" spread. When both the strike prices and expiration dates are different, it is known as a "diagonal" spread.

These terms seem to have come from the original spread order tickets used by floor traders operating on the Chicago Board Options Exchange or CBOE. The option order tickets were designed so that the expiration month of an option had to be marked horizontally on the ticket, while the two strike prices were written vertically, with one situated on top of the other.

Option spread trades are also characterized by whether they were established for a net credit or a net debit from the trader's perspective. For example, a credit spread trade generally involves the trader simultaneously buying one less valuable option leg and selling another more valuable option leg, so that the net premium of the two option positions is a credit and the trader receives money for the spread.

In contrast, a debit-spread trade is entered for a net debit and so the trader will need to pay out premium to establish the position. Thus, a debit spread generally involves the trader simultaneously selling one less valuable option leg and buying another more valuable option leg, so that the net premium of the two option positions is a debit and the trader pays money for the spread.

Another popular type of put or call spread is known as the ratio spread. Ratio spreads typically involve the simultaneous or legged spreading of one option against another with different principal amounts for each leg. Such ratio strategies are popular with traders who wish to reduce the premium they pay up front to enter into an option position.

Vertical Spreads

A vertical call spread is when a trader buys or sells a call option of a lower strike price and simultaneously sells or buys a call with a higher strike price, all for the same expiration date. They could also do a similar vertical put spread by buying one put and selling another put of a different strike price, but the same expiration.

The vertical spread is a limited risk position which is at most worth only the difference between the strikes less the premium paid. For example, a EUR/USD 1.3000 – 1.3250 strike Euro call/U.S. Dollar put spread is only worth at most 0.0250 or 250 pips. Therefore, any amount paid for that spread must be deducted from the maximum value of the spread, which is 0.0250, in order to obtain its maximum net profit. If a trader is selling the vertical spread, then their maximum gain would be the premium received, while their losses would be limited to the difference between the strikes, less the premium.

As an example given a spot rate of 1.3000, a trader might pay 0.0150 or 150 pips for the 1.3000 Euro call and receive 0.0058 or 58 pips for the 1.3250 Euro call, both expiring in one month's time, which would result in a net cost of 92 pips. The maximum risk on this vertical call spread would be the 92 pips paid, with the maximum value being 250 pips, which is the difference between the Euro call strike prices. Thus, the net maximum profit would be 250 minus 92 or 158 pips.

If the option trader is correct, and the vertical spread's value goes to the maximum of 250 pips at expiration after a market rise, the trader can liquidate the position for a 158 pip profit. If the trader is incorrect and the market falls, they can either liquidate the call spread for a loss or take the profit on the short option and sell an option in the next expiration cycle, thereby converting the position into a short calendar spread.

Additional follow up strategies can vary widely depending on the trader's objectives, positioning and market moves. For example, a trader can roll the higher Euro call strike up, by buying back the short 1.3250 Euro call and selling a call with a higher strike, say 1.3500. Another follow up possibility could involve buying the short 1.3250 Euro call back and simultaneously selling the underlying exchange rate to create a synthetic long Euro put position out of the remaining long Euro call struck at 1.3000.

Buying a Vertical Call Spread

One of the most popular option strategies for taking advantage of an upside move in an exchange rate consists of the Vertical Call Spread. The strategy involves buying a call option and simultaneously selling another option of the same expiration, but with a higher strike price.

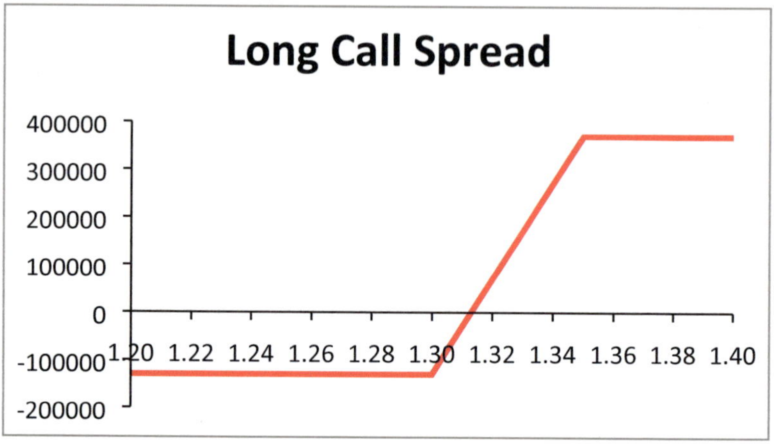

Figure #5: Profit and Loss diagram of a long one month 1.3000 to 1.3500 vertical call spread in the EUR/USD currency pair.

As the above option diagram illustrates, the risk for a vertical call spread is represented by the area below the zero line and is limited to the amount paid for the spread. The profit potential is also limited by the upper strike above which the profit line levels out.

For example, given a EUR/USD spot rate of 1.3000 and implied volatility of 10 percent, consider the long vertical call spread consisting of a purchased EUR/USD two month 1.3000 Euro call/U.S. Dollar put option priced at 215 pips spread against a short two month 1.3250 Euro call/U.S. Dollar put priced at 115 pips. Buying that vertical call spread involves paying a net price of 100 pips, which would cost $100,000 in premium on a principal amount of 10,000,000 Euros.

The maximum risk on the above long vertical call spread is the 100 pips paid for it initially. Furthermore, at most, the vertical call spread is only worth the difference between the strikes minus the initial cost of the spread. In this case, that profit potential would be the 250 pip strike spread minus the 100 pips price = 150 pips maximum profit potential. This means that the trader using this strategy would be risking 100 pips to make a maximum of 150 pips.

Selling a Vertical Call Spread

A short vertical call spread position involves selling a near the money call and buying a further out of the money call for the same expiration date. The sale of a vertical call spread has a similar risk profile as the purchase of the vertical call spread, except reversed around the X-axis. The risk on the position is limited to the difference between the strikes minus the amount of credit taken in at the onset, while the profit is limited to the original credit at which the position was initially established for.

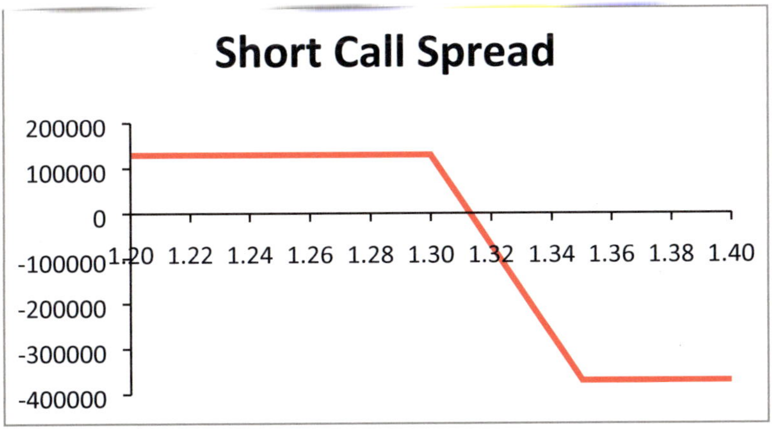

Figure #6: Profit and Loss diagram of a short one month 1.3000 to 1.3500 vertical call spread in the EUR/USD currency pair.

As shown in the above option profit and loss diagram, the risk profile for the short vertical call option spread is a mirror image of the long vertical call spread reflected at the X-axis, with the risk limited to the difference between the strikes less the premium received, and the maximum profit equal to the original premium received.

Going short the vertical call spread is optimal for a trader when their expectation is for the exchange rate to weaken over the time frame of the spread. If the spot rate stays below the lower strike price, the position will gain its maximum profit, with the position losing money only after the exchange rate rises toward the upper strike by more than the number of pips initially received. The maximum loss occurs above the upper call strike price.

For example, given a EUR/USD spot rate of 1.3000 and implied volatility of 10 percent, consider the short vertical call spread consisting of a sold EUR/USD two month 1.3000 Euro call/U.S. Dollar put option priced at 215 pips spread against a long two month 1.3250 Euro call/U.S. Dollar put priced at 115 pips. Selling that vertical call spread involves receiving a net price of 100 pips, which would yield $100,000 in premium on a principal amount of 10,000,000 Euros.

The maximum risk on the above short vertical call spread is the 250 pips difference between the strike prices, less the 100 pips initially received for selling it, or a net risk of 150 pips maximum loss realized if the market rises above the upper call strike price. Furthermore, at most, this short vertical call spread is only worth the 100 pips received. This means that the trader using this short vertical call spread strategy would be receiving 100 pips up front to risk a maximum of 150 pips.

Buying a Vertical Put Spread

The mechanics of a long vertical put spread are identical to the long vertical call spread, with the difference being that the risk/reward profile is geared towards the strategy benefitting from a downward move in the exchange rate. The long vertical put strategy involves buying a put option and simultaneously selling another put option with a lower strike price for the same expiration date.

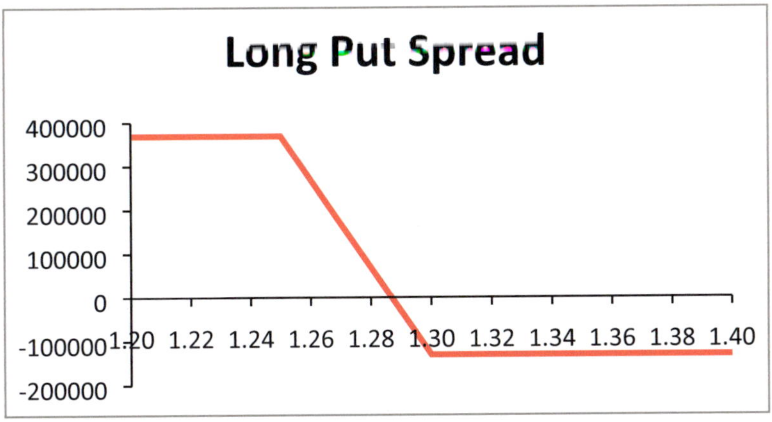

Figure #7: Profit and Loss diagram of a long one month 1.3000 to 1.2500 vertical put spread in the EUR/USD currency pair.

As can be discerned in the above option diagram, the long vertical put spread has its maximum risk limited to the premium paid for it when the exchange rate is above the upper put strike price. Its maximum profit potential occurs when the exchange rate is at or below the lower put strike price.

For example, given a EUR/USD spot rate of 1.3000 and implied volatility of 10 percent, consider the long vertical put spread consisting of a purchased EUR/USD two month 1.3000 Euro put/U.S. Dollar call option priced at 211 pips spread against a short two month 1.3250 Euro put/U.S. Dollar call priced at 108 pips. Buying that vertical put spread involves paying a net price of 103 pips, which would cost $103,000 in premium on a principal amount of 10,000,000 Euros.

The maximum risk on the above long vertical put spread is the 103 pips paid for it initially. Furthermore, at most, the vertical put spread is only worth the difference between the strikes minus the initial cost of the spread. In this case, that profit potential would be the 250 pip strike price difference minus the 103 pip price = 147 pips maximum profit potential. This means that the trader using this strategy would be risking 103 pips to make a maximum of 147 pips.

Selling a Vertical Put Spread

A short vertical put spread position involves selling a near the money put and buying a further out of the money put for the same expiration date. The sale of a vertical put spread has a similar risk profile as the purchase of the vertical put spread, except reversed around the X-axis. The risk on the position is limited to the difference between the strikes minus the amount of credit taken in at the onset, while the profit is limited to the original credit at which the position was initially established for.

Going short the vertical put spread is optimal when the expectation is for the exchange rate to strengthen over the time frame of the spread. By staying above the higher put strike price, the position will gain its maximum profit, with the position losing money only after the exchange rate drops more than the number of pips received below the upper put strike price.

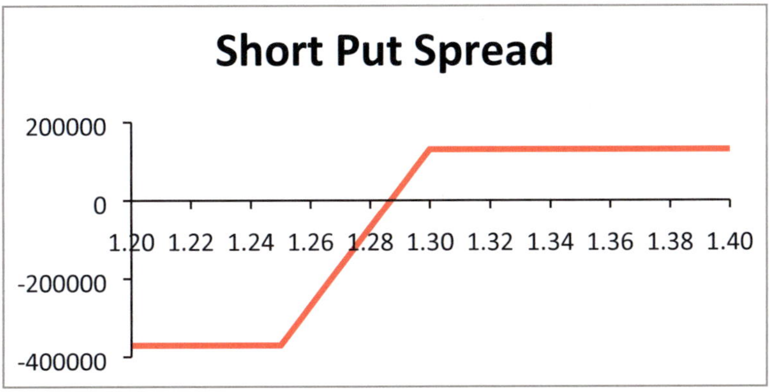

Figure #8: Profit and Loss diagram of a short one month 1.3000 to 1.2500 vertical put spread in the EUR/USD currency pair.

As shown in the above option diagram, the risk profile for the short vertical put option spread is a mirror image of the long spread reflected around the X-axis of the graph, with its risk limited to the difference between the strikes less the premium received expressed in pips, while the maximum profit is limited to the original credit received.

For example, given a EUR/USD spot rate of 1.3000 and implied volatility of 10 percent, consider the short vertical put spread consisting of a sold EUR/USD two month 1.3000 Euro put/U.S. Dollar call option priced at 211 pips spread against a long two month 1.2750 Euro put/U.S. Dollar call priced at 108 pips. Selling that vertical euro put spread involves receiving a net price of 103 pips, which would yield $103,000 in premium on a principal amount of 10,000,000 Euros.

The maximum risk on the above short vertical call spread is the 250 pips difference between the strike prices, less the 103 pips initially received for selling it, or a net risk of 147 pips maximum loss realized if the market falls above the lower put strike price. Furthermore, at most, this short vertical put spread is only worth the 103 pips received. This means that the trader using this short vertical put spread strategy would be receiving 103 pips up front to risk a maximum of 147 pips.

Horizontal, Calendar or Time Spreads

A horizontal spread — sometimes also called a calendar or time spread — typically involves buying a call or put for one expiration date and simultaneously selling a call or put for another expiration date. In general, a long horizontal spread involves selling a shorter dated option and buying a longer dated one, while a short horizontal spread involves buying a shorter dated option and selling a longer dated option.

The reasoning behind entering into a long time spread is that the underlying exchange rate should increase in the case of calls or decrease in the case of puts by a certain amount, thereby leaving the short term short option side of the position to expire worthless while the longer term long position is left with some remaining time and/or intrinsic value. This would allow the trader to take advantage of a subsequent rise in the exchange rate in the case of a call, or a decline if the trader was holding a put.

The long time spread trader can make considerable profit on option premium if the near term option in a time spread is not exercised. This would be the case if the exchange rate stayed above the strike price in the case of a put time spread and above the strike in the case of a call time spread. The trader can then roll the remaining long option position out using another calendar spread and begin the process in the next expiration cycle.

A time spread can also be shorted, by selling the further out expiration option and buying the near term option. The typical reasoning behind using this strategy is an anticipation of a decline in volatility, so this strategy might be used by a professional option market maker to speculate on volatility movements. If the currency rate hits a lull in trading and stays within a limited range for a certain period of time, then option implied volatility drops, thereby making the short longer term option position lose value relative to the near term option position.

Buying a Horizontal Call Spread

A long horizontal call spread involves selling a shorter dated call option and buying a longer dated call option. This option strategy could be used by a trader with the view that the underlying exchange rate will decrease initially by a certain amount, thereby leaving the short term short call option side of the position to expire worthless at its expiration.

Once the short-term option has expired, the longer term long call position is left with some remaining time and/or intrinsic value. This would allow the trader to take advantage of a subsequent rise in the exchange rate in the case of a call, or it could be converted to a put by selling the underlying currency pair. Such a position could also usually benefit from an overall rise in implied volatility, since longer-term options have a higher volatility than shorter-term options.

An example of a long horizontal call spread could involve a trader selling a one month 1.3000 Euro

Call/U.S. Dollar put for 149 pips and buying a two month 1.3000 Euro Call/U.S. Dollar put for 216 pips. The net price would be 67 pips. If after one month, the spot rate has fallen to 1.2900, the short option expires worthless and the trader is left holding the long 1.3000 Euro Call/U.S. Dollar put, which expires in one month and might be worth 109 pips. If the spot rate then rises to 1.3500 after the second month has passed, the second option is exercised and worth 500 pips, so the net profit on the position would be 433 pips.

Selling a Horizontal Call Spread

A short horizontal call spread involves buying a shorter dated call option and selling a longer dated call option. This option strategy might be used by a trader who thought that implied volatility would decrease over a one month time frame. If volatility does in fact decline as expected by the time the initial option expires, the remaining option can then be repurchased at a lower volatility and time value.

To show a profit, the spot rate needs to move rapidly in either direction to reduce the time value on both options, and if the short-term volatility rises relative to long-term volatility, then that also benefits the position. The short calendar spread profits from the difference between the faster decay of the short-term options' lower premium versus the longer term options' higher premium as spot moves.

An example of a short horizontal call spread could involve a trader buying a one month 1.3000 Euro Call/U.S. Dollar put for 149 pips and selling a two month 1.3000 Euro Call/U.S. Dollar put for 216 pips, with implied volatility at 10 percent for both options. The net price received would be 67 pips.

If the spot rate moves sharply to 1.3500 after two days and one month volatility increases to 11 percent, with two month at 10.2 percent, then the short longer term call is worth 557 pips, while the long shorter term call is worth 522 pips, for a net price to unwind the strategy of 35 pips.

Buying a Horizontal Put Spread

A long horizontal call spread involves selling a shorter dated call option and buying a longer dated call option. This option strategy could be used by a trader with the view that the underlying exchange rate will decrease initially by a certain amount, thereby leaving the short term short call option side of the position to expire worthless at its expiration.

Once the short-term option has expired, the longer term long call position is left with some remaining time and/or intrinsic value. This would allow the trader to take advantage of a subsequent rise in the exchange rate in the case of a call, or it could be converted to a put by selling the underlying currency pair. Such a position could also usually benefit from an overall rise in implied volatility, since longer-term options have a higher volatility than shorter term options.

An example of a long horizontal call spread could involve a trader selling a one month 1.3000 Euro Call/U.S. Dollar put for 149 pips and buying a two month 1.3000 Euro Call/U.S. Dollar put for 216 pips. The net price would be 67 pips. If after one month, the spot rate has fallen to 1.2900, the short option expires worthless and the trader is left holding the long 1.3000 Euro Call/U.S. Dollar put, which expires in one month and might be worth 109 pips. If the spot rate then rises to 1.3500 after the second month has passed, the second option is exercised and worth 500 pips, so the net profit on the position would be 433 pips.

Selling a Horizontal Put Spread

A short horizontal call spread involves buying a shorter dated call option and selling a longer dated call option. This option strategy might be used by a trader who thought that implied volatility would decrease over a one month time frame. If volatility does in fact decline as expected by the time the initial option expires, the remaining option can then be repurchased at a lower volatility and time value.

To show a profit, the spot rate needs to move rapidly in either direction to reduce the time value on both options, and if the short-term volatility rises relative to long term volatility, then that also benefits the position. The short calendar spread profits from the difference between the faster decay of the short-term options' lower premium versus the longer term options' higher premium as spot moves.

An example of a short horizontal call spread could involve a trader buying a one month 1.3000 Euro Call/U.S. Dollar put for 149 pips and selling a two month 1.3000 Euro Call/U.S. Dollar put for 216 pips, with implied volatility at 10 percent for both options. The net price received would be 67 pips.

If the spot rate moves sharply to 1.3500 after two days and one month volatility increases to 11 percent, with two month at 10.2 percent, then the short longer term call is worth 557 pips, while the long shorter term call is worth 522 pips, for a net price to unwind the strategy of 35 pips.

Diagonal Spreads

Time, calendar or horizontal spreads can also incorporate different strike prices. This type of option spread strategy is commonly known as a "diagonal" spread because it has a horizontal component consisting of different expirations and a vertical component consisting of different strike prices. The differing time and strike price elements involved in a diagonal spread give the overall position an added element for profit on movements in the underlying exchange rate and implied volatility.

The primary advantage of using a diagonal spread strategy involves the staggering of the strike prices. This can allow a trader to short a near term out of the money option to help finance a purchased medium term at the money option. The higher probability of the near term option expiring worthless often means that the long medium term option can be converted into a vertical spread once the near term option expires that would be cheaper than if entered into initially. This opportunity gives this diagonal spread strategy high marks for potential profits, while at the same time putting a limit on potential losses since the longer-term option acts as a hedge for the shorter term option.

The profit and loss profile of a diagonal spread is limited to the difference between the strikes and the amount paid, or the credit taken in minus the difference between the strikes. The profile changes significantly if the short side of the spread expires worthless, leaving the trader with a long call or put position with a different expiration date.

At this point, the option trader can choose to liquidate some or all of their long option position; sell another option to establish a spread to offset some of the risk and obtain some premium income; reverse the position by converting the remaining option from a put to a call or vice versa by taking an opposite position in the underlying exchange rate; or use a partial or delta hedge to reduce their position's sensitivity to spot movements.

Ratio Spreads

Ratio spreads typically involve the simultaneous or legged spreading of one option against another with different principal amounts for each leg. Ratio spreads can be vertical, horizontal or diagonal, but the examples here will focus on vertical ratio spreads for simplicity.

Premium credit or premium neutral ratio spread option positions are a popular structure since the overall premium received is either positive or zero and this feature can substantially increase the attractiveness of establishing the option position.

Long Call Ratio Spread

The long call ratio spread consists of a purchased close to the money call option spread against a greater amount of sold call options with a strike price set further out of the money. Such a strategy is typically used to express a limited bullish view.

As the option profit and loss diagram below illustrates, the long 1:3 ratio call spread incurs unlimited risk above the higher short strike price. This is because two calls would not be covered in the case of sharp upward move in the underlying exchange rate. Furthermore, the maximum profit would be seen at the higher strike price, with the profit decreasing down to zero at and below the lower call strike price.

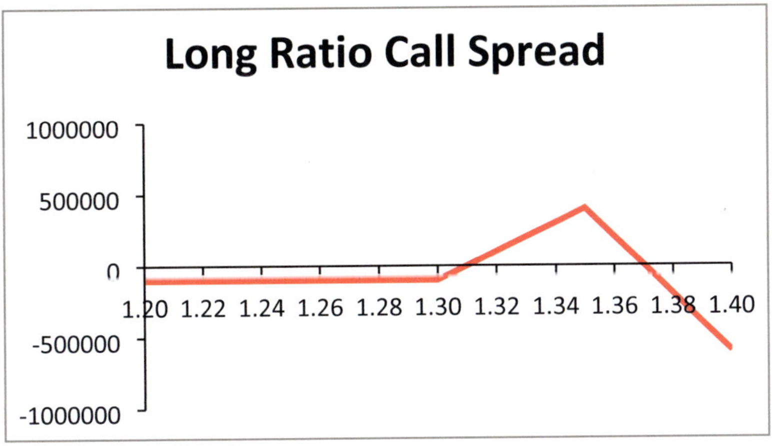

Figure #9: Profit and Loss diagram of a long vertical 1:3 ratio 1.3000 to 1.3500 call spread.

For example, a long ratio call spread trader might buy 10,000,000 euros of a 1.3000 EUR Call/USD Put and simultaneously sell 30,000,000 euros of a 1.3500 EUR Call/USD Put, with a three month expiration. The cost of buying the 1.3000 EUR call is offset by the premium received from selling three times the amount of the 1.3500 EUR call. In this case, the price of the purchased 1.3000 euro call is a 261 pip debit, which is fully offset by three sold 1.3500 euro calls at 87 pips each that equals a total credit of 261 pips.

Using European style options and with the underlying EUR/USD exchange rate at 1.3500 at the options' expiration date — which is the point of maximum profit on the ratio spread — the 10,000,000 Euro call option bought for 261 pips would now be worth 500 pips while the three short 1.3500 EUR call/USD put options would expire worthless. Thus, this would net the trader a 239 pip profit on the long 1.3000 trade or $239,000 plus the 261 pips total credit taken in from the three short 1.3500s or another $261,000, making the net profit at the 1.3500 strike price the combined sum of $500,000.

Alternatively, if the underlying exchange rate is below 1.3500, say at 1.3300 for example, then the long 1.3000 EUR call/USD put would be worth 300 pips for a net profit of 300-261=39 pips, plus the 261 pips credit from the sale of the three 1.3500 euro calls, making the net profit a total of 300 pips or $300,000.

Furthermore, if the exchange rate rallied to 1.3600 by expiration, then the three short 1.3500 euro calls would be worth 100 pips X 3 = 300 pips, and the long 1.3000 euro call position would be worth 500 pips, which would still result in a profit of 200 pips or $200,000 on the trade.

Nevertheless, if the exchange rate reaches 1.3750 at expiration, the long 1.3000 call covers one short 1.3500 call for a 500 point net gain, but the remaining two short 1.3500 calls would be worth 250 pips each X 2 = 500 pips. The position therefore breaks even at 1.3750 and begins to lose money if the EUR/USD exchange rate ends up anywhere above that level at expiration.

Short Call Ratio Spread

The short call ratio spread consists of a sold close to the money call option spread against a greater amount of purchased call options with a strike price set further out of the money. Such a strategy could be used to express a view where the market might fall somewhat or rise dramatically.

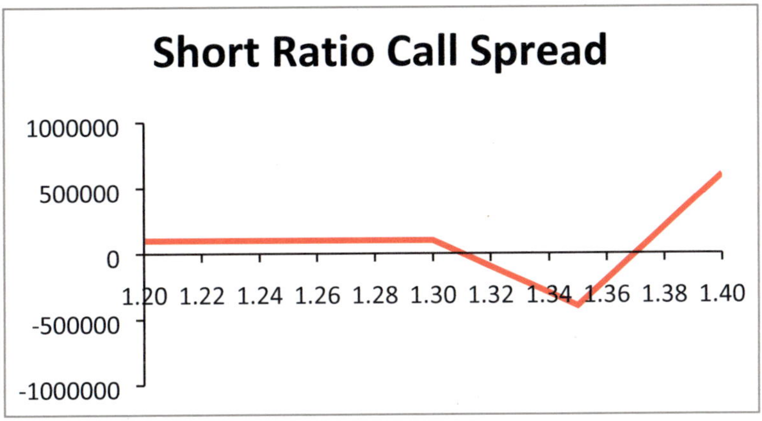

Figure #10: Profit and Loss diagram of a short vertical 1:3 ratio 1.3000 to 1.3500 call spread.

As depicted above, the short call ratio spread option profit and loss diagram looks like the mirror image of the long call ratio spread diagram reflected around the horizontal X axis. In the case of a short call ratio spread, a closer to the money strike price call is sold against a greater amount of an out of the money strike price call option. For example, this could involve buying three out of the money calls struck at 1.3500 and selling one closer to the money call struck at 1.3000 all expiring in three months' time.

Nevertheless, the risk profile on the above short call ratio spread position does not look as favorable to most traders as the long position. To begin with, the position will only pay off if the underlying exchange rate ends up over the 1.3750 breakeven level at expiration. With the position established at the 1.3000 level and with three months until expiration, the likelihood of the rate closing above that figure might be rather low, depending on current volatility levels.

As the above option diagram illustrates, the profit and loss for the short call ratio spread position at expiration in the direction of declining exchange rates below the short 1.3000 call's strike price has limited risk since none of the calls will be exercised.

For exchange rates situated above that 1.3000 call strike price, losses will initially accrue down to a maximum of 500 pips at the 1.3500 strike price as the short 1.3000 call gains in value. After that point, the position will appreciate in value with a doubled slope that reflects the existence of two net long call options. The position eventually breaks even at the 1.3750 level if initially established for a zero net premium.

Long Ratio Put Spread

The risk profile of the long ratio put spread is the mirror image of the long call ratio spread reflected around the vertical axis. The main objective behind using this bearish strategy is to profit from a limited downward move in the exchange rate. The position is established by buying a close the money put and selling a greater about of further out of the money puts.

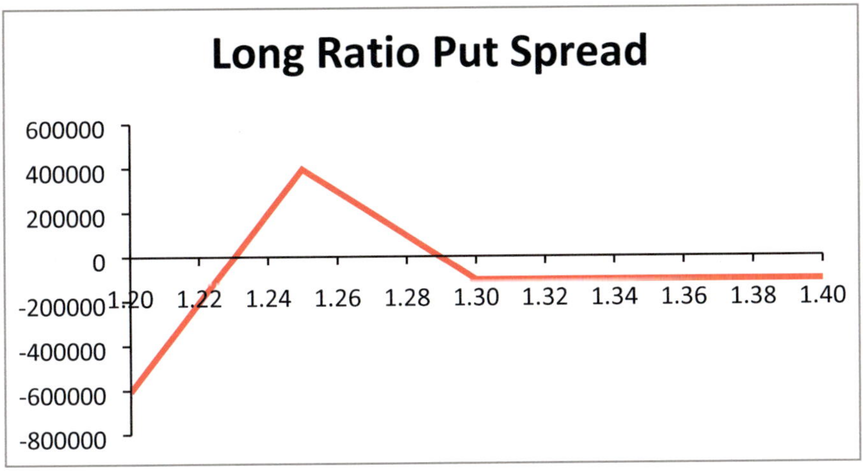

Figure #11: Profit and Loss diagram of a long vertical 1:3 ratio 1.3000 to 1.2500 put spread.

For example, a ratio put spread trader might buy 10,000,000 euros of a 1.3000 Euro Put/U.S. Dollar Call and simultaneously sell 30,000,000 euros of a 1.2500 Euro Put/U.S. Dollar Call, all with a three month expiration date when the EUR/USD spot rate is at 1.3000.

Using these parameters, the cost of buying the 1.3000 euro put is mostly offset by the premium received from selling three times the amount of the 1.2500 euro put. In this case, the price of the 1.3000 euro put is 257 pips, which is offset by the sale of three 1.2500 euro puts at 78 pips each, which equals 234 pips. At these prices, the long ratio put spread on a 1 by 3 basis would cost the trader a net amount of 23 pips or $23,000 to establish.

As the above option diagram illustrates, the profit and loss profile for this long ratio put spread position shows unlimited risk starting to emerge below the 1.2500 strike level, with gains noted from the 1.3000 strike level down to 1.2500. At the 1.2500 level — the level of this strategy's maximum profit — the short 1.2500 puts are worthless, but the long 1.3000 put is worth 500 pips, thereby giving the trader a net profit of 500 pips minus the initial -23 pips paid for the position for a maximum potential gain of 477 pips. Above the 1.3000 strike price, the entire position expires worthless, with the trader having lost a total of 23 pips, which is the amount that was initially paid for the position.

The profit zone for this strategy occurs when the exchange rate ends up between 1.2500 and 1.3000, with the trader's maximum profit seen at 1.2500. The downside risk increases with a doubly negative slope under the 1.2500 strike, because the trader is effectively naked short two put options at that strike price. These options can only be hedged by buying another put or by selling the EUR/USD currency pair, which would then leave the position with unlimited risk to the upside.

Short Ratio Put Spread

The short put ratio spread option diagram is the mirror image of the long put spread diagram reflected around the horizontal X axis. In the case of a short put ratio spread, a higher strike put is sold against a greater amount of a lower put strike.

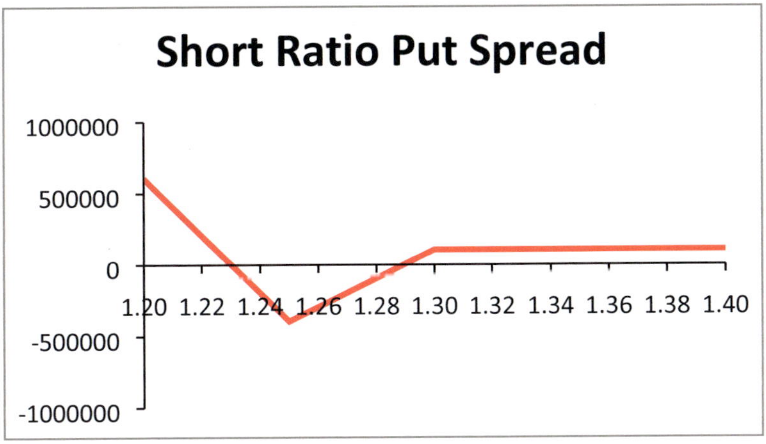

Figure #12: Profit and Loss diagram of a short vertical 1:3 ratio 1.3000 to 1.2500 put spread.

The above option diagram shows a short put ratio spread that involves buying three out of the moneys puts and selling one short at the money put. As you can see, the profit and loss profile for this strategy shows more risk and less reward near the current spot rate than the corresponding long ratio put spread position.

For example, a short ratio put spread trader might sell 10,000,000 euros of a 1.3000 Euro Put/U.S. Dollar Call and simultaneously buy 30,000,000 euros of a 1.2500 Euro Put/U.S. Dollar Call, all with a three month expiration date when the EUR/USD spot rate is at 1.3000.

Using these parameters, the credit from selling the 1.3000 euro put is mostly used to purchase three times the amount of the 1.2500 euro puts. In this case, the 1.3000 euro put sale brings in 257 pips, which is used to purchase three 1.2500 euro puts at 78 pips each, which equals 234 pips. At these prices, the short ratio put spread on a 1 by 3 basis would yield the trader a net credit of 23 pips or $23,000 to establish.

Once more, the risk profile on the short ratio put spread does not look as favorable as the long ratio put spread position, despite taking in an initial credit of +23 pips. The profit area on the short ratio put spread diagram is limited to 23 pips above the 1.3000 put strike price. Losses then accrue below the 1.2977 level down to a maximum of 477 pips at the 1.2500 strike price. At that point, those losses start to erode, with unlimited profits accruing at a double slope toward the strategy's lower breakeven level of 1.2262.

Straddles

The name of the straddle strategy has its origin in the shape of its profit and loss diagram, which shows two lines projecting diagonally in a V shape from a common inflection point, which is the straddle's strike price. These lines point either above the X axis to infinity in the case of a long straddle or below the X axis to infinity in the case of a short straddle. In other words, the graph's inflection point is placed below the graph's Y axis zero line when the trader is long the straddle, and above it when the trader is short the straddle. The displacement from the Y axis zero point is equal to the total premium either paid for the long straddle position or received for the short straddle position.

Long Straddle

The long straddle position typically consists of a long call and a long put of the same strike price and expiration date. For example, simultaneously buying a 1.3750 EUR call/USD put and a 1.3750 EUR put/USD call on the EUR/USD exchange rate expiring in one month's time would be establishing a long one month straddle position in the EUR/USD currency pair. In the forex market, straddles are typically established either at the money forward, with their strike prices equal to the forward rate, or at the money spot, with their strike prices equal to the current spot rate.

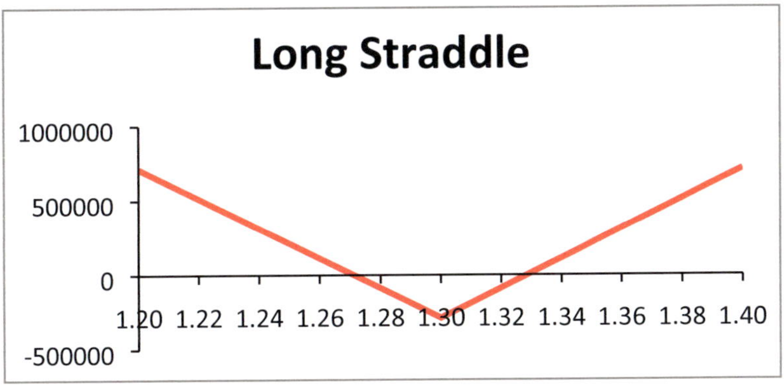

Figure #13: Profit and Loss diagram of a long 1.3000 straddle.

As the above illustration shows, the maximum risk in the position consists of the trader's initial cost for both the EUR put and the EUR call. The two arrows show the unlimited profit potential in the event of a major move in the EUR/USD currency pair within the active time frame of the option prior to its expiration.

The straddle is generally bought by option traders that are expecting a large move in the exchange rate in either direction. If the exchange rate rises by the strategy's expiration date, the EUR call will show a profit and the EUR put will expire worthless. The opposite would be true in the case of the exchange rate showing a decline, because the EUR put will then have value, but the EUR call will expire worthless.

Short Straddle

The short straddle consists of a short call and a short put of the same strike price and expiration date. For example, simultaneously selling a 1.3750 EUR call/USD put and a 1.3750 EUR put/USD call on the EUR/USD exchange rate expiring in one month's time would be establishing a short one month straddle position.

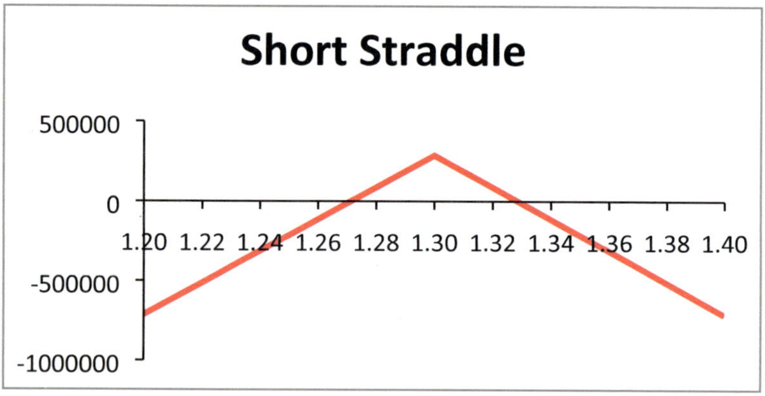

Figure #14: Profit and Loss diagram of a short 1.3000 straddle.

As the above illustration shows, the maximum gain in the position consists of the amount of premium the trader initially received for both the EUR put and the EUR call. The two downward pointing arrows show the unlimited loss potential in the event of a major move in the EUR/USD currency pair within the active time frame of the option prior to its expiration.

Option traders will often sell a straddle to generate income during periods when the underlying exchange rate is locked in a limited trading range. This strategy works well with near term at the money straddles in which the rate of premium decay over time is at its maximum. Nevertheless, if the exchange rate rises by the strategy's expiration date, the sold EUR call will show a loss but the sold EUR put will expire worthless. The opposite would be true in the case of the exchange rate showing a decline, because the short EUR put will then show a loss, but the short EUR call will expire worthless.

Delta Hedged Straddle Strategies

Straddles can also be traded on a delta neutral basis against the fluctuations observed in the underlying exchange rate. This is a way for an option trader to take a bet on what actual volatility will be observed in the future versus the implied volatility level at which the straddle is currently priced. If the trader thinks implied volatility is too low or too high, they can then respectively buy or sell the straddle and actively rebalancing their portfolio in the spot or forward market as the straddle's delta fluctuates with movements in the underlying exchange rate. If the trader is long the straddle, such rebalancing activities will typically be profitable, while if they are short the straddle, such rebalancing will usually be done at a loss.

For example, an at the money straddle will have two 0.50 delta options, if the rate moves significantly in one direction, the delta on one side of the straddle will be higher and the trader can buy or sell the corresponding difference in the spot market, locking in a profit on a portion of that side of the straddle

If the rate moves in the contrary direction once the trader has partially hedged one side, then the trader can take a profit on the spot transaction. If the rate continues in the other direction, the trader is completely hedged on the partial short spot trade and can sell an additional spot amount until the option/exchange rate ratio is 1:1.

Strangles

Strangles have a very similar risk profile and trading objective as Straddles, with the primary difference being that the risk/reward is spread over more than one strike price. In other words, the Strangle strategy consists of a long or short call and a long or short put with two different strike prices.

In most cases, both options comprising the Strangle are out of the money, with the underlying exchange rate trading somewhere in between the strikes at the time of execution. If the in the money options are used instead of the out of the money options, the resulting strangle is known as a Guts or Guts Strangle.

The graphic representation of the profit and loss profile for a Strangle is similar to the diagram for a Straddle, with the main difference being that instead of a single point from where the arrows originate, they now originate from either side of a flat line extending between the two strike prices.

Long Strangle

The graph below illustrates the risk and reward profile of the long Strangle position. Potential losses are represented by the region where the line is situated on the negative side between the two strike prices. The lines go into positive profit territory beyond both of the strike prices once the initial premium paid has been earned back.

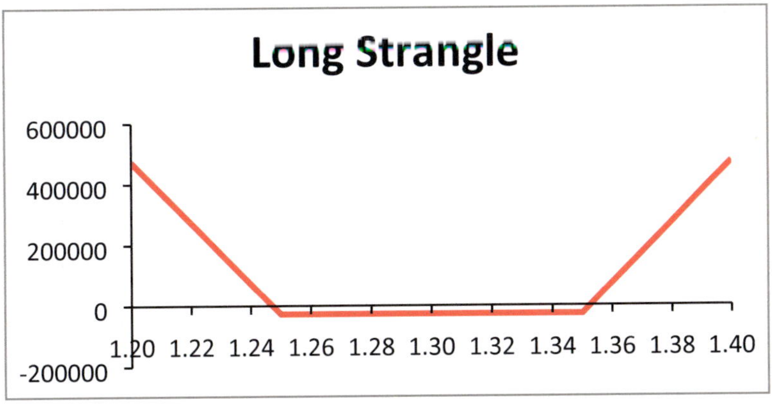

Figure #15: Profit and Loss diagram of a long 1.2500 to 1.3000 strangle.

Long Strangles cost less, but offer a lower return and an increased risk of expiring worthless than a Long Straddle. This is because the likelihood of an exchange rate trading within a limited range is generally higher than for the rate to have a spike of two big figures or more in a limited amount of time.

Going long a Strangle will generally have a much lower dollar cost than buying a Straddle since both options would be out of the money. Also, a long Straddle position would offer a trader the chance to benefit from a significant move in either direction.

Using the long Strangle as a trading position is similar to the strategy used for a long Straddle. Taking a long Strangle position in a currency pair is a sound strategy if a significant move in either direction is expected, and a limited amount of risk is to be assumed.

Nevertheless, the wider the Strangle's strike prices are situated from each other means that the overall price is lower, but a larger move in the underlying exchange rate is required to show a profit. The lower up front cost of a long Strangle would be the most compelling reason for a trader to position in this way versus a long Straddle.

Follow-up strategies for the long Strangle are similar to the long Straddle. One way of taking profits is to just liquidating the long Strangle position as soon as a significant market move has occurred in order to minimize the growing effect of time decay as the position approaches its expiration.

Another technique involves legging out of the long strangle position in a ranging market by selling back the long call if the market rises and/or selling back the long put if the market falls.

Short Strangle

The diagram below illustrates the risk and reward profile of the short Strangle position. Profit is represented by the line on the plus side between the two strike prices, with the lines going into the negative loss region on either side of the strike prices once the initial premium received has been consumed.

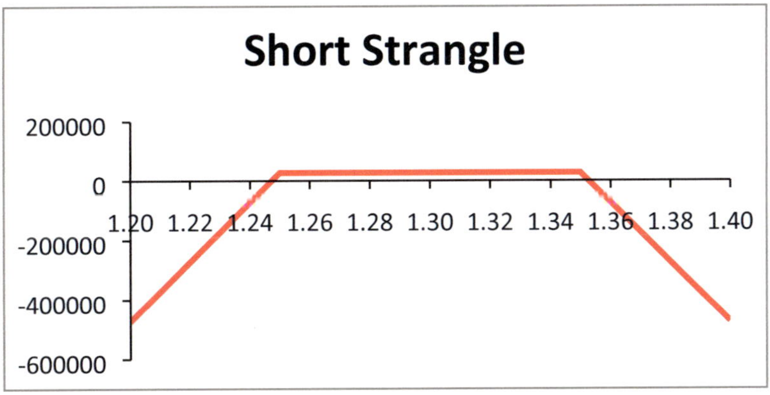

Figure #16: Profit and Loss diagram of a short 1.2500 to 1.3500 strangle.

Notably, shorting the Strangle, while providing time decay income as it moves closer to expiration, is still a potentially costly position to hold if not hedged with other options or a position in the underlying currency pair. This is due to the fact that unlimited loss potential exists in both directions outside the spot range situated between the two strike prices.

Nevertheless, the short Strangle position gives the trader a significant up front premium income with less risk than a short Straddle — although with less favorable time decay and less premium received.

Follow-up strategies for the short Strangle are similar to the short Straddle, with some variation due to the spread in strike prices. One way of taking profits is to just liquidating the position close to expiration after significant time decay has reduced its premium cost.

Another technique involves legging out of the short strangle position in a ranging market by buying back the short call if the market declines or buying back the short put if the market rises. Furthermore, if one side of the strangle retains a considerable amount of premium close to expiration, then an offsetting position can be taken in either the underlying currency pair or the option can be closed out.

Butterflies

The Butterfly spread is a popular neutral option strategy that can be achieved by combining both a bull and a bear spread using four options.

The long put or call Butterfly spread consists of going long two options, one with a higher strike and one with a lower strike, while simultaneously shorting two options of a middle strike price situated between the two long option strikes.

Butterfly spreads can be done completely with puts or completely with calls. A butterfly spread can also be constructed by spreading a long or short straddle against a short or long strangle, in which case it consists of both puts and calls. This latter type of spread is sometimes called an Iron Butterfly if the wing strikes of the Strangle are both roughly equidistant from the central strike price of the Straddle.

From a trading perspective, long Butterfly strategies are typically aimed at taking advantage of a flat or range bound market, while short butterfly strategies benefit from a significant move in the underlying currency pair. Butterfly strategies are more of a trading strategy, and so they are rarely used by hedgers.

Butterfly spreads can also be legged into. For example, a bullish trader might buy a call spread by purchasing an at the money call and selling an out of the money call with a higher strike price. They could then wait for the underlying market to appreciate closer to the upper short call strike price before selling a second call spread with the sold call's strike price set equal to the upper strike price of the initial purchased call spread and the purchased call strike price set out of the money at a higher level. The resulting legged position would be a long butterfly with better breakeven levels than if the long butterfly spread had been sold initially.

Whether established as a long or short position, butterfly spreads have limited risk of loss and limited potential for profit. In the case of a short Iron Butterfly, this risk is equal to the amount of premium initially paid for the spread, while the profit is capped at the difference between the middle and outer strike prices less the initial premium paid.

In contrast, a long Iron Butterfly's risk is limited to the difference between two strike prices, less the amount of premium received up front when the spread was transacted. The long Iron butterfly's profit potential is capped at the amount of premium initially received when purchased.

The Long Butterfly Strategy

No matter whether established using all calls, all puts or as a straddle/strangle spread, the long Butterfly strategy is typically directionally neutral with respect to the underlying currency pair. The long Butterfly strategy is typically used by a trader expecting a quiet market without much directional movement. As the graph below shows, the long Butterfly strategy has both limited upside and limited downside potential.

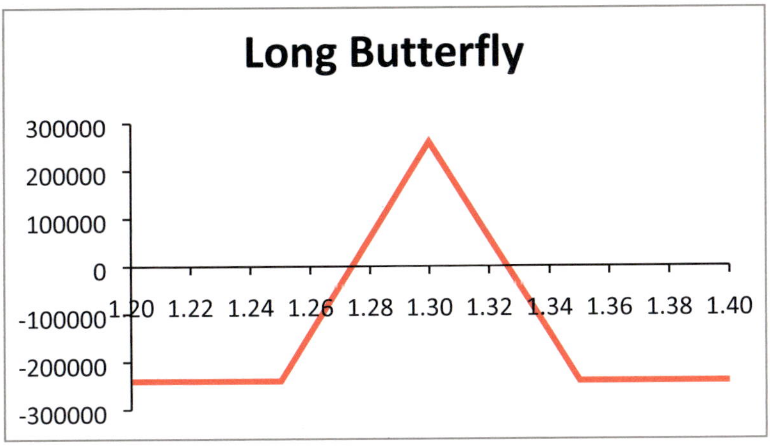

Figure #17: Profit and Loss diagram of a long 1.2500 to 1.3000 to 1.2500 Butterfly spread.

In the case of a long Iron butterfly spread consisting of a sold straddle and a purchased strangle, the optimum level for the underlying exchange rate at expiration would be at the center strike price. This result would leave the two sold middle strike options at the money, while the long higher strike call and the long lower strike put would both expire worthless. In this case, the maximum profit potential would be the premium initially received for buying the Iron Butterfly spread.

The same risk profile is evident in the call and put long Butterfly spreads, which both have the middle strike price level offering the highest return at expiration.

For example, consider the case of a long EUR/USD Butterfly spread with the underlying EUR/USD spot rate at 1.3000 expiring in one month. A trader could enter into this position by selling two 1.3000 EUR calls/USD puts and buying one 1.2750 EUR call/USD put and one 1.3250 EUR call/USD put all expiring in one month's time.

The trader in this example might instead pay a total of 64 U.S. Dollar pips for the long Butterfly spread by selling two 1.3000 calls at 148 pips each and simultaneously buying one 1.2750 call for 303 pips and one 1.3250 call for 57 pips. The trader in this situation would receive a total of 296 for the short call position, and would pay a total of 360 for the 1.2750 call and 1.3250 call positions, making a net cost to the trader of 64 pips on the spread as an up front payment.

Based on a principal amount of 10,000,000 Euros for the 1.2750 and 1.3250 calls and 20,000,000 Euros for the 1.3000 calls, it would cost the trader $64,000 to establish this long Butterfly position using those prices. The maximum risk for this long 1.27510-1.3000-1.3250 call Butterfly position would consist of the difference between the center and outer strikes minus the original cost of the position expressed in U.S. Dollar pips.

To establish a similar long Butterfly spread using puts, the trader would sell two 1.3000 Euro puts at 148 pips each, and buy a 1.2750 Euro put at 55 pips and a 1.3250 Euro put at 306 pips. The analogous long Iron Butterfly strategy would involve selling a 1.3000 Euro call at 148 pips and a 1.3000 Euro put at 148 pips, and buying a 1.3250 Euro call at 57pips and a 1.2750 Euro put at 55 pips.

The Short Butterfly Strategy

Like the long Butterfly strategy, the all call, all put or straddle/strangle short Butterfly spread is typically directionally neutral with respect to the underlying currency pair. In contrast, a trader's expectation in using the short Butterfly strategy is usually that the exchange rate will trade either well below or well above the middle strike price. As the graph below shows, the short Butterfly strategy has both limited upside and limited downside potential.

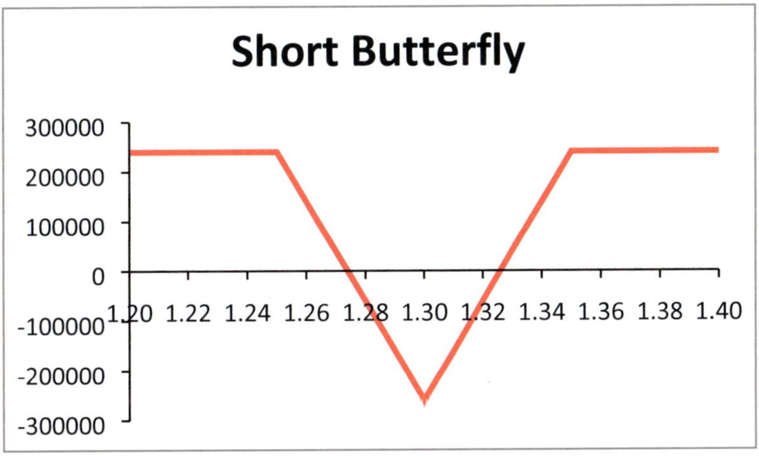

Figure #18: Profit and Loss diagram of a short 1.2500 to 1.3000 to 1.2500 Butterfly spread.

For example, consider a long straddle/short strangle short Iron Butterfly spread consisting of a purchased at the money call and put, spread against a sold out of the money call and out of the money put, all in equal amounts. If the market in the underlying ends up well below the lowest put strike price, then the transaction is profitable by an amount equal to the distance between the lower and middle put strike prices, less the premium initially paid up front for the short Iron Butterfly spread strategy.

If the market ends up at the center strike price at expiration, then the loss equals the premium paid initially for the short Butterfly. If the market ends up well above the highest call strike price, then the trading strategy is profitable by an amount equal to the distance between the middle and upper call strike prices, less the premium initially paid up front for the short Iron Butterfly spread.

Another example would be a short one month Butterfly position established using calls. Consider the case of a short EUR/USD Butterfly spread with the underlying EUR/USD spot rate at 1.3000 expiring in one month. A trader could enter into this position by buying two 1.3000 EUR calls/USD puts and selling one 1.2750 EUR call/USD put and one 1.3250 EUR call/USD put all expiring in one month's time.

The trader in this example might pay a total of 64 U.S. Dollar pips for the short Butterfly spread by buying two 1.3000 calls at 148 pips each and simultaneously selling one 1.2750 call for 303 pips and one 1.3250 call for 57 pips. The trader in this situation would pay a total of 296 for the long call position, and would receive a total of 360 pips for the 1.2750 call and 1.3250 call positions, making a net credit to the trader of 64 pips on the spread paid to them up front.

Based on a principal amount of 10,000,000 Euros for the 1.2750 and 1.3250 calls and 20,000,000 Euros for the 1.3000 calls, the trader would receive $64,000 to establish this short Butterfly position using those prices. The maximum risk for this short 1.27510-1.3000-1.3250 call Butterfly position would consist of the 250 pip difference between the center and outer strikes minus the original 64 pip credit of the position, or 186 pips.

Entering into a corresponding short Butterfly using puts would involve buying two 1.3000 Euro puts at 148 pips and selling a 1.2750 Euro put at 55 pips and a 1.3250 Euro put at 306 pips for a net credit of 65 pips. The corresponding short Iron Butterfly would involve buying a 1.3000 Euro call for 148 pips and a 1.3000 Euro put for 148 pips, and selling a 1.3250 Euro call for 57 pips and a 1.2750 Euro put for 55 pips, for a net cost of 184 pips.

Condors

The option spread trading strategy known as the Condor is similar to the Butterfly spread, with the primary difference being that the Condor is spread over four strike prices instead of over three strikes. The strategy takes its name from the similarity in the graph to a large bird with outspread wings.

The long Condor spread's similarity to the long Butterfly spread includes the trader's objectives for the strategy, which is that the exchange rate will end up within a limited trading range at expiration. In the long Condor's case, this hoped for result would have the exchange rate situated between the two middle strikes in the position that would each expire worthless in the case of an Iron Condor.

Like the Butterfly spread, the Condor strategy can again involve both a bull and a bear call spread or bull and bear put spread. Using the previous strike prices for a Condor in the EUR/USD currency pair, a long call Condor expiring in one month's time could consist of long one 1.2750 Euro call, one short 1.3000 Euro call, one long 1.3500 Euro call and one short 1.3250 Euro call.

The Iron Condor strategy is analogous to the Iron Butterfly strategy in that a closer to the money Strangle is spread against a further out of the money Strangle.

The Long Condor Trading Strategy

The long Condor trading strategy can be established using all calls, all puts or as a straddle/strangle spread known as an Iron Condor. In each case, the long Condor option trading strategy is typically directionally neutral with respect to the underlying currency pair, but it is entered into expecting nothing more than a relatively minor exchange rate move.

The graph below illustrates the limited risk, limited profit possibilities of the long Condor position, where the trader has sold the options with strike prices closer to the spot rate and bought the options with strike prices further away from the spot rate.

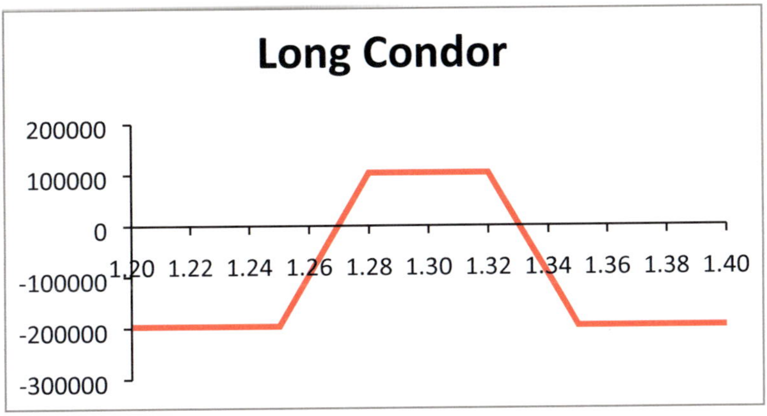

Figure #19: Profit and Loss diagram of a long 1.2500 to 1.2750 to 1.3250 to 1.3500 Condor spread.

The above profit and loss graph illustrates the long Condor's similarity to the long Butterfly spread, as well as its differences. The main difference between the two strategies is that instead of the maximum profit being the point over one central strike, as in the long Butterfly spread, the long condor's maximum profit is flat over a two strike price range.

The maximum profit for the long Iron Condor strategy is limited to the net amount received for the position when established and is achieved between the two middle strike prices.

If the currency pair rises, the maximum risk in the long Iron Condor position is the difference between the highest and next highest strikes minus the initial price received for the position expressed in U.S. Dollar pips.

If the currency pair falls, the maximum risk in the long Iron Condor position is the difference between the lowest and next lowest strikes minus the initial price received for the position expressed in U.S. Dollar pips.

For example, consider the case of a one month long 1.2750-1.3000-1.3250-1.3500 Iron Condor in the EUR/USD currency pair with the exchange rate now at 1.3000. The 1.2750 Euro put is bought for 54 pips, and the 1.3500 call is bought for 17 pips. On the short side, the 1.3000 put is sold for 148 pips, while the 1.3250 call is sold for 58 pips. All options are transacted in equal amounts, so the net credit of the entire position is 135 pips.

The maximum profit for the above example would be 135 pips, provided the exchange rate is between 1.3000 and 1.3250 at expiration. If the exchange rate is above or below the two middle strikes, the position's profit begins to erode, with a maximum loss potential of 115 pips equal to the difference between the inner and outer strikes less the 135 pip credit received for the position.

The long Condor can be used to adjust an option portfolio trader's existing position by helping neutralize their overall position's long gamma exposure if the Condor is bought in the near term against an option position further out in time. By itself, the long Condor is an excellent limited risk-trading vehicle to profit from an expected range trading environment for a credit compared to other option strategies.

In addition to allowing the trader to take advantage of a ranging market in the underlying exchange rate, the long condor is also a short volatility play that can be held in a volatile market with relative safety. It can also be legged into, thereby increasing the potential for trading gains.

The Short Condor Trading Strategy

Irrespective of whether it is established using all calls, all puts or as a straddle/strangle spread, the short Condor option trading strategy is typically directionally neutral with respect to the underlying currency pair, but it is entered into expecting a substantial exchange rate move.

To enter into a short Condor spread, a trader generally buys the options with a strike price nearer to the prevailing exchange rate and sells the options with strike prices further away from the exchange rate. Compared to the long Condor, the resulting profit and loss diagram is reversed around the horizontal X axis as shown below.

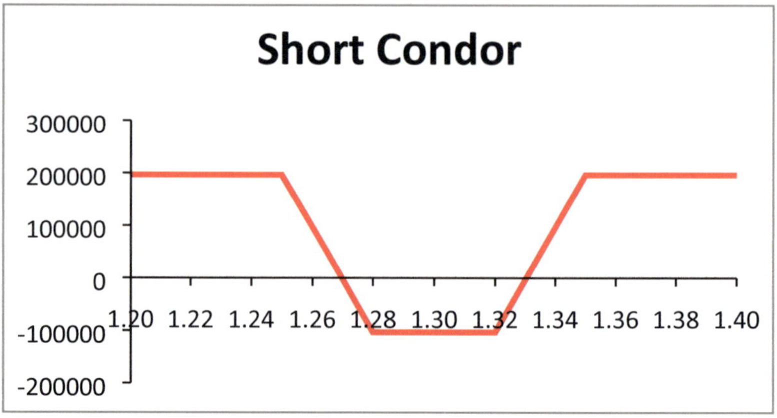

Figure #20: Profit and Loss diagram of a short 1.2500 to 1.2750 to 1.3250 to 1.3500 Condor spread.

The above profit and loss graph illustrates the short Condor's similarity to the short Butterfly spread, as well as its differences. The main difference between the two strategies is that instead of the maximum loss being the point at one central strike, as in the short Butterfly spread, the short condor's maximum loss is flat over a two strike price range.

When selling the put, call or Iron Condor, a trader is typically expecting the market to make a substantial move in either direction. Selling the put Condor has the same risk profile as the short call Condor and the short Iron Condor.

For example, consider the case of a one month 1.2750-1.3000-1.3250-1.3500 Iron Condor in the EUR/USD currency pair with the exchange rate now at 1.3000. The 1.2750 Euro put is sold for 54 pips, and the 1.3500 call is sold for 17 pips. On the long side, the 1.3000 put is bought for 148 pips, while the 1.3250 call is bought for 58 pips. All options are traded in equal amounts, so the net cost of the entire position is 135 pips.

The maximum loss for the above example would be 135 pips, provided the exchange rate is between 1.3000 and 1.3250 at expiration. If the exchange rate is above or below the two middle strikes, the position begins to make money, with a maximum profit potential of 115 pips equal to the difference between the inner and outer strikes less the 135 pips paid for the position.

Depending on an option portfolio trader's existing position, the short Iron Condor spread could help neutralize the overall position's short gamma exposure if the Condor is sold in the near term against an option position further out in time. By itself, the short Condor is an excellent trading vehicle to profit from an expected range breakout for a relatively low cost and limited risk profile compared to other option strategies.

In addition to allowing the trader to take advantage of a large swing in the underlying exchange rate, the short condor is also a long volatility play that can be held in a volatile market. It can also be legged into, thereby increasing the profit making possibilities.

Conversions, Reversals and Box Spreads

Because of the flexibility afforded by the use of currency options, an artificial forward position can be established using forex options making it possible to arbitrage such options against the real forward exchange rate.

For example, for a long position equivalent to an exchange rate, the trader could buy a call and sell a put. This position would give the trader the right to buy the exchange rate at the strike via the call position, and would obligate the trader to buy the exchange rate at the strike via the short put, effectively making the trader long the synthetic exchange rate.

For this reason, market makers and dealers will use conversions, reversals and box spreads for lending and borrowing at money market rates. By trading in the spot and forward market against their option position, the dealer or market maker can avoid paying wider option price spreads.

Conversions

Establishing a risk neutral arbitrage position by buying a currency pair forward and simultaneously selling a base currency call and buying a base currency put — all in equal base currency amounts and with the same delivery date — is called a conversion.

For example, consider the situation where a trader wishes to enter into a one month conversion position in the EUR/USD currency pair that is currently trading for value spot at 1.3000. They could purchase EUR/USD one month forward for 1.3002, and then simultaneously sell a one month

Euro Call/U.S. Dollar put struck at 1.3000 for 150 pips and buy a one month 1.3000 Euro put/U.S. Dollar call for 148 pips. While they pay away two pips to establish the forward contract, they receive two pips from the option positions. This conversion arbitrage position makes the trader neutral with respect to spot movements.

Conversions can set up for substantial credits in volatile markets, although the risk and dealing spreads involved in establishing these positions if legged into is sometimes not worth the potential rewards. If the position is traded through a dealer as part of a complementary strategy, then conversions are more viable.

Some swing traders use the conversion arbitrage relationship to convert a put into a call when their market view shifts.

Reversals or Reverse Conversions

The opposite of a Conversion is known as a Reversal or Reverse Conversion. The Reversal involves establishing an arbitrage position by selling a currency pair forward and simultaneously selling a base currency put and buying a base currency call — all in equal base currency amounts and with the same delivery date. The Reversal arbitrage is always characterized by a short position in the underlying exchange rate.

In the forex market, being short a base currency put and long a base currency call in equal amounts effectively makes the trader long the underlying exchange rate. Accordingly, traders can quickly hedge their option positions and create a Reversal position by selling the relevant currency pair in the same amount as the option positions.

To determine the option synthetic exchange rate the trader would add the difference of the call premium minus the short put premium to the strike price.

For example, with the spot EUR/USD exchange rate trading at 1.3000 and the one month forward rate at 1.3002, the one month 1.3000 Euro call/U.S. Dollar put can be sold for 150 pips, while the one month 1.3000 Euro put/U.S. Dollar call can be bought for 148 pips. Based on these prices, selling the Euro call and buying the Euro put would yield a 2 pip credit, resulting in a synthetic forward exchange rate 1.3002. If the trader then sells the underlying one month forward contract anywhere over 1.3002, then they have effectively established a profitable and risk free Reversal arbitrage position.

Box Spreads

Another form of arbitraging currency options involves simultaneously buying or selling a bull base currency call spread and a bear base currency put spread, with both vertical spreads having the same expiration, strike prices and base currency amounts. This arbitrage strategy is commonly known as a Box Spread.

The Box Spread is only worth the difference between the strikes, so selling the spread for more than the difference in strike prices would be a profitable riskless arbitrage opportunity for a trader. Conversely, buying the Box Spread for less than the difference between the strikes would also constitute an arbitrage due to the fact that at expiration the box will be worth more.

Box spreads are also sometimes used by market makers and dealers to borrow and lend money at the prevailing money market rates since such spreads can be established for a credit or a debit.

Furthermore, since these spreads are not readily available to trade as spreads, some traders will leg into them trading one side, the call spread, for example, and then transacting the put side. Depending on the volatility in the underlying currency pair and the liquidity in its options market, a box spread can usually be established without too many problems.

Nevertheless, when executing a four way position like the Box Spread, it is usually better to get the two sides done at one time that have minimal exposure to the underlying. Trying to trade each of the four options individually could be counterproductive and leave the trader with a losing arbitrage, thereby locking in a loss for their trading account.

Risk Reversals

The long risk reversal position consists of a short out of the money put and a long out of the money call with the same expiration date. The inverse position, short an out of the money call and long an out of the money put with the same expiration date is referred to as a short risk reversal.

Typically, this type of position is established for even money or zero cost, which means that premium is neither paid for the position nor taken in as a credit, with the sale of the short option completely paying for the purchase of the long option.

In addition, professional forex option traders often quote options in implied volatility terms based on their Delta risk management parameter. For a risk reversal, a common quotation request would be for a 25 Delta risk reversal where the asking party buys a 25 Delta out of the money call and sells a 25 delta out of the money put.

The response from the market marker is typically expressed as the implied volatility spread for the 25 Delta risk reversal. Thus, if they would sell the 25 Delta call for an 11% implied volatility and buy the 25 Delta put for a 10.9% implied volatility, then the 25 Delta risk reversal would be quoted as 0.1% in implied volatility terms.

The Long Risk Reversal Strategy

By itself, the long risk reversal strategy makes a trader long the underlying at the long call strike price, or long the underlying at the short put strike price. Thus, it has unlimited profit potential above the purchased call strike, and unlimited loss potential below the sold put strike, with a flat profile in between those strikes, as illustrated in the diagram below.

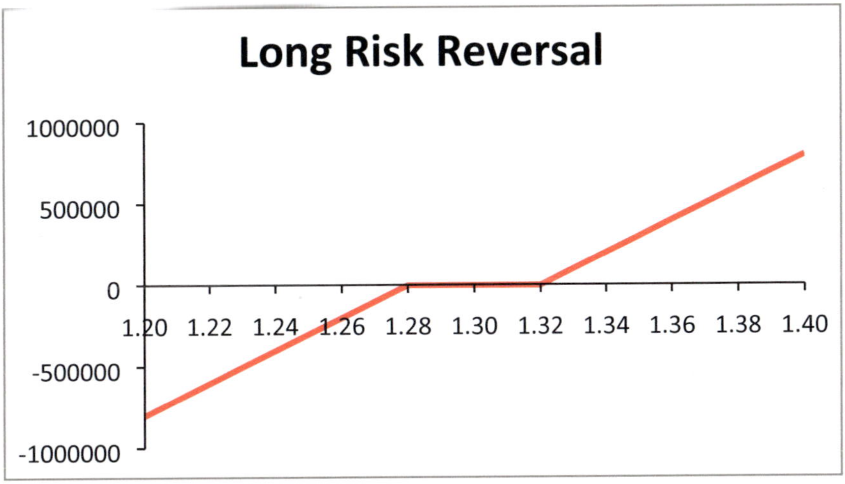

Figure #21: Profit and Loss Profile of a Long 1.2750 to 1.3250 Risk Reversal Strategy.

The above graph illustrates the unlimited profit potential of the long 1.3250 call and the unlimited risk of the uncovered short 1.2750 put, with a neutral line denoting the lack of risk or profit between the two strike prices at 1.2750 and 1.3250. Thus, at expiration, the zero cost risk reversal mimics an outright long or outright short position in the underlying exchange rate outside of the range defined by the put and call strike prices.

The Short Risk Reversal Strategy

In contrast, the short risk reversal strategy makes a trader short the underlying at the long put strike price, or short the underlying at the short call strike price. Thus, it has unlimited profit potential below the purchased put strike, and unlimited loss potential above the sold call strike price, with a flat profile in between those strikes, as illustrated in the diagram below.

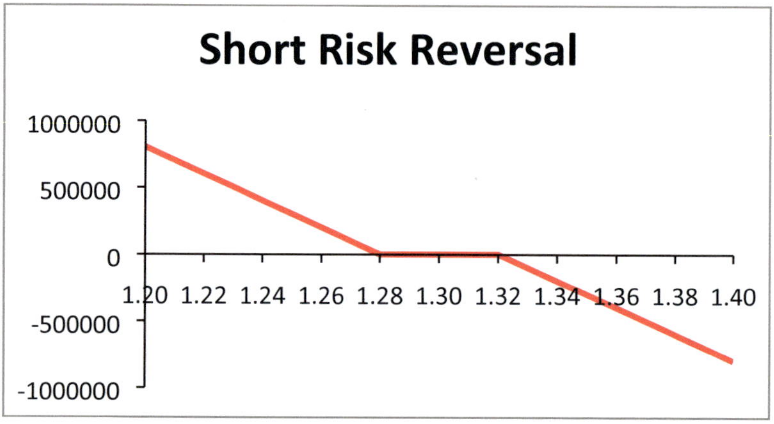

Figure #22: Profit and Loss Profile of a Short 1.2750 to 1.3250 Risk Reversal Strategy.

When combined with an underlying spot or forward position, the risk reversal gives a trader a speculative position over a particular exchange rate range limited by the strike prices of the long and short options.
The same is true for the collar spread often used by hedgers. In the foreign exchange option market, risk reversals and collars are often directly quoted in terms of the option's implied volatility.

If the position costs the trader an initial debit to establish, then the position is known as a *positive* risk reversal. The positive risk reversal is an indicator of the volatility skew of the options, since the cost of the position implies that call volatility would be higher than put volatility, indicating bullish sentiment in the market. Conversely, if the position generates a credit upon establishing, then the position is known as a *negative* risk reversal with the volatility skew indicating bearish sentiment in the underlying exchange rate.

While the zero cost risk reversal appears to require no capital outlay to establish, the naked short portion of the position will generally tie up a large amount of capital to hold in terms of the margin required unless bank credit lines can be utilized. This may not be a problem for a dealer or market maker trading the position as part of their option book and using credit lines, but for an individual or retail trader, the margin cost of holding the short option position could be prohibitive.

Furthermore, smaller traders looking for a long or short exchange rate position may do better by simply trading the underlying currency pair since dealing spreads for spot quotes are typically tighter than for the options required to execute a risk reversal strategy.

Chapter 6: Exotic Forex Option Trading Strategies

Using Exotic Forex Options to Trade Currencies

The use of exotic currency options allows forex traders numerous additional ways to take risk and express a detailed market view with an exotic option strategy.

The various exotic trigger options — such as knock outs, knock ins and one touch binaries — have useful applications for strategic currency traders, especially for those that employ technical analysis extensively to formulate their market views. In addition to trigger and binary options, average rate and basket exotic options add additional risk taking possibilities for a currency trader, with their special underlying assets being an average exchange rate or a basket of currencies.

Basically, the use of exotic options in forex trading helps widen the choices a currency trader has to express a market view to include numerous combinations. Such variations can help the trader take a vast number of directional, trigger, and premium trading positions over just about any foreseeable time frame.

For example, technical traders can often identify support or resistance points on currency charts that allow them to reduce their cost of buying an option by strategically placing a knock out trigger beyond those levels that makes it less likely to be triggered than its price would indicate.

A strategic trader might also be able to select a suitable exotic option to sell that will probably never be exercised in the case of a knock in option or which is likely to get cancelled prior to expiration by having its trigger rate hit like a knock out option or a one touch binary option.

At expiration binary options also provide strategic forex traders with a way to express a simple bet on the forex market. They can buy an at expiration binary option with an upfront payment that has a known pay out if their view is correct. This allows them to profit from a correct market view, without having the complication of unlimited profit potential or the added expense of paying for it up front by buying a vanilla forex option.

Binary Options for Strategic Directional Trading

Directional trading using binary currency options is generally a relatively straightforward endeavor due to the all or nothing aspect of the derivative's payout. A binary currency option has a well defined risk profile with downside risk limited to the premium paid and upside potential limited to the payout of the option.

In many cases, binary forex options can be traded as a short term directional strategy, with hourly, daily or weekly expirations available on all of the major, and some of the minor, currency pairs from numerous online binary option brokers. These binary options are available to retail and institutional traders alike, but can usually only be purchased with the required premium payment due up front.

A long-term binary option strategy can also usually be implemented via a major bank or financial institution that runs an exotic option market-making book. Nevertheless, such over the counter binary option transactions are typically based on credit lines that will need to be established before any binary option trading can take place. Some exchanges have been experimenting with offering binary currency options, such as the Chicago IMM. Binaries with longer-term expirations will generally involve paying a higher premium since they have greater time value.

Another interesting feature of binary forex options is that they are not always referred to as calls or puts, but instead are often referred to as up or down binaries. Thus, a simple bullish directional trading strategy would consist of buying an up or call binary or selling a down or put binary. Similarly, a bearish directional trading strategy would consist of buying a down or put binary or selling an up or call binary.

The advantage of using a forex binary call or put option versus a regular call or put option on an exchange rate is that the trader will receive a fixed return at expiration if their view is correct regardless of how much the exchange rate has fluctuated or moved in the meantime. A regular call or put option may retain premium until expiry, but it may or may not produce a significant return depending upon how much the option ends up in the money. This sort of variable return seen with vanilla forex options may not suit a speculative trader who simply wants to make a bet that the exchange rate will be above or below a particular strike price, and get a fixed payout if their view ends up being correct. In that case, a binary option could very well be a more suitable speculative vehicle.

Regular up or down binary currency options are also sometimes known as high or low binary options. These exotic forex options typically have a strike price and an expiration date and time. If the trader is correct on their market view and the spot rate ends up on the anticipated side of the strike price, the trader is paid the agreed upon payout as a fixed return on their premium invested to buy the binary. Conversely, if the trader incorrectly calls the market, then their entire investment is usually lost, although some such binary options can be structured to return a modest consolidation payout if the trader's view turns out to be wrong.

Long Binary Call for a Bullish View

For a bullish outlook on an exchange rate, the purchase of a long binary up, high or call option would be the most appropriate. For example, consider the case of a trader who is expecting the EUR/USD exchange rate to appreciate two full big figures or 200 U.S. Dollar pips within the next two days when the underlying exchange rate is trading at 1.3000. An up binary with a two day expiry and a strike price of 1.3200 could be the appropriate vehicle for their wager on the market.

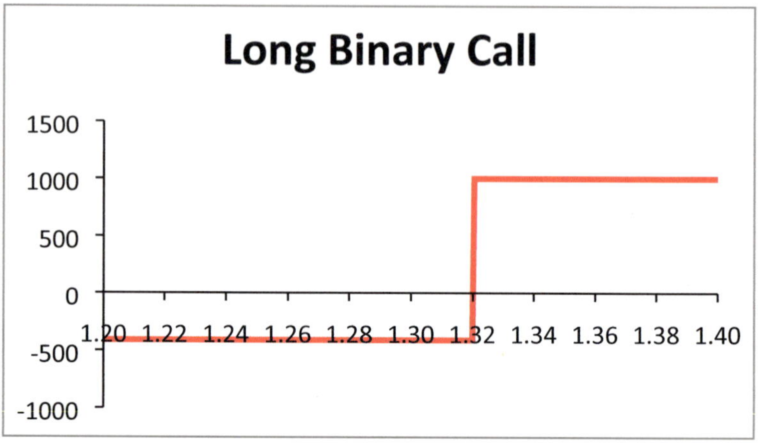

Figure #1: The at expiration profit and loss diagram of a long 1.3200 binary Euro call option with a $1,000 payout that was purchased for $410.

If they wished to have the 1.3200 up binary pay out $1,000 if the EUR/USD exchange rate ends up over 1.3200 at expiration in two days' time, then the binary will cost some fraction of the $1,000 payout amount. The amount of premium charged by the market maker will depend on the probability that the underlying market could close above the 1.3200 strike price of the up binary option contract, which would be based upon the forex option market's implied volatility for that time frame.

The market maker would determine the premium amount by using a pricing model and offer the option to the client. Furthermore, if the market maker thought that the 1.3200 strike price of the up binary could easily be exceeded because of a looming central bank decision, for example, the offer price of the option could be higher than its theoretical fair value.

Assuming the binary market maker believes there is a 41 percent chance the underlying rate could be over 1.3000, given a market implied volatility of 10 percent, they might quote a fair value offer of $410 for the $1,000 payout 1.3200 strike binary call option expiring in two days. Nevertheless, if the market maker believes the probability of the underlying rate rising in the next two days is higher than the option's fair value would indicate due to an upcoming event, then the binary option's price could be marked up accordingly. For example if the market maker believes that there is actually a 50 percent chance for the option to be in the money, they might price the binary at $500 instead of at $410.

In either case, if the EUR/USD rate is above the 1.3200 level when the option expires, the option holder receives the full $1,000 payout. Their profit on the transaction would then be the $1,000 received minus the premium initially paid for the option. Thus, if they paid $410 for the binary, their net profit would be $590, but if they paid $500, then their net profit would only be $500. Of course, if the underlying exchange rate fails to close above the 1.3200 strike price at expiration, then the binary option expires worthless and its holder forfeits the full amount they paid for the binary call.

If the bullish trader bought a one touch binary instead of an at-expiration binary option, then they would receive their payout if the market touched their trigger level at any time prior to the binary's expiration.

Short Binary Call for a Bearish View

For a bearish outlook on an exchange rate, the sale of a binary call option could be an appropriate strategy for a strategic trader. For example, consider the case of a bearish trader who was expecting the EUR/USD exchange rate to stay below the 1.3200 level over the next two days. If the underlying exchange rate is trading at 1.3000, a short binary call with a two day expiry and a strike price of 1.3200 could be an appropriate vehicle for their wager on the market's direction. They could choose the sold binary call's payout based on what they could comfortably afford to lose on the trade if their view turned out to be incorrect.

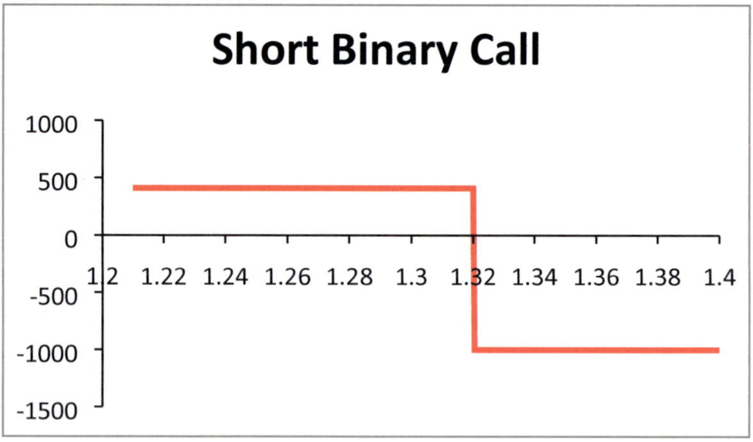

Figure #2: The at expiration profit and loss diagram of a short 1.3200 binary Euro call option with a $1,000 payout that was sold for $410.

If the trader wished to risk $1,000, then a binary call option with a 1.3200 strike price, a payout of $1,000 and with the underlying EUR/USD exchange rate trading at 1.3000 with two days to expiry and implied volatility at 10 percent might be trading around its fair value at the $410 level, which is only a portion of the $1,000 contract payout amount.

The premium amount received by the trader for selling this 1.3200 binary Euro call option will depend on the probability that the underlying exchange rate might close above the strike price. The market marker buying the option would determine that amount and make a bid on the binary option to their client. If the market maker thought that the EUR/USD spot rate would hold below the 1.3200 strike for two days, then they might bid a lower price for the binary call option than its fair value.

For example, if the market maker thinks there is only a 35 percent chance that the underlying spot rate could be over 1.3200, they might make a bid of only $350 for the $1,000 payout binary call option struck at 1.3200. If the market maker believes the probability of the underlying rate closing higher than the strike is higher, like 50 percent for example, then they might show a better bid for the binary option of $500.

In either case, if the EUR/USD spot rate is below the 1.3200 strike price level when the binary call option expires, then the speculative option trader who sold it keeps the amount received for it, i.e. the $350, $410 or $500 in premium that they initially received for the sold option. If the exchange rate closes above the strike price, then the option trader must pay the market maker the binary payout of $1,000, so their net loss is $1,000 less the initial premium received for selling the binary option.

If the bearish trader sold a one touch binary instead of an at-expiration binary option, then they would need to make its payout if the market touched the option's trigger level at any time prior to expiration.

Long Binary Put for a Bearish View

If a trader wishes to take a bearish outlook on the exchange rate for a currency pair, they could purchase a down, low or put binary option as an appropriate speculative vehicle.

For example, consider the case of a trader who is expecting the EUR/USD exchange rate to fall two big figures or 200 U.S. Dollar pips within the next two days when the underlying exchange rate is trading at 1.3000. A down or low binary Euro put with a two day expiry and a strike price of 1.2800 could be a suitable betting vehicle for their bearish market view.

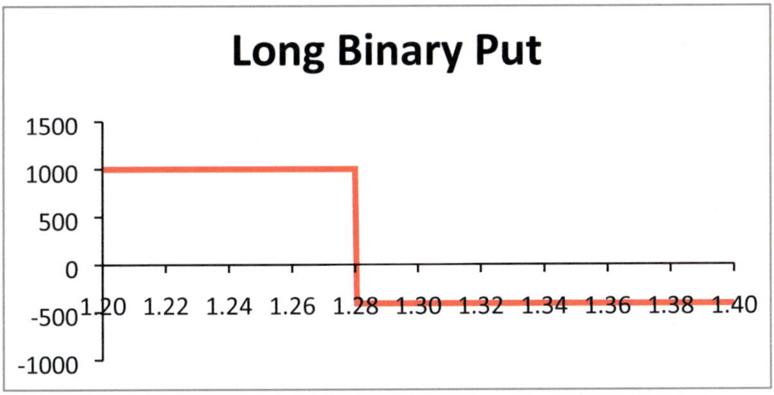

Figure #3: The at expiration profit and loss diagram of a long 1.2800 binary Euro put option with a $1,000 payout that was purchased for $410.

If they wished to have the 1.2800 down binary pay out $1,000 if the EUR/USD exchange rate ends up below 1.2800 at expiration in two days' time, then the binary will cost some fraction of the $1,000 payout amount. Again, the amount of premium charged by the market maker will depend on the probability that the underlying market could close below the 1.2800 strike price of the down binary option contract, which would be based upon the forex option market's implied volatility for that time frame.

The market maker would determine the premium amount by using a pricing model and offer the option to the client. Furthermore, if the market maker thought that the market could easily fall below the 1.2800 strike price of the down binary because of an upcoming key data release, for example, the offer price of the option could be higher than its theoretical fair value.

Given that the binary market maker believes there is a 41 percent chance that the underlying rate could be under 1.2800, and assuming a market implied volatility of 10 percent, they might quote a fair value offer of $410 for the $1,000 payout 1.2800 strike binary Euro put option expiring in two days.

Nevertheless, if the market maker believes the probability of the underlying rate falling in the next two days is higher than the option's fair value would indicate due to an upcoming event, then the binary option's price could be marked up accordingly. For example if the market maker believes that there is actually a 50 percent chance for the option to be in the money, they might offer the binary at $500 instead of at its theoretical value of $410.

Anyway, if the EUR/USD rate is below the 1.2800 level when the binary put option expires, the option trader receives the full $1,000 payout for their correct market view. Their profit on the transaction would then be the $1,000 received minus the premium initially paid for the option. Thus, if they paid $410 for the binary, their net profit would be $590, but if they paid $500, then their net profit would only be $500. Should the underlying exchange rate fail to close below the 1.2800 strike price at expiration, then the binary option expires worthless and the trader will forfeit the full amount they paid for the binary put.

If the bearish trader bought a one touch binary instead of an at-expiration binary option, then they would receive their payout if the market touched their trigger level at any time prior to the binary's expiration.

Naked Short Binary Put for a Bullish View

A trader looking to take a bullish view on an exchange rate with limited risk could contemplate selling a binary put option. Their reward for doing so would be the initial premium received for selling the binary put.

For example, consider the case of a bullish trader who was expecting the EUR/USD exchange rate to stay above the 1.2800 level over the next two days. If the underlying exchange rate is trading at 1.3000, a short binary Euro put with a two day expiry and a strike price of 1.2800 could be an appropriate vehicle for their wager on the market's upward direction.

With such a short binary put strategy, the trader could even safely tolerate a mild drop to 1.2800 without having the short binary option exercised against them. They could choose the sold binary put's payout based on what they could comfortably afford to lose on the trade if their bullish view turned out to be incorrect.

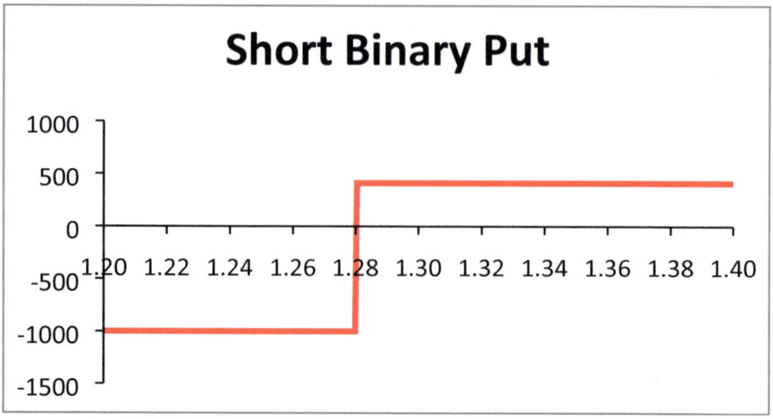

Figure #4: The at expiration profit and loss diagram of a short 1.2800 binary Euro put option with a $1,000 payout that was sold for $410.

If the speculator wished to risk $1,000 on this trade, then a binary put option with a 1.2800 strike price and a payout of $1,000, with the underlying EUR/USD exchange rate trading at 1.3000, and with two days to expiry and implied volatility at 10 percent might be trading around its fair value at the $410 level, which is only a fraction of the $1,000 contract payout amount.

In general, the sum received by the trader for selling this 1.2800 binary put option will depend on the probability that the underlying exchange rate might close below the strike price. The market marker buying the option would determine that amount and make a bid on the binary option to their client. If the market maker thought that the EUR/USD spot rate would hold above the 1.2800 strike for two days, then they might bid a lower price for the binary put option than its fair value.

For example, if the market maker thinks there is only a 35 percent chance that the underlying spot rate could be below 1.2800, they might make a bid of only $350 for the $1,000 payout binary put option struck at 1.2800. If the market maker believes the probability of the underlying rate closing below the strike is higher, like 50 percent for example, then they might show a higher bid for the binary put option of $500.

Either way, if the EUR/USD spot rate is above the 1.2800 strike price level when the binary call option expires, then the speculative option trader who sold it keeps the amount they received for it, i.e. the $350, $410 or $500 in premium that they initially got for the sold option. If the exchange rate closes below the strike price, then the strategic trader who sold the option must pay the market maker the binary payout of $1,000, so their net loss is $1,000 less the initial premium received for selling the binary option.

If the bullish trader sold a one touch binary instead of an at-expiration binary option, then they would need to make its payout if the market touched the option's trigger level at any time prior to expiration.

Knock Out Options for Strategic Directional Trading

Knock Out options are a type of barrier option that cease to exist if their barrier is reached prior to expiration. They have numerous interesting applications in directional trading, and they can help a strategic trader express a market view with considerable specificity. A purchased Knock out currency option has a well-defined risk profile with downside risk limited to the premium paid and unlimited upside potential as long as its trigger remains untouched at expiration. A sold Knock out currency option has unlimited downside risk unless its barrier is touched, and gains are limited to the premium initially received for selling it.

Since Knock Out options are considered exotic currency options, they typically do not trade on exchanges. Thus, the strategic trader wishing to incorporate them into their trading portfolio will typically need to contact a market maker in the Over the Counter market. This often makes Knock Out options more of a product for institutional traders, large corporations and high net worth individuals, rather than for smaller retail traders.

The following sections will describe how to use Knock Out options to express a particular bullish or bearish market view.

Long Knock Out Call for a Bullish View

A knock out call is also sometimes called a down and out option. This type of exotic option shares all of the elements of a plain vanilla call option, but it has the added feature of a knock out trigger that can render the option worthless if the underlying spot exchange rate trades at or through the knock out trigger level. The knock out call buyer's risk, as with any option purchase, is limited to the amount of the premium they initially paid for the option.

The speculator with a bullish perspective on an underlying exchange rate would purchase a knock out call and would receive most of the benefits of a plain vanilla call as long as the option did not get cancelled prior to expiration. Additionally, the knock out feature reduces the cost of the knock out call option, which in turn moves the trader's breakeven point on the strategy closer to the option's strike price.

In the event that the spot rate never trades at the trigger level, a bullish speculator who purchased the knock out call would have a significant profit potential if the exchange rate appreciates above the call's strike price, without ever trading at its trigger level.

Nevertheless, if the spot rate trades at the call option's trigger level before expiration, then the option contract is rendered null and void and is effectively cancelled, regardless of where the spot rate trades afterwards.

The knockout call option strategy's disadvantage is the risk of the option being knocked out in the event the underlying rate depreciated to the trigger level before the option's expiration date.

Generally, the original buyer of the knock out option contract gets to set four of the five parameters of the contract: the notional amount, the call strike price, the trigger level, and the option's expiration date. The seller of the option — who is generally an over the counter market maker working at a major financial institution — then determines the option premium.

The cost of the knock out call option and its strike price will determine the profit and loss profile on the trade. The cost of the knock out call option largely depends on the distance between the option's strike price and the forward rate, but it is also sensitive to the distance between the option's trigger level and the prevailing spot rate.

Increasing or decreasing the difference between the current spot price and the knock out call option's trigger level will make the exotic option's premium respectively cheaper or more expensive. A similar effect occurs when the difference between the strike price and forward rate is varied.

If the trader wants to pay a lower premium on the option when they have a strong view that the market will appreciate substantially in the near future, the most common way for them to lower the option premium cost by changing its parameters is to move the trigger level closer to the current exchange rate level. This change would make the probability of a knock out that would cancel the option more likely, and so it would increase the chances that the buyer would lose their premium without obtaining any potential benefits from the call option. Conversely, if the trader prefers to lower their risk of being knocked out on the long knock out call trade, then the trigger point could be moved further away from the spot rate. Generally, with the trigger point further away, the premium the trader will pay for the option increases.

For example, consider the case of a bullish technical trader who thinks the EUR/USD currency pair will appreciate significantly above the 1.3200 level over the coming month, as long as the spot market does not trade below technical support they have identified at the 1.2800 level. In this case, they might purchase a Euro Call/U.S. Dollar Put with a strike price of 1.3200 and a knockout level of 1.2800 expiring in 30 days.

With one month EUR/USD implied volatility at 10 percent and the spot rate at 1.3000, such an option would cost roughly 0.0062 points or 62 pips. Thus, the trader would need to pay a premium of $62,000 for a10,000,000 euro notional amount of this option.

The diagram below shows what the profit and loss profile of this option would be if the option is not knocked out with a solid line and uses a dashed line to illustrate the net loss that would result if the option is cancelled prematurely if its trigger level trades prior to expiration.

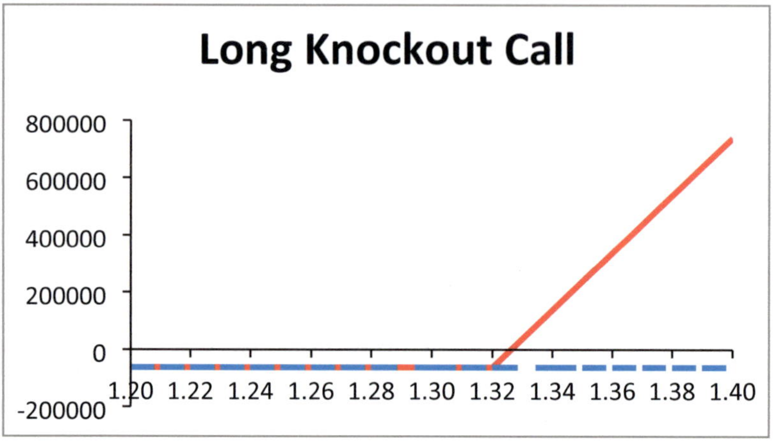

Figure #5: The at expiration profit and loss diagram of a long 1.3200 knock out Euro call/U.S. Dollar Put option with a knock out level of 1.2800 in an amount of 10,000,000 euros and costing 62 pips for a total premium paid out of $62,000.

The trader might compare this knock out option's cost of 62 pips to the cost of 71 pips for the otherwise identical vanilla 1.3200 Euro call/U.S. Dollar put with the same expiration date. In this case, adding the knock out feature at the 1.2800 trigger level reduces the one month 1.3200 Euro call option's theoretical value by 9 pips, or by $9,000 on a 10,000,000 euro notional amount.

Naked Short Knock Out Call for a Bearish View

In the situation where a speculative trader has a bearish view on the exchange rate for a currency pair, the sale of a knock out call could be an appropriate strategy if managed properly. The further out of the money the trigger level is fixed on the short option contract, the less probability of the option getting knocked out. Therefore, when selling a knock out call, the trigger point element will be a key-determining factor in the pricing of the option.

Ideally, when selling a knock out call based on a bearish perspective, the trigger point could be placed at a level that is deemed very likely to trade in the near future to knock out the option. For example, this trigger could be put at a level comfortably above any strong technical support points seen on the chart for the underlying exchange rate.

If the trader has only a mildly bearish expectation, the trigger level could be set closer to the prevailing exchange rate, but the option premium received would be notably less. Nevertheless, if the speculator is very bearish on the underlying, the trigger point could be placed lower, thereby making the option's sale more lucrative in terms of the premium received for it.

For example, consider the case of a bearish technical trader who thinks that the EUR/USD currency pair will be unlikely to rise above the 1.3200 level over the coming month, and that the rate is also likely to quickly trade down to the 1.2800 level. In this case, they might sell a Euro Call/U.S. Dollar Put with a strike price of 1.3200 and a knockout level of 1.2800 expiring in 30 days.

With one month EUR/USD implied volatility at 10 percent and the spot rate at 1.3000, such an option would bring in roughly 0.0062 points or 62 pips. Thus, the trader would receive a premium of

$62,000 for a10,000,000 euro notional amount of this option.

The diagram below shows what the profit and loss profile of this short knock out option would be if the option is not knocked out with a solid line. It also displays a dashed line to illustrate the net gain that would result if the option is cancelled prematurely if its trigger level trades prior to expiration.

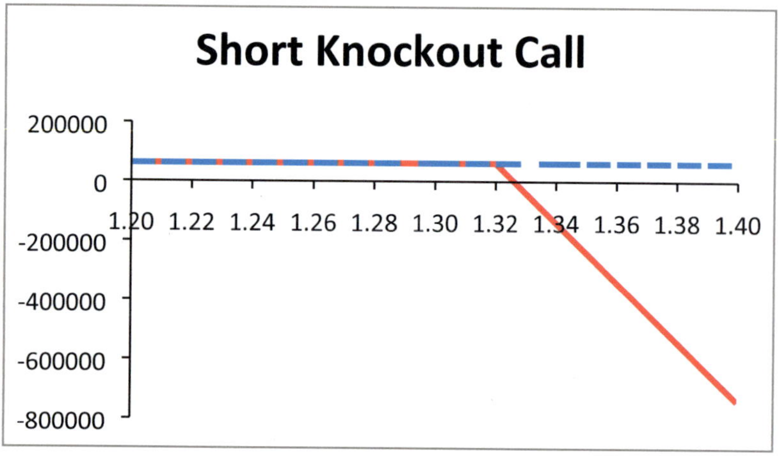

Figure #6: The at expiration profit and loss diagram of a short 1.3200 knock out Euro call/U.S. Dollar Put option with a knock out level of 1.2800 in an amount of 10,000,000 euros and yielding 62 pips for a total premium received of $62,000.

The trader might compare this sold knock out option's yield of 62 pips to the yield of 71 pips for the otherwise identical vanilla 1.3200 Euro call/U.S. Dollar put with the same expiration date. In this case, adding the knock out feature at the 1.2800 trigger level reduces the one month 1.3200 Euro call option's theoretical value by 9 pips, or by

$9,000 on a 10,000,000 euro notional amount, but if their bearish market view is correct, the option may be cancelled quickly.

Long Knock Out Put for a Bearish View

Exotlc option traders sometimes call a knock out put option an up and out option. This type of exotic option is similar to a plain vanilla put option, with the exception that it has a knock out trigger that can cause the option to immediately expire worthless if the underlying spot exchange rate trades at or through the knock out trigger level. The risk that a knock out put buyer takes, as with any option purchase, is limited to the amount of the premium they initially paid for the bearish option strategy.

A speculative trader wishing to take a bullish view on an underlying exchange rate could purchase a knock out put. In doing so, they would receive most of the benefits of owning a plain vanilla put provided that the option did not get cancelled or knocked out prior to expiration. Also, the knock out feature reduces the cost of the knock out put option, and therefore moves the trader's breakeven point on their bearish strategy nearer to the option's strike price.

If the spot rate never trades at the trigger level, a bearish speculator who purchased the knock out put would have a significant profit potential if the exchange rate depreciates below the put's strike price, without ever trading at its trigger level, which should be placed strategically above the spot rate.

Nonetheless, should the spot rate trade up to the put option's trigger level prior to expiration, then the option contract immediately expires and is effectively cancelled, no matter where the currency pair's spot rate subsequently trades.

The long knockout put option strategy's main disadvantage is the risk of the option being knocked out in the event the underlying rate appreciates to the trigger level before the option's expiration date.

In general, the original buyer of the knock out option contract gets to set the parameters of the contract, including the notional amount, the put strike price, the trigger level above the market, and the option's expiration date. The option market maker then determines the option's premium based on market parameters like implied volatility, interest rates and the spot rate.

The premium or cost paid for the knock out put option and its strike price will determine the profit and loss profile on the trade. The cost of the knock out put option largely depends on the distance between the option's strike price and the forward rate, but it is also sensitive to the distance between the option's trigger level and the prevailing spot rate.

A higher or lower difference between the prevailing spot price and the trigger level of the knock out put will make the exotic option respectively less or more expensive. This same effect is observed when the difference between the strike price and the forward rate is changed.

When a trader wants to reduce the premium paid on the knock out put option, especially if they have a strongly bearish view on the market, they often move the option's trigger level lower, and hence nearer to that of the prevailing exchange rate. This change would make the probability of a knock out that would cancel the option more likely, and so it would increase the chances that the buyer would lose their premium without obtaining any potential benefits from being able to exercise the put option. On the other hand, if the bearish trader wants to reduce the risk of being knocked out on the long knock out put trade, then they could move the trigger point upwards and further away from the spot rate. Generally, with the trigger point being moved further away, the premium the trader will pay for the option increases, although the price of the analogous vanilla put option is an upward limit.

As an illustration, consider the case of a bearish technical trader who thinks the EUR/USD currency pair will depreciate significantly below the 1.2800 level over the coming month, as long as the spot market does not trade above technical resistance they have identified at the 1.3200 level. In this case, they might purchase a Euro Put/U.S. Dollar Call with a strike price of 1.2800 and a knockout level of 1.3200 expiring in 30 days.

If one month implied volatility for EUR/USD is trading at 10 percent and the spot rate is at 1.3000, such an option would cost roughly 0.0062 points or 62 pips. This means the trader would pay a premium of $62,000 to buy a10, 000,000 Euro notional amount of this option.

The graph below shows what the profit and loss profile of this option would look like if the option is not knocked out with a solid line. The graph uses a dashed line to illustrate the net loss that would result if the option is cancelled prematurely if its 1.3200 trigger level trades prior to expiration.

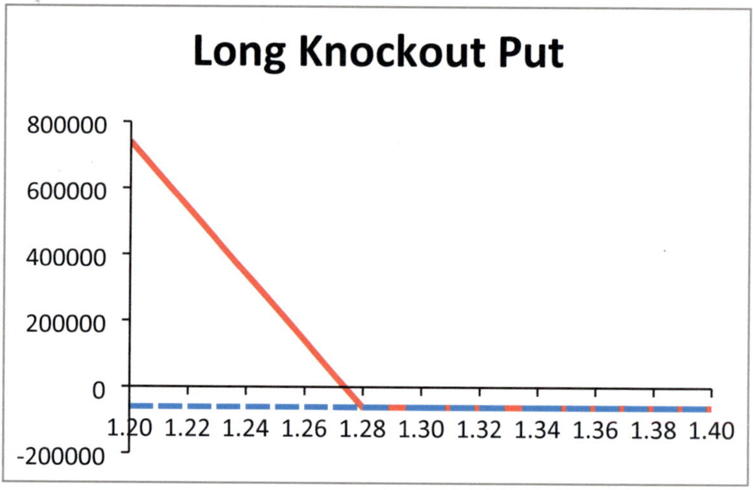

Figure #7: The at expiration profit and loss diagram of a long 1.2800 knock out Euro put/U.S. Dollar Call option with a knock out level of 1.3200 in an amount of 10,000,000 euros and costing 60 pips for a total premium paid out of $60,000.

For comparison purposes, this knock out option's cost of 60 pips can be related to the cost of 69 pips for the otherwise identical vanilla 1.2800 Euro put/U.S. Dollar call expiring on the same date. In this example, the addition of the knock out feature at the 1.3200 trigger level decreases the theoretical value of the one month 1.2800 Euro put option by 9 pips, which would be $9,000 for a 10,000,000 Euro notional amount.

Naked Short Knock Out Put for a Bullish View

When a speculative trader wishes to take a bearish view on a currency pair's exchange rate, they could sell a knock out put option. The more out of the money that the trigger level is set on the short put option, the less likely the option is to get knocked out. Thus, when shorting a knock out put, the trigger level will be an important factor determining the price of the option.

When selling a knock out put based on a bullish market view, the trigger point can be placed at a level that is deemed very likely to trade in the near future so that the option is knocked out quickly. For example, the trader could set the trigger at a level comfortably below any strong technical resistance points seen on the underlying currency pair's exchange rate chart. If all goes well, normal fluctuations in the exchange rate will result in the option's early cancellation by hitting the trigger prior to expiration.

A trader with only a mildly bullish view could set the trigger level closer to the prevailing exchange rate, but the option premium they receive for it would be significantly reduced. Furthermore, speculators with a very bullish view on the underlying could place their knockout put trigger level higher, thereby making the option's premium higher and its sale more lucrative.

For illustration purposes, consider the situation where a bullish technical trader has the view that the EUR/USD currency pair will be unlikely to fall below the 1.2800 level over the coming month, and that the rate is also likely to quickly trade up to the 1.3200 level in the near future. In this situation, they might short a Euro Put/U.S. Dollar Call with a strike price of 1.2800 and a knock out level of 1.3200 expiring in 30 days.

If one month EUR/USD implied volatility is trading at 10 percent and the spot rate is situated at 1.3000, such an option would bring in roughly 0.0060 points or 60 pips. This means the trader would take in a premium of $60,000 for a10,000,000 Euro face amount of this knock out option.

The figure below shows with a solid line what the profit and loss profile of this short knock out put option would be if the option is not knocked out. It also displays a dashed line to show the net profit that the trade would yield if the option gets cancelled early by having its 1.3200 trigger level trade before it expires.

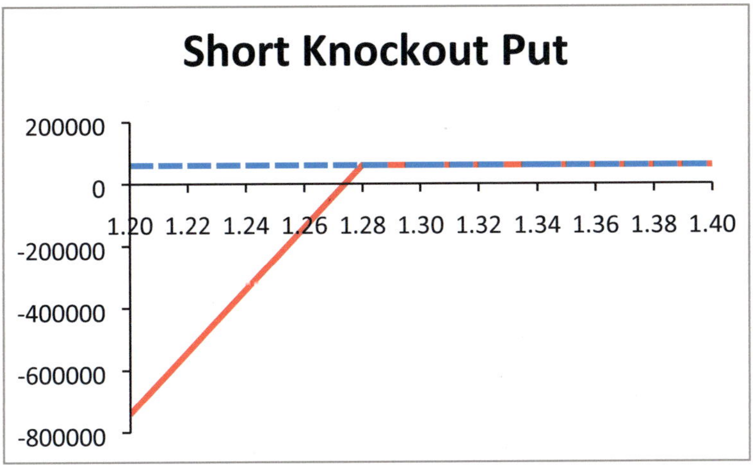

Figure #8: The at expiration profit and loss diagram of a short 1.2800 knock out Euro Put/U.S. Dollar Call option with a knock out level of 1.3200 in an amount of 10,000,000 euros and yielding 60 pips for a total premium received of $60,000.

This trade maximum return of 60 pips might be compared to the yield of 69 pips for the otherwise identical vanilla 1.2800 Euro Put/U.S. Dollar Call expiring on the same date. By adding the knock out feature at the 1.2800 trigger level, the price of a one month 1.2800 Euro put option is reduced by 9 pips, or by $9,000 on a 10,000,000 Euro notional amount, but if the trader's bullish market view turns out to be right, then the option could quickly be cancelled.

Knock In Options for Strategic Directional Trading

Knock In options are a type of barrier option that only come into existence if their barrier is reached prior to expiration. They have numerous interesting applications in directional trading, and they can help a strategic trader express a market view with considerable specificity.

A purchased Knock In currency option has a well-defined risk profile with downside risk limited to the premium paid and unlimited upside potential as long as its trigger has been touched by expiration. A sold Knock In currency option has unlimited downside risk if its barrier is touched, and gains are limited to the premium initially received for selling it.

Since Knock In options are considered exotic currency options, they typically do not trade on exchanges. This means that the strategic trader wishing to incorporate them into their trading portfolio will typically need to contact a market maker in the Over the Counter market. As a result, this situation often makes Knock In options more of a product for institutional traders, large corporations and high net worth individuals, rather than for smaller retail traders.

The following sections will describe how to use Knock In options to express a particular bullish or bearish market view.

Long Knock In Call for a Bullish View

A Knock in Call option shares all of the elements of a plain Vanilla Call option, but it only comes into existence if the underlying spot exchange rate trades at or through the knock in trigger level incorporated into the option contract. In the event that the knock in trigger level is never reached by the time it expires, the knock in option is permanently voided and has no payout. The reason the Knock in is referred to as such is the fact that the option trigger must be reached for the option to exist, so the option gets knocked into existence when the underlying market trades at the trigger level.

As is the case with a Knock out option, the knock in feature generally reduces the premium of the exotic knock in Call option versus that of a plain Vanilla Call. The strategy behind the use of a Knock in Call for a bullish outlook on an exchange rate is that the trader is expecting the underlying rate to move lower to the option's knock in level first, which triggers the option into existence, and for the spot rate to then trade higher to end up above the Knock in Call option's strike price by its expiration date.

The principal reason for a speculator to use a Knock in Call versus a plain Vanilla Call is the reduced premium they will need to pay due to the Knock in feature. As in other purchased options, the risk for the buyer of a Knock in Call option is limited to their initial cash outlay for the position. Their positive returns will only start to accrue once the option is knocked in and the underlying exchange rate then appreciates above the Knock in Call option's strike price.

The main disadvantage of using this strategy is the risk of the Knock in Call option not being triggered by the underlying exchange rate falling to the trigger level before the option's expiration date. The buyer of the Knock in Call option sets four parameters of the contract consisting of: the currency pair, the notional amount of one currency, the Call strike price, the knock in trigger level and the option's expiration date. The market maker selling this exotic option then typically determines the option premium based on the market determined implied volatility for that expiration date, the prevailing spot rate and the forward rate.

To reduce the premium of a Knock in Call option, the strategic trader can either raise the strike price or lower the trigger level, since the notional amount and option terms are generally fixed. Therefore, setting the trigger level further from the prevailing exchange rate — and hence less likely to be touched so that the option comes into existence — or setting the strike price higher — and hence more out of the money and less likely to be exercised — would be the easiest way to adjust the option premium lower.

If the Knock in Call's strike price is set further out of the money, then the trader should be expecting a suitably greater amount of appreciation in the underlying exchange rate so that they can break even after paying the Knock in call option's initial premium cost. Therefore, the differences between the strike price, the trigger level and the current level of the underlying exchange rate, as well as the implied volatility, make up the major factors used when determining the Knock in call option's premium.

Follow up strategies for the Knock in Call option include changing the terms of the option contract to maximize the trader's profit after a move. Keeping the term and amounts of the option fixed, a move lower in the spot rate could be an opportunity to move the strike price of the Knock in Call lower. If the spot rate moved higher, then the trigger level could be adjusted higher, thereby making it more likely to be triggered bringing the option into existence. Both of these adjustments would require the payment of additional premium.

As an example, consider the case of a bullish technical trader who thinks the EUR/USD currency pair will appreciate significantly above the 1.3200 level over the coming month, but that it will first retrace down to technical support they have identified at the 1.2800 level. In this case, they might purchase a Euro Call/U.S. Dollar Put with a strike price of 1.3200 and a knock in level of 1.2800 expiring in 30 days.

With one month EUR/USD implied volatility at 10 percent and the spot rate at 1.3000, such an option would cost roughly 0.0008 points or 8 pips. Thus, the trader would need to pay a premium of $8,000 for a10,000,000 euro notional amount of this option.

The diagram below shows what the profit and loss profile of this option would be if the option is not knocked in with a solid line and uses a dashed line to illustrate the net return that would result if the Knock in call option comes into existence if its trigger level trades prior to expiration.

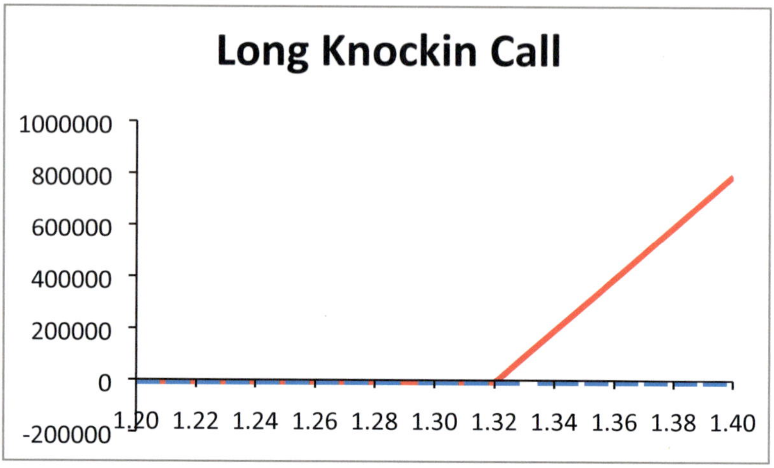

Figure #9: The at expiration profit and loss diagram of a long 1.3200 knock in Euro Call/U.S. Dollar Put option expiring in one month with a knock in level of 1.2800 in an amount of 10,000,000 euros and costing 8 pips for a total premium paid out of $8,000.

The trader might compare this Knock in option's cost of 8 pips to the cost of 71 pips for the otherwise identical vanilla 1.3200 Euro call/U.S. Dollar put with the same expiration date. In this case, adding the knock in feature at the 1.2800 trigger level reduces the one month 1.3200 Euro Call option's theoretical value by 63 pips, or by $63,000 on a 10,000,000 euro notional amount.

Short Knock In Call for a Bearish View

In the case of the speculator having a bearish perspective on an exchange rate, the sale of a Knock in Call option could be appropriate. The closer to the money the trigger level is set on the option contract, the greater the probability of the option getting triggered and coming into existence. Therefore, when selling a Knock in call, the trigger level will be an important strategic element determining the success of the strategy and it is also a key input into the pricing of the Knock in option.

With a bearish market view in mind, the trigger point of the Knock in Call should be placed safely away from the present level of the underlying exchange rate. Ideally, this trigger will be placed above a key resistance level or below a key support level that is deemed less likely to trade from a technical perspective. Nevertheless, the further away the trigger is placed from the prevailing spot rate, the lower the option premium that will be received for selling the Knock in Call since the chances of the option being knocked into existence is reduced.

If the speculator is strongly bearish, the trigger point of the sold Knock in Call could be placed above the current spot rate. This would make the premium received for the option higher since the Knock in Call would be closer to the money or even in the money when knocked in and would therefore increase the strategy's yield, if the bearish view turns out to be correct. This sort of Knock in option is sometimes called a Reverse Knock in option or an Up and In call option.

In the case of a mildly bearish view, the knock in trigger level could be set below the prevailing exchange rate, so that the Knock in Call option would be further out of the money if it gets triggered into existence.

For example, consider the case of a technical trader who thinks the EUR/USD currency pair will probably end up below the 1.3200 spot level over the coming month, but that it might rally above that level if the market fails to trade below key support they have identified at the 1.2800 level. In this case, they might sell a Euro Call/U.S. Dollar Put with a strike price of 1.3200 and a knock in level of 1.2800 expiring in 30 days.

With one month EUR/USD implied volatility at 10 percent and the spot rate at 1.3000, such an option would yield roughly 0.0008 points or 8 pips. Thus, the trader would receive a premium of $8,000 for a10,000,000 euro notional amount of this option.

The graph show below illustrates what the profit and loss profile of this short exotic option would be if the option is not knocked in with a solid line, and it uses a dashed line to show the net return that would result if the Knock in Call option comes into existence if its 1.2800 trigger level trades prior to expiration.

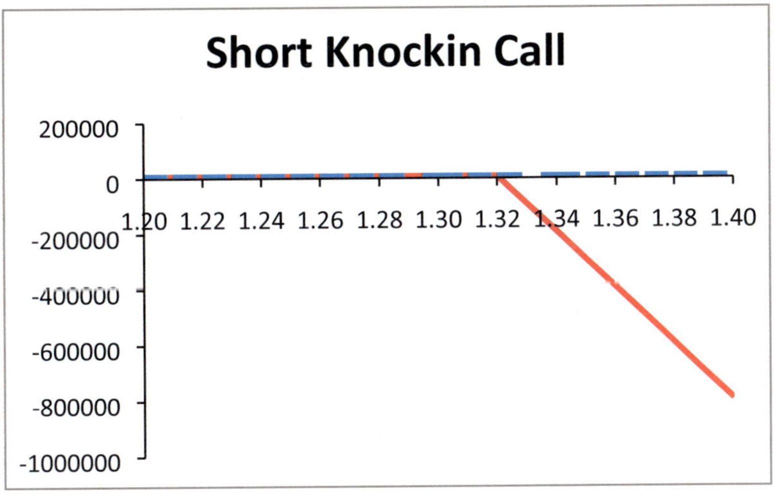

Figure #10: The at expiration profit and loss diagram of a short 1.3200 knock in Euro Call/U.S. Dollar Put option expiring in one month with a knock in level of 1.2800 in an amount of 10,000,000 euros and yielding 8 pips for a total premium received of $8,000.

The trader might compare the 8 pip yield from selling this Knock in option to the yield of 71 pips for selling the otherwise identical vanilla 1.3200 Euro call/U.S. Dollar put with the same expiration date. By including the knock in feature at the 1.2800 trigger level, the premium received for the one month 1.3200 Euro Call option is reduced by 63 pips, or by $63,000 on a 10,000,000 euro notional amount.

Long Knock In Put for a Bearish View

A Knock in Put option shares all of the elements of a plain Vanilla Put option, but it only comes into existence if the underlying spot exchange rate trades at or through the knock in trigger level incorporated into the option contract. In the event that the knock in trigger level is never reached by the time it expires, the Knock in Put option is permanently voided and has no payout.

The knock in feature generally reduces the premium of the exotic Knock in Put option versus that of a plain Vanilla Put. The strategy behind the use of a up and in Knock in Put for a bearish outlook on an exchange rate is that the trader is expecting the underlying rate to move higher to the option's knock in level first, which triggers the option into existence, and for the spot rate to then trade lower to end up below the Knock in Put option's strike price by its expiration date.

The principal reason for a speculator to use a Knock in Put versus a plain Vanilla Put is the reduced premium they will need to pay due to the Knock in feature. The risk for the buyer of a Knock in Put option is limited to their initial cash outlay for the position. Their gains will only start to accrue once the option is knocked in and the underlying exchange rate then depreciates below the Knock in Put option's strike price.

The main disadvantage of using this strategy is the risk of the Knock in Put option not being triggered by the underlying exchange rate rising to the trigger level before the option's expiration date. Thus, the trader's bearish view might have been correct, but the option will not exist to exercise for a profit.

The buyer of the Knock in Put option sets five parameters of the contract consisting of: the currency pair, the notional amount of one currency, the Put strike price, the knock in trigger level, and the option's expiration date. The market maker selling this exotic option then typically determines the option premium based on the market determined implied volatility for that expiration date, the prevailing spot rate and the forward rate.

To reduce the premium of a Knock in Put option, the strategic trader can either lower the strike price or raise the trigger level, since the notional amount and other option terms are generally fixed. Therefore, setting the trigger level further from the prevailing exchange rate — and hence less likely to be touched so that the option comes into existence — or setting the strike price lower — and hence more out of the money and less likely to be exercised — would be the easiest way to adjust the option premium lower.

If the Knock in Put's strike price is set further out of the money, then the trader should be expecting a suitably greater amount of depreciation in the underlying exchange rate so that they can break even after paying the Knock in Put option's initial premium cost.

Follow up strategies for the Knock in Put option include changing the terms of the option contract to improve the bearish position's profit potential after an adverse move. Keeping the term and amounts of the option fixed, a move higher in the spot rate could be an opportunity to roll the strike price of the

Knock in Put higher. If the spot rate moved lower, then the knock in level could be adjusted lower, thereby making it more likely to be triggered and bring the option into existence. Both of these adjustments would require the payment of additional premium.

As an example, consider the case of a bearish technical trader who thinks the EUR/USD currency pair will depreciate significantly below the 1.2800 level over the coming month, but that it will first rally higher to technical resistance they have identified at the 1.3200 level. In this case, they might purchase an up and in Euro Put/U.S. Dollar Call with a strike price of 1.2800 and a knock in level of 1.3200 expiring in 30 days.

With one month EUR/USD implied volatility at 10 percent and the spot rate at 1.3000, such an option would cost roughly 0.0008 points or 8 pips. Thus, the trader would need to pay a premium of $8,000 for a10,000,000 euro notional amount of this option.

The diagram below shows what the profit and loss profile of this option would be if the option is not knocked in with a solid line and uses a dashed line to illustrate the net return that would result if the Knock in Put option comes into existence if its trigger level trades prior to expiration.

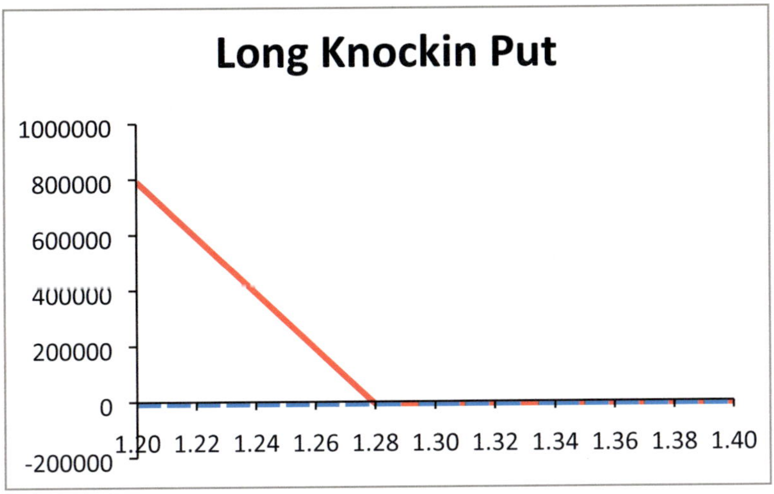

Figure #11: The at expiration profit and loss diagram of a long 1.2800 knock in Euro Put/U.S. Dollar Call option expiring in one month with a knock in level of 1.3200 in an amount of 10,000,000 euros and costing 8 pips for a total premium paid out of $8,000.

The trader might compare this Knock in option's cost of 8 pips to the cost of 68 pips for the otherwise identical Vanilla 1.2800 Euro Put/U.S. Dollar Call with the same expiration date. In this case, adding the knock in feature at the 1.3200 trigger level reduces the one month 1.2800 Euro Put option's theoretical value by 60 pips, or by $60,000 on a 10,000,000 euro notional amount.

Short Knock In Put for a Bullish View

In the case of the speculator having a bullish perspective on an exchange rate, the sale of a Knock in Put option could be appropriate. The closer to the money the trigger level is set on the option contract, the greater the probability of the option getting triggered and coming into existence. Therefore, when selling a Knock in Put, the trigger level will be an important strategic element determining the success of the strategy and it is also a key input into the pricing of the Knock in option.

With a bullish market view in mind, the trigger point of the short Knock in Put should be placed safely away from the present level of the underlying exchange rate. Ideally, this trigger will be placed above a key resistance level that is deemed less likely to trade from a technical perspective. Nevertheless, the further away the trigger is placed from the prevailing spot rate, the lower the option premium that will be received for selling the Knock in Put since the chances of the option being knocked into existence is reduced.

In the case of a mildly bullish view, the knock in trigger level could be set above the prevailing exchange rate, so that the Knock in Put option would be further out of the money if it gets triggered into existence.

Nevertheless, if the speculator is strongly bullish, the trigger point of the sold Knock in Put could be placed below the current spot rate. This would make the premium received for the option higher since the Knock in Put would be closer to the money or even in the money when knocked in and would therefore increase the strategy's yield, if the bullish view turns out to be correct. This sort of

Knock in option is sometimes called a Reverse Knock in Put option or a Down and In Put option.

For example, consider the case of a technical trader who thinks the EUR/USD currency pair will probably end up above the 1.2800 spot level over the coming month, especially if the market rallies above strong resistance noted at 1.3200. In this case, they might sell a Euro Put/U.S. Dollar Call with a strike price of 1.2800 and a knock in level of 1.3200 expiring in 30 days.

With one month EUR/USD implied volatility at 10 percent and the spot rate at 1.3000, such an option would yield roughly 0.0008 points or 8 pips. Thus, the trader would receive a premium of $8,000 for a10,000,000 euro notional amount of this option.

The graph show below illustrates what the profit and loss profile of this short exotic option would be if the option is not knocked in with a solid line, and it uses a dashed line to show the net return that would result if the Knock in Put option comes into existence if its 1.3200 trigger level trades prior to expiration.

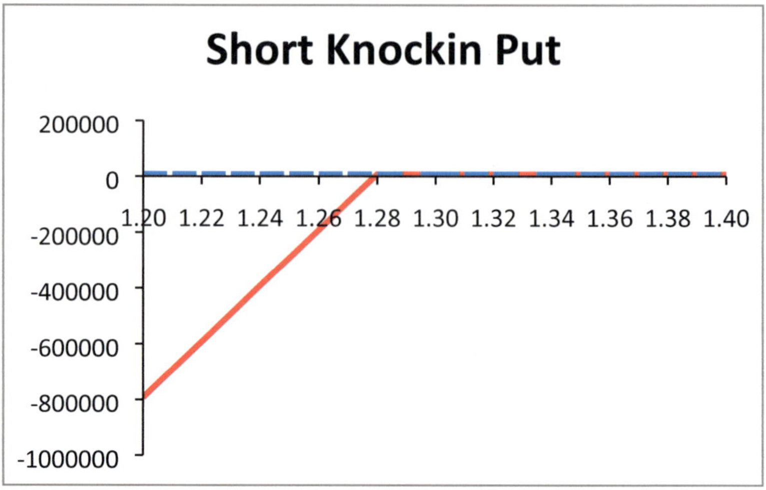

Figure #12: The at expiration profit and loss diagram of a short 1.2800 knock in Euro Put/U.S. Dollar Call option expiring in one month with a knock in level of 1.3200 in an amount of 10,000,000 euros and yielding 8 pips for a total premium received of $8,000.

The trader might compare the 8 pip yield from selling this Knock in option to the yield of 68 pips for selling the otherwise identical vanilla 1.2800 Euro Put/U.S. Dollar Call with the same expiration date. By including the knock in feature at the 1.3200 trigger level, the premium received for the one month 1.2800 Euro Put option is reduced by 60 pips, or by $60,000 on a 10,000,000 euro notional amount.

Average Rate Options for Strategic Directional Trading

An Average Rate or Asian option is a cash settled exotic derivative in which the payout is calculated at expiration by comparing a fixed strike with an average of the underlying exchange rate accumulated over the life of the option, instead of comparing the strike price with the underlying exchange rate itself at expiration. Like with Vanilla options, an Average Rate option's strike price is predetermined.

The average of the underlying exchange rate is calculated by taking observations of the exchange rate on certain specified days — a minimum of two would be required — during the life of the option. These observations are usually called "fixings", and an Average Rate option can have different weightings assigned to each fixing date, or all fixing dates could have the same weighting, which is the typical default weighting method.

The level of the exchange rate at each fixing is then averaged at expiration and compared to the strike price of the option. Several different averaging methods can be used, although a simple arithmetic average is the most common, which involves adding up all of the observations and then dividing by the number of observations. If the averaged rate computed from the fixings is better than the prevailing exchange rate at expiration, then the option is exercised by its holder, who receives a cash payout from its writer.

Since Average Rate options are considered exotic currency options, they typically do not trade on exchanges. Thus, the strategic trader wishing to incorporate them into their trading portfolio will typically need to contact a market maker in the Over the Counter market. This usually makes Average Rate options more of a product for institutions traders, large corporations and high net worth individuals, rather than for smaller retail traders.

The following sections will describe how to use Average Rate options to express a particular bullish or bearish market view.

Long Average Rate Call Option for a Bullish View

A bullish directional trader might consider buying an Average Rate Call option, especially if they wish to smooth out the risk of a sharp corrective movement that could otherwise wipe out their accumulated profits if it occurs close to expiration. The underlying averaged exchange rate is usually computed at expiration and compared to the Average Rate Call's strike price to determine the amount of its cash payoff, if any.

When such an Average Rate Call option ends up in the money at expiration by having had its strike price set at a level below the underlying average exchange rate, its holder receives the difference between the strike price and the average underlying exchange rate multiplied by the option's base currency notional amount.

If the observed average rate is lower than the Average Rate Call's strike price, then the option holder receives zero payout, and the option expires worthless.

A trader looking to profit from a significant and protracted move in an exchange rate would probably be better off buying a Knock Out or plain Vanilla Call option, versus an Average Rate Call option, since their return would be higher. Nevertheless, the main reason a bullish trader might consider buying an Average Rate Call option is that the option premium might be significantly lower than the Vanilla Call option, depending on the number of fixings involved.

Another reason for a bullish speculator to use an Average Rate Call option would be to avoid the risk of a retracement coming late in the option's lifetime that might otherwise reduce or even eliminate any accrued profits on a Vanilla or Knock out Call position. Even if such a retracement might cause the Vanilla or Knock out Call option of the same strike price to expire out of the money, the Average Rate Call option may have retained some accumulated value relative to the average of the observed fixings.

Like other options, the risk on the purchase of an Average Rate Call option is limited to the amount of money invested. When purchasing an Average Rate Call, the buyer generally establishes the option's expiration date, strike price, currency pair and its notional currency amount, as well as the fixing source and frequency of the observations to be used in the averaging process. In general, the more fixing dates during the life of the option, the lower the Average Rate Call option's premium will be. The fixing dates do not need not be spaced out evenly over the Average Rate Call option's lifetime, although they usually are for the sake of convenience and simplicity when pricing the option.

The price of an Average Rate Call option can be compared to that of a series of Vanilla Call options with the same strike price and with expirations matching the fixing dates and amounts matching the weightings. Nevertheless, the Average Rate Call option will always have a lower premium than the series of plain Vanilla Call options.

As an example, consider the case of a bullish trader who thinks the EUR/USD currency pair will move sharply upwards to consolidate over the coming month, although they are concerned that it might also retrace some of its early gains as the option approaches its expiration. In this case, they might buy an Average Rate Euro Call/U.S. Dollar Put with a strike price of 1.3000 and daily fixings expiring in 30 days.

With one month EUR/USD implied volatility at 10 percent and the spot rate at 1.3000, such an option would cost roughly 0.0084 points or 84 pips. Thus, the trader would pay a premium of $84,000 for a10,000,000 euro notional amount of this option.

The graph show below illustrates what the profit and loss profile of this long Average Rate Call option would be at expiration at varying levels of the underlying average rate.

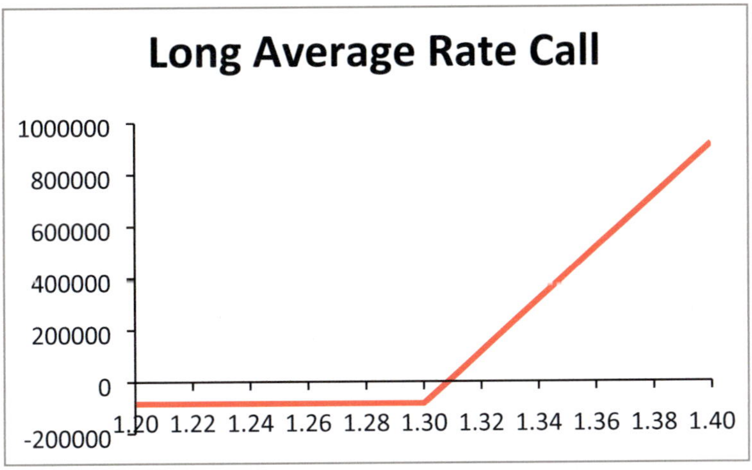

Figure #13: The at expiration profit and loss diagram of a long 1.3000 Average Rate Euro Call/U.S. Dollar Put option expiring in one month with daily fixings in an amount of 10,000,000 euros and costing 84 pips for a total premium paid of $84,000.

The trader might compare the 84 pip cost of buying this Average Rate option to the cost of 149 pips for buying the otherwise identical vanilla 1.3000 Euro call/U.S. Dollar put with the same expiration date. By including the averaging feature, the premium paid for the one month 1.3000 Euro Call option is reduced by 65 pips, or by $65,000 on a 10,000,000 euro notional amount.

Note that if the EUR/USD exchange rate did in fact quickly move higher and then stay there for most of the month, that even if it then retraced lower by the option's expiration date, the Average Rate option would have accumulated more intrinsic value than its Vanilla equivalent upon expiration.

Short Average Rate Call Option for a Bearish View

The sale of an Average Rate Call option may suit a speculator expecting a decline in an exchange rate, although the premium received for it will typically be considerably less than if the trader had sold a plain Vanilla Call instead. The main benefit to selling an Average Rate Call when bearish is that the risk on the position is generally lower due to the averaging process involved compared to that of a Vanilla Call option, which would be valued against the prevailing exchange rate at expiration.

If the exchange rate were to fall initially as expected, but then spike higher by the option's expiration, the short Vanilla option might end up in the money and be exercised against the seller, but the Average Rate Call might remain out of the money and expire worthless.

The Average Rate Call seller will typically specify the expiration date, strike price and notional amount of the option, while the market maker buying it will compute the premium for the option based on current market parameters that include the spot rate, forward rate and implied volatility. Furthermore, the premium received for the Average Rate Call sale will generally be less than that received for a plain Vanilla Call option with the same parameters, and the premium will decrease along with the number of fixings or observation points to be made during the lifetime of the Average Rate option.

Shorting an Average Rate Call basically limits the amount of profit for the seller to the premium taken in initially, while losses on the position can be unlimited if the relevant average of the underlying exchange rate rises above the strike price at expiration.

For illustrative purposes, consider the case of a bearish trader who thinks the EUR/USD currency pair will move lower over the coming month, although they are concerned that it might also retrace some of its early losses as the option approaches its expiration. In this case, they might sell an Average Rate Euro Call/U.S. Dollar Put with a strike price of 1.3000 and daily fixings expiring in 30 days.

With one month EUR/USD implied volatility at 10 percent and the spot rate at 1.3000, such an option would yield roughly 0.0084 points or 84 pips. Thus, the trader would receive a premium of $84,000 for selling a10,000,000 euro notional amount of this option.

The graph show below illustrates what the profit and loss profile of this short Average Rate Call option would be at expiration at varying levels of the underlying average rate.

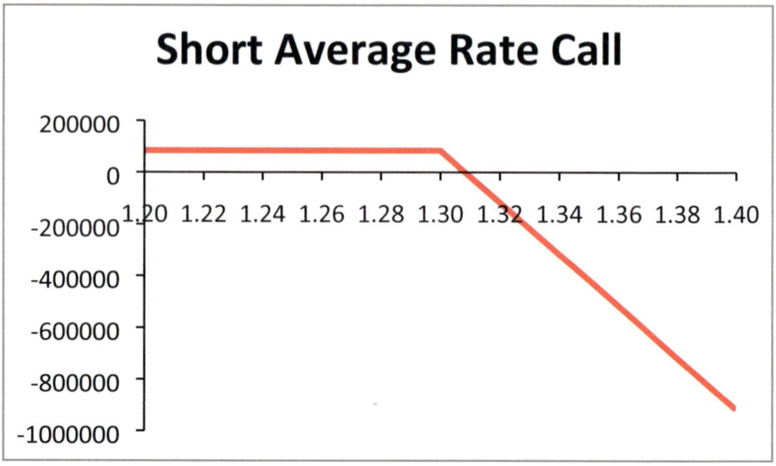

Figure #14: The at expiration profit and loss diagram of a short 1.3000 Average Rate Euro Call/U.S. Dollar Put option expiring in one month with daily fixings in an amount of 10,000,000 euros and yielding 84 pips for a total premium received of $84,000.

The trader might compare the 84 pips received for selling this Average Rate Call option to the premium of 149 pips received for selling the otherwise identical vanilla 1.3000 Euro Call/U.S. Dollar Put with the same expiration date. By including the averaging feature, the premium received for the one month 1.3000 Euro Call option is reduced by 65 pips, or by $65,000 on a 10,000,000 euro notional amount.

Note that if the EUR/USD exchange rate did in fact move quickly lower and then stay lower for most of the month, that even if the rate then bounced higher above the strike price by the option's expiration date, the Average Rate option would have accumulated less intrinsic value, if any, compared with its Vanilla equivalent upon expiration.

Long Average Rate Put Option for a Bearish View

An Average Rate Put option ends up in the money at expiration if its strike prIce Is greater than the underlying average exchange rate. In this case, its holder receives the difference between the strike price and the average underlying exchange rate multiplied by the option's base currency notional amount. If the observed average rate is higher than the Average Rate Put's strike price, then the option holder receives zero payout, and the option expires worthless.

A trader with a bearish view looking to profit from a significant and protracted down move in an exchange rate would probably be better off buying a Knock Out or plain Vanilla Put option, versus an Average Rate Put option, since their return would probably be higher. Nevertheless, the main reason a bearish trader might consider buying an Average Rate Put option is that the option premium might be significantly lower than the Vanilla Put option, depending on the number of fixings involved.

A bearish speculator might also use an Average Rate Put option to avoid the risk of a market rally coming late in the option's lifetime that might otherwise reduce or even eliminate any accrued profits on a Vanilla or Knock out Put position. Even if such a rally might cause the Vanilla or Knock out Put option with the same strike price to expire out of the money, the Average Rate Put option may have retained some accumulated value relative to the average of the observed fixings.

Like other options, the risk on the purchase of an Average Rate Put option is limited to the amount of money invested. When purchasing an Average Rate Put, the buyer generally establishes the option's expiration date, strike price, currency pair and its notional currency amount, as well as the fixing source and frequency of the observations to be used in the averaging process.

The price of an Average Rate Put option can be compared to that of a series of Vanilla Put options with the same strike price and with expirations matching the fixing dates and amounts matching the weightings. Nevertheless, the Average Rate Put option will always have a lower premium than the series of plain Vanilla Put options.

As an example, consider the case of a bearish trader who thinks the EUR/USD currency pair will move sharply downwards to consolidate its losses over the coming month, although they are concerned that it might also rally to retrace some of its early losses as the option approaches its expiration. In this case, they might buy an Average Rate Euro Put/U.S. Dollar Call with a strike price of 1.3000 and daily fixings expiring in 30 days.

With one month EUR/USD implied volatility at 10 percent and the spot rate at 1.3000, such an option would cost roughly 0.0082 points or 82 pips. Thus, the trader would pay a premium of $82,000 for a10,000,000 euro notional amount of this option.

The graph show below illustrates what the profit and loss profile of this long Average Rate Put option would be at expiration at varying levels of the underlying average rate.

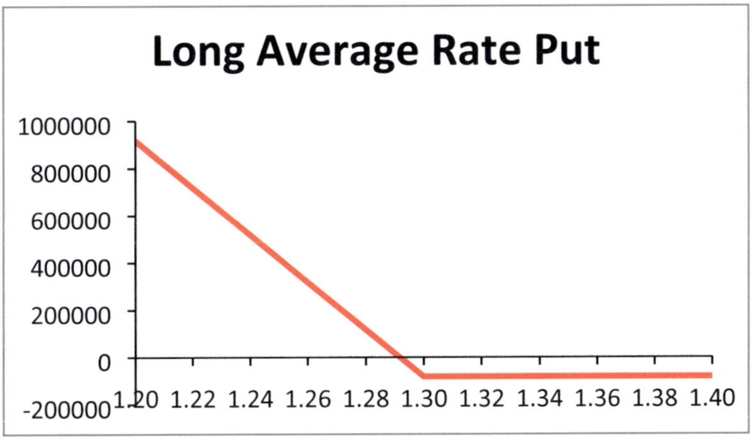

Figure #15: The at expiration profit and loss diagram of a long 1.3000 Average Rate Euro Put/U.S. Dollar Call option expiring in one month with daily fixings in an amount of 10,000,000 euros and costing 82 pips for a total premium paid of $82,000.

The bearish trader might compare the 82 pip cost of buying this Average Rate option to the cost of 148 pips for buying the otherwise identical vanilla 1.3000 Euro Put/U.S. Dollar Call with the same expiration date. By including the averaging feature, the premium paid for the one month 1.3000 Euro Call option is reduced by 66 pips, or by $66,000 on a 10,000,000 euro notional amount.

Note that if the EUR/USD exchange rate did in fact quickly move lower and then stay there for most of the month, that even if it then rallied higher by the option's expiration date, the Average Rate Put option would have accumulated more intrinsic value than its Vanilla Put equivalent upon expiration.

Short Average Rate Put Option for a Bullish View

Selling an Average Rate Put option may suit a speculator expecting a rise in an exchange rate, especially if the risk of a retracement lower near expiration is seen, although the premium received for it will typically be considerably less than if the trader had sold a plain Vanilla Put instead. The main benefit to selling an Average Rate Put when bullish is that the risk on the position is generally lower due to the averaging process involved compared to that of a Vanilla Put option, which would be valued against the prevailing exchange rate at expiration.

If the exchange rate were to rise initially as expected but then crash lower by the option's expiration date, then the short Vanilla Put option might end up in the money and be exercised against the strategic seller, but the Average Rate Put might remain out of the money and expire worthless.

The Average Rate Put seller will typically specify the expiration date, strike price, currency pair and notional amount of the option, while the market maker buying it will compute the premium for the option based on current market parameters that include the spot rate, forward rate and implied volatility. In addition, the premium received for the Average Rate Put sale will generally be less than that received for a plain Vanilla Put option with the same parameters, and the premium will decrease along with the number of fixings or observation points to be made during the lifetime of the Average Rate option.

Selling an Average Rate Put option basically limits the amount of profit for the seller to the premium taken in initially, while losses on the position can be unlimited if the relevant average of the underlying exchange rate falls below the strike price at expiration.

For example, consider the case of a bullish trader who thinks the EUR/USD currency pair will move higher over the coming month, although they are concerned that it might also drop to retrace some of its early gains as the option approaches its expiration. In this case, they might sell an Average Rate Euro Put/U.S. Dollar Call with a strike price of 1.3000 and daily fixings expiring in 30 days.

With one month EUR/USD implied volatility at 10 percent and the spot rate at 1.3000, such an option would yield roughly 0.0082 points or 82 pips. Thus, the trader would receive a premium of $82,000 for selling a10,000,000 euro notional amount of this option.

The graph show below illustrates what the profit and loss profile of this short Average Rate Put option would be at expiration at varying levels of the underlying average rate.

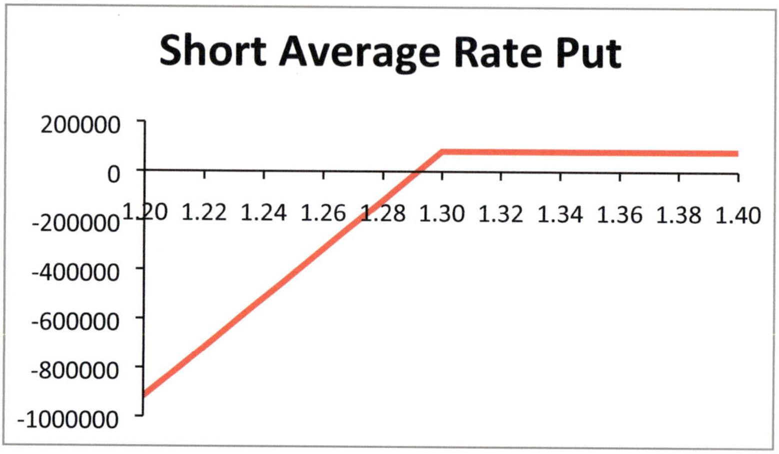

Figure #16: The at expiration profit and loss diagram of a short 1.3000 Average Rate Euro Put/U.S. Dollar Call option expiring in one month with daily fixings in an amount of 10,000,000 euros and yielding 82 pips for a total premium received of $82,000.

The trader might compare the 82 pips received for selling this Average Rate Put option to the premium of 148 pips received for selling the otherwise identical vanilla 1.3000 Euro Put/U.S. Dollar Call with the same expiration date. By including the averaging feature, the premium received for the one month 1.3000 Euro Put option is reduced by 66 pips, or by $66,000 on a 10,000,000 euro notional amount.

If the EUR/USD exchange rate did in fact move quickly higher and stay higher for most of the month as expected, then even if the exchange rate subsequently dropped below the strike price by the option's expiration date, the Average Rate Put option would have accumulated less intrinsic value, if any, compared with its Vanilla Put option equivalent upon expiration.

Average Strike Options for Strategic Directional Trading

An Average Strike Rate option or ASRO is a derivative in which the payout is calculated at expiration by comparing the underlying exchange rate to an average strike price. The strike price of the option is calculated over the life of the option instead of it having a fixed, pre-determined strike price like normal Vanilla options. Average Strike options can be cash settled or physically settled.

As with average rate options, the average strike is calculated from the spot rate observed on pre-arranged dates known as "fixings". Average Strike options might also have their strike prices computed with a given degree of moneyness from the spot rate at the fixing, such as a two percent out of the money spot averaged strike price.

Typically, an Average Strike option's fixings are given an equal weight for each date when computing the averaged strike price on an arithmetical basis. This simple averaging process generally involves adding up the fixing observations and dividing by the number of observations to obtain the option's strike price. Nevertheless, some Average Strike options also include a weighing element that allows for adjustment of the importance of each observation to the overall average. Traders generally use Average Strike options instead of Vanilla options for speculative purposes because of their lower premium when compared to Vanilla options.

Most of the elements required for pricing an Average Strike option are the same as with most other options. For forex Average Strike options, these include the currency pair, the notional amount and the option's expiration date. The fixing method is also specified, and even though the strike price is not known in advance, traders can also specify what degree of moneyness the strike price should have relative to the observed fixings.

The market maker for the Average Strike option will determine the spot, forward and implied volatility for the option in order to compute its theoretical value and therefore determine an appropriate premium for the option. The implied forward exchange rate reflects and is computed from the interest rate differential between the two currencies, and it directly affects the price of the option.

Due to the averaging process involved in determining the strike price, an at the money Average Strike option's premium will generally be lower than the premium for an equivalent plain Vanilla at the money option with the same maturity.

Nevertheless, how much cheaper an Average Strike option might be relative to a Vanilla option depends on the number of fixing periods in the contract, with more fixings typically reducing the price more.

Long Average Strike Call Option for a Bullish View

For a speculator with a bullish view on an exchange rate, buying an Average Rate Call option might suit their needs, although they need to understand how the strike price averaging process might affect their returns. By purchasing an Average Strike Call option, the trader might reduce their profit potential, so they might be better off buying a Knock out, Knock in or plain Vanilla Call option instead. The chief advantage of buying an Average Strike Call consists of the lower premium of the option due to the lower volatility of the average used to compute its strike price.

In terms of its appropriateness for a strategic forex trader, an Average Strike Call might make sense for a technical trader who sees the market entering the consolidation phase of a bullish flag or pennant pattern after its initial sharp spike upwards. Anticipating another sharp rally after more consolidation at current levels, they could buy an Average Strike Call with fixing observations to be made during the expected remainder of the consolidation phase. Observations made at these lower levels will then set an attractive average strike price that should be considerably in the money relative to the final price at or near expiration after the bullish flag or pennant pattern completes with a final sharp move to the upside. This Average Strike Call option will also be considerably cheaper than a comparable Vanilla Call option.

As an example, consider the case of a bullish technical trader who observes a bull flag forming on the daily charts for the EUR/USD currency pair, and so they think EUR/USD will probably consolidate for a four week period before moving sharply upwards toward the end of the coming month. In this scenario, they might buy an Average Strike Euro Call/U.S. Dollar Put with an at the money spot strike price to be determined by an arithmetic equally-weighted average of daily EUR/USD spot fixings observed during the next four weeks and that will expire in 30 days.

Given one month EUR/USD implied volatility at 10 percent and the spot rate at 1.3000, such an Average Strike Call option might cost roughly 0.0084 points or 84 pips. Thus, the trader would pay a premium of $84,000 for a10,000,000 euro notional amount of this option.

The graph show below illustrates what the profit and loss profile of this long Average Strike Call option would be at expiration at varying levels of the underlying average rate.

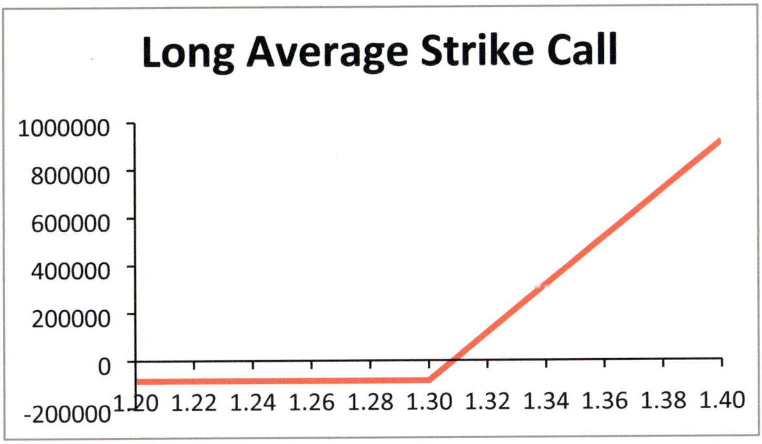

Figure #17: The at expiration profit and loss diagram of a long Average Strike Euro Call/U.S. Dollar Put option expiring in one month with daily strike price fixings that averaged to 1.3000 in an amount of 10,000,000 euros and costing 84 pips for a total premium paid of $84,000.

The trader might compare the 84 pip cost of buying this Average Strike option to the cost of 149 pips for buying the otherwise identical vanilla 1.3000 Euro call/U.S. Dollar put with the same expiration date. By including the averaging feature on the option's strike price, the premium paid for the one month 1.3000 Euro Call option is reduced by 65 pips, or by $65,000 on a 10,000,000 euro notional amount.

Note that if the EUR/USD exchange rate did in fact stabilize around current levels and then move quickly higher toward the end of the option's one month lifetime, that the Average Strike Call option would have cost considerably less than an equivalent Vanilla Call initially purchased with the same strike price.

Short Average Strike Call Option for a Bearish View

Speculators with a bearish outlook on an exchange rate could consider selling an Average Strike Call option. This would limit their gains to the premium received, and would have a lower maximum profit compared to an equivalent Vanilla Call sale of the same maturity and notional amount.

Nevertheless, the Average Strike Call sale strategy could be viable in a bearish exchange rate outlook, especially where the trader expects the market to stabilize initially before falling toward the end of the option's lifetime.

The primary advantage of shorting an Average Strike Call option is that the risk involved in the sale declines over time if the exchange rate stays stable. This risk drops further as the exchange rate moves progressively lower.

The main disadvantage of selling an Average Strike Call is that the strike price will trail the underlying exchange rate. This can progressively lower the Average Strike Call option's strike price in a declining market, which can result in potentially unlimited losses if a sharp upward spike in the exchange rate were seen as the option's expiration date approaches.

As an illustrative example, consider the case of a bearish trader who thinks the EUR/USD currency pair will stabilize or even rise in the near term and then move lower as the coming month concludes. In this case, they might sell an Average Strike Euro Call/U.S. Dollar Put with an at the money spot strike price determined by an arithmetic average of daily fixings and expiring in 30 days.

With one month EUR/USD implied volatility at 10 percent and the spot rate at 1.3000, the sale of such an option might yield roughly 0.0084 points or 84 pips. If so, the trader would receive a premium of $84,000 for selling a10,000,000 euro notional amount of this option.

The graph show below illustrates what the profit and loss profile of this short Average Strike Call option would be at expiration at varying levels of the underlying spot rate, if its averaged strike price turned out to be 1.3000.

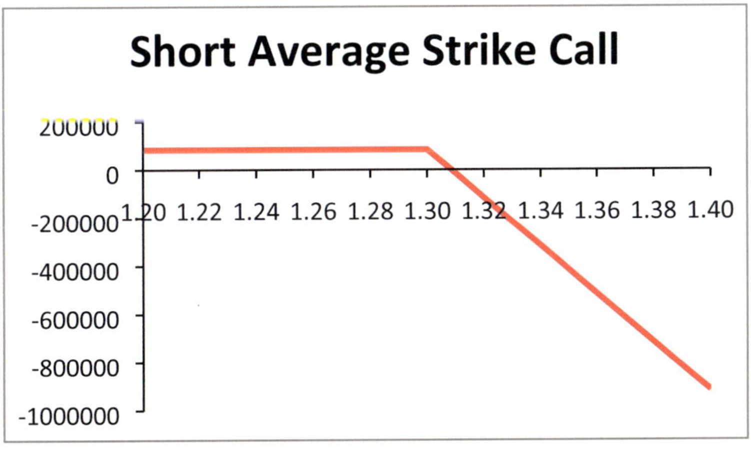

Figure #18: The at expiration profit and loss diagram of a short Average Strike Euro Call/U.S. Dollar Put option with a final strike price of 1.3000 computed from daily fixings observed over a one month period in an amount of 10,000,000 euros and yielding 84 pips for a total premium received of $84,000.

The trader could compare the 84 pips received for selling this Average Strike Call option to the premium of 149 pips received for selling the otherwise identical Vanilla 1.3000 Euro Call/U.S. Dollar Put with the same expiration date. By including the averaging feature on the strike price, the premium received for the one month 1.3000 Euro Call option is reduced by 65 pips, or by $65,000 on a 10,000,000 euro notional amount.

Note that even if the EUR/USD exchange rate did in fact rise against the position, as long as it subsequently fell below the averaged strike price by the option's expiration date, the Average Strike Call option would have accumulated no intrinsic value, but its Vanilla equivalent would be in the money upon expiration.

Long Average Strike Put Option for a Bearish View

An Average Strike Put option ends up in the money if its averaged strike price computed from a series of observations or fixings is greater than the underlying exchange rate at expiration. In this case, its holder receives the difference between the averaged strike price and the underlying exchange rate multiplied by the option's base currency notional amount. If the observed exchange rate at expiration is higher than the Average Strike Put's averaged strike price, then the option holder receives zero payout, and the option expires worthless.

A trader with a bearish view looking to profit from a significant and protracted down move in an exchange rate would probably be better off buying a Knock Out or plain Vanilla Put option, versus an Average Strike Put option, since their return would probably be higher. Nevertheless, the main reason a bearish trader might consider buying an Average Strike Put option is that the option premium might be significantly lower than the Vanilla Put option, depending on the number of fixings involved.

A bearish speculator might also use an Average Strike Put option to benefit from a situation where the market might stabilize — or even initially rally — but then fall significantly by the option's expiration date. This scenario might make the averaged strike price better than the spot rate when the option was initially transacted, and its lower up front price would then improve the trade's breakeven relative to a Vanilla Put. Such an initial rally might also eliminate any potential profits on a Knock out Put position if the market traded up to the trigger level to knock it out of existence.

Like other options, the risk on the purchase of an Average Strike Put option is limited to the amount of money invested. When purchasing an Average Strike Put, the buyer generally establishes the option's expiration date, strike price, currency pair and its notional currency amount, as well as the fixing source and frequency of the observations to be used in the averaging process. An Average Strike Put option will always have a lower premium than a plain Vanilla Put option of the same expiration and moneyness.

As an example, consider the case of a bearish trader who thinks the EUR/USD currency pair will consolidate or even rally in the near term before then moving sharply downwards toward the end of the coming month. In this case, they might buy an Average Strike Euro Put/U.S. Dollar Call expiring in 30 days with an arithmetic average of equally weighted daily fixings used to determine its strike price.

With one month EUR/USD implied volatility at 10 percent and the spot rate at 1.3000, such an option could cost roughly 0.0082 points or 82 pips. If so, the trader would pay a premium of $82,000 for a10,000,000 euro notional amount of this option.

The graph show below illustrates what the profit and loss profile of this long Average Strike Put option would be at expiration at varying levels of the underlying exchange rate if its average strike price turned out to be 1.3000.

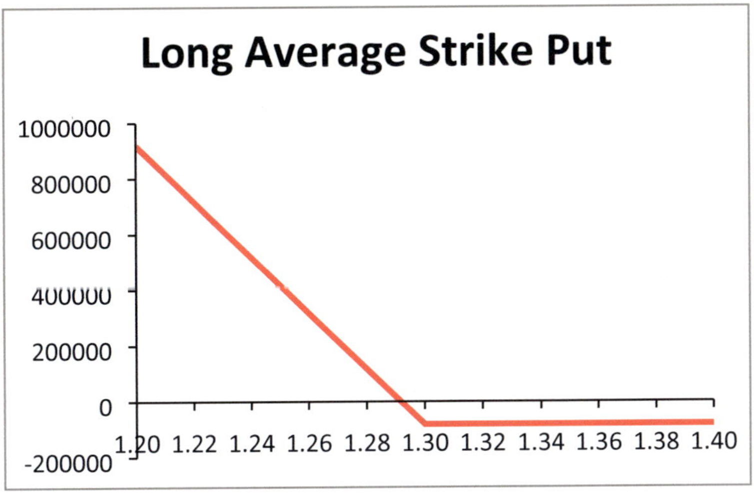

Figure #19: The at expiration profit and loss diagram of a long Average Strike Euro Put/U.S. Dollar Call option expiring in one month with a final strike price of 1.3000 determined by daily fixings in an amount of 10,000,000 euros and costing 82 pips for a total premium paid of $82,000.

The bearish trader might compare the 82 pip cost of buying this Average Strike option to the cost of 148 pips for buying the otherwise identical vanilla 1.3000 Euro Put/U.S. Dollar Call with the same expiration date. By including the averaging feature on the option's strike price, the premium paid for the one month 1.3000 Euro Call option is reduced by 66 pips, or by $66,000 on a 10,000,000 euro notional amount.

Note that if the EUR/USD exchange rate did in fact rally initially and then declined sharply near the end of the option's one month lifetime, that an at the money spot Average Strike Put option would probably have a higher strike price than the initial spot rate and hence might accumulate more intrinsic value than its Vanilla Put equivalent upon expiration.

Short Average Strike Put Option for a Bullish View

Selling an Average Strike Put option may suit a speculator expecting a rise in an exchange rate, especially if the trader sees significant risk of a near term decline, followed by a greater rally as the option nears its expiration date. The transaction's profit potential is limited to the premium initially received, which will typically be considerably less than if the trader had sold a plain Vanilla Put instead.

The main benefit to selling an Average Strike Put when bullish is that the risk on the position is generally lower when compared to that of a fixed strike Vanilla Put option due to the averaging process applied to its strike price. Furthermore, if the exchange rate were to fall initially as expected but then spike higher by the option's expiration date, then a short at the money spot Vanilla Put option with a fixed strike price might still end up in the money and be exercised against the strategic seller. In contrast, an at the money spot Average Strike Put's strike price would be adjusted downwards over its lifetime, and so it might remain out of the money and expire worthless in this scenario.

The Average Strike Put seller will typically specify the expiration date, the moneyness of the strike price, the currency pair and the notional amount of the option. The market maker buying the exotic option will compute the premium for the option based on current market parameters that include the spot rate, forward rate and implied volatility. In addition, the premium received for the Average Strike Put sale will generally be less than that received for a plain Vanilla Put option with the same parameters. The price of an Average Strike Put will also decrease with an increase in the number of fixings or observation points used to compute its strike price to be made during the lifetime of the Average Strike option.

As with a sold Vanilla option, selling an Average Strike Put option basically limits the amount of profit for the seller to the premium that was taken in initially. Similarly, losses on the short Average Strike Put position can be unlimited if the spot rate at expiration ends up below its averaged strike price determined from its series of fixing observations made during the exotic option's lifetime.

For example, consider the case of a bullish trader who thinks the EUR/USD currency pair will move higher over the coming month, although they are concerned that it might drop initially before then rallying toward the end of the month. In this case, they might sell an at the money spot Average Strike Euro Put/U.S. Dollar Call expiring in 30 days with daily strike price fixings to be equally weighted and arithmetically averaged.

With one month EUR/USD implied volatility at 10 percent and the spot rate at 1.3000, such an option might yield roughly 0.0082 points or 82 pips. If so, the trader would receive a premium of $82,000 for selling a10,000,000 euro notional amount of this option.

The graph show below illustrates what the profit and loss profile of this short Average Strike Put option would be at expiration at varying levels of the underlying exchange rate assuming the averaged strike price turned out to be 1.3000.

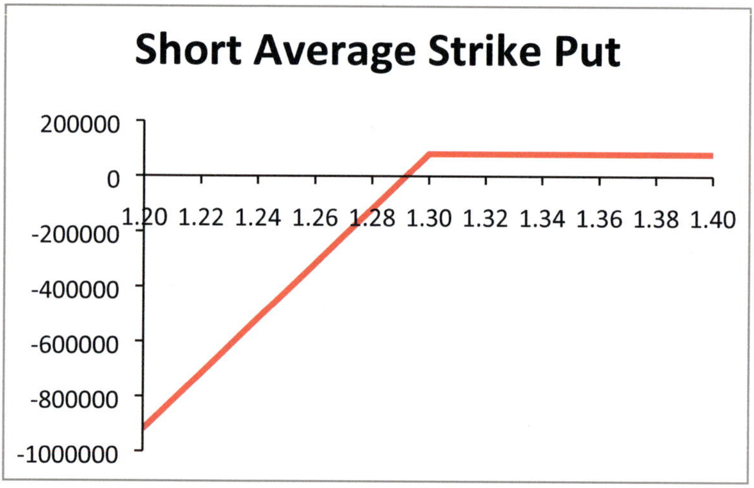

Figure #16: The at expiration profit and loss diagram of a short Average Strike Euro Put/U.S. Dollar Call option expiring in one month with daily strike price fixings averaged to yield a 1.3000 strike in an amount of 10,000,000 euros and yielding 82 pips for a total premium received of $82,000.

The trader might compare the 82 pips received for selling this Average Strike Put option with an ultimate strike price of 1.3000 to the premium of 148 pips received for selling the otherwise identical vanilla 1.3000 Euro Put/U.S. Dollar Call with the same expiration date. By including the strike averaging feature, the premium received for the one month 1.3000 Euro Put option is reduced by 66 pips, or by $66,000 on a 10,000,000 euro notional amount.

If the EUR/USD exchange rate did in fact move lower for most of the month as expected, then as long as the exchange rate subsequently rallies above the averaged strike price by the option's expiration date, the Average Rate Put option would have accumulated no intrinsic value, but its Vanilla Put option equivalent may well be in the money upon expiration.

Basket Options for Strategic Directional Trading

A forex Basket option is an exotic derivative whose value is based on that of an underlying basket made up of several different currencies. Basket forex options can work as a speculative vehicle when priced correctly and when the trader has an accurate outlook on one currency quoted against a group or basket of others. Basket options can consist of any group of counter currencies that can be quoted against any denominating or base currency.

Sophisticated speculators can use these Basket options when they have a particular opinion on the correlated movements of various counter currency exchange rates quoted against one base currency, which is typically a major currency like the U.S. Dollar or Euro.

Obtaining an upper limiting value for the price of a multi-currency basket option involves using the implied volatilities of each currency pair's vanilla options contained in the basket with an equivalent expiration and degree of moneyness to compute and then sum up their premium costs in base currency terms from their individual prices weighted by the amount of each counter currency contained in the basket.

Since this approximation does not take into account cross currency correlations between component currencies in the basket, the price thereby obtained is considered an upper limit for the Basket option's value. More accurate values for basket options which have one denominating base currency can be obtained by using the implied correlations calculated from the implied volatilities for each different currency pair involved in the basket.

As with other exotics, the buyer of a Basket option will need to specify the option expiration date, its moneyness, and the notional amount of each currency in the basket, while the seller generally uses market determined parameters like implied volatility and prevailing spot and forward rates to fix the Basket Call's premium cost.

Long Basket Call Option for a Bullish View

For a bullish outlook on a basket of currencies – which would also be a bearish view on the denominating base currency, a speculator could purchase a Basket Call – which would also be a Put on the base currency.

As an example, consider the situation of a speculator that thinks the U.S. Dollar is likely to depreciate against a basket consisting of the world's other major currencies over the coming month. They could purchase a one month Basket Call/U.S. Dollar Put option with an at the money spot strike price. In this case, the basket option's underlying basket of currencies could consist of the Euro, the Japanese Yen, the Pound Sterling, the Swiss Franc, the Australian Dollar, the Canadian Dollar and the New Zealand Dollar, all in 1,000,000 U.S. Dollar equivalent amounts with a one month expiration date.

In the above example, a decline in the U.S. Dollar's value against most or all of the other seven major currencies by the Basket option's expiration date would be the optimum scenario for a positive payout on the Basket Call/U.S. Dollar Put option, although the trader could still potentially profit from favorable movements in a majority of the currency pairs involved.

As with most other long option strategies, buying the Basket Call/U.S. Dollar Put would limit the speculator's risk to the amount of premium paid for its initial purchase, and their upside potential would be unlimited.

Short Basket Call Option for a Bearish View

Selling a Basket Call/U.S. Dollar Put option on a basket of currencies quoted versus the U.S. Dollar might be a suitable strategy for a speculator who thinks the basket of currencies is likely to depreciate or remain relatively stable versus the U.S. Dollar by the option's expiration date.

As with most other sold options, the trader's profit potential for a Basket Call option sale is limited to the premium initially received for it. This premium will typically be somewhat less than if the trader had instead sold a series of plain Vanilla counter currency Calls/base currency Puts in the notional amounts of each counter currency in the basket.

Speculators that sell Basket currency options generally need to have a good idea on the direction of a currency against a basket of currencies. This is due to the fact that their loss potential is unlimited if the U.S. Dollar falls substantially against the counter currencies such that the Basket Call/U.S. Dollar Put option's strike price ends up in the money.

Chapter 7: Hedging Currency Exposures with Vanilla Forex Options

Currency Risk Hedging Principles

Fluctuations in foreign exchange rates can be advantageous for those with currency exposures, as any profitable forex trader can attest. Furthermore, options offer a perfect hedging vehicle for just about any outright long or short foreign exchange position, and they offer numerous ways to offset direct foreign exchange exposures strategically.

Nevertheless, those corporations, investors and individuals with significant forex market exposure incidental to their primary business activities, may wish to find ways to reduce, minimize and/or optimize their forex market risks. With this objective in mind, the use of vanilla currency options is an essential and well established part of the forex risk management arsenal employed by many multinational corporations, international fund managers and even private investors.

Such hedgers often buy options outright to protect their business related currency exposures against forex market risks, especially when such currency exposures have an element of uncertainly. Furthermore, they also often sell covered forex options either to provide them with additional income or to finance the purchase of protective options that limit their downside risk.

The advantages of using currency options to hedge a foreign exchange exposure are often weighed against the benefits of using forward market hedges instead. Forward hedges are typically considered ideal when protecting a known currency cash flow destined to occur at some known point in the future and when no exposure to forex market fluctuations is desired.

Option hedges start to become more attractive than forwards when some element of uncertainly is involved in the hedging process. For example, the amount to be hedged may be uncertain. In this case, a purchased forex option could be used to protect the currency exposure amount that may not materialize, while a forward contract could protect the exposure amount that is reasonably expected to occur.

Using forex options as a hedge can also be very beneficial when a hedger believes that the underlying currency pair may move in a favorable direction for their exposure. For example, if they have a long exposure in the base currency and think it is likely to appreciate in the future, then hedging by selling a forward contract would eliminate any potential for future gain on their exposure. By purchasing a protective base currency put instead, the hedger can leave their long exposure's profit potential unlimited if the base currency rises as expected, while still having covered their downside risk if their market view turns out to be incorrect.

A follow up strategy for this purchased option hedge could consist of rolling the protective long put up to a higher strike as the market continues advancing. This would be done by executing a put spread where the hedger simultaneously sells their existing out of the money put and buys a closer to the money put with a higher strike. Using rolling put spreads like this to lock in gains on underlying exposure could help protect the exposure's past gains in case of an unfavorable retracement.

One particular advantage of a corporate hedger strategically allowing the profit potential of an underlying exposure to remain unlimited is that it could improve their business position relative to other companies that have hedged their analogous exposures completely using forwards. Such companies can no longer use the more favorable exchange rate to their competitive advantage in the marketplace for their products by increasing their profit margins and/or reducing their prices like the corporation that hedges using options can. Essentially, once a forward is used to hedge a significant currency exposure, the hedger will be locked into a price and no longer able to participate in any currency appreciation.

Furthermore, quite a number of major international corporations have seen their stock prices adjusted sharply lower after announcing significant foreign exchange losses. Given the broad spectrum of option and forward hedging products available today to a corporate finance department, a decision to leave a significant currency exposure completely unhedged would probably not be seen as a prudent or sensible risk management strategy. In addition, overlooking a significant currency exposure that should have been hedged would probably be considered negligent, especially if significant forex market losses occurred as a result of the oversight.

Just about every large multinational corporation doing business abroad has or employs — through a bank or other financial institution — a finance department that manages their foreign currency exposure. The difference that foreign currency translation makes to the corporate bottom line of large multinational companies that do business in various nations and currencies, such as Apple Inc. or Exxon, can be enormous. The fact is that many businesses experience foreign currency transaction and translation risks in their activities outside of their official domicile. For example, these foreign currency exposures might include foreign sales, the employment of foreign manufacturing resources, the international purchase of commodities or other products, and the acquisition of foreign companies.

Although forex forwards have been in use for decades as hedges, many of the more financially sophisticated of these companies now also use currency options as part of their risk management programs, especially where participation in some beneficial moves is considered desirable or when contingent currency risks need to be protected against.

Buying Downside Protection

Perhaps the most conservative currency option hedging strategy involves purchasing an option to protect an underlying currency exposure from adverse exchange rate moves. Commonly known as buying downside protection or insurance, this hedge strategy typically involves paying an upfront premium to purchase a protective option with a strike price set at an acceptable exchange rate level for the corporation's budget.

The main benefit of purchasing currency options as downside protection lies in the possibility of allowing profits to accrue on the underlying exposure, while at the same time limiting losses beyond the strike price of the purchased option, Of course, such benefits are reduced by the option hedge's initial cost expressed in pips.

Nevertheless, with the magnitude of movement possible in the foreign exchange market, a long-term currency exposure without an adequate hedge could prove disastrous to a corporation, institution or individual. This is especially true in the case of an exchange rate that fluctuates in a wide range with high actual volatility An adequate long protective option strategy could provide a valid foreign currency downside hedge in any of a number of risk scenarios.

The following sections will cover the various types of long option strategies used to hedge underlying currency exposures.

Call Option Buying to Hedge an Underlying Short Exposure

As illustrated in Figure #1 below, a long call hedge for an underlying short exposure has a limited risk equal to the premium paid for it, while the profit potential is unlimited in the direction of falling exchange rates once the option's breakeven point has been attained. The kink in the curve is at the long call option's strike price.

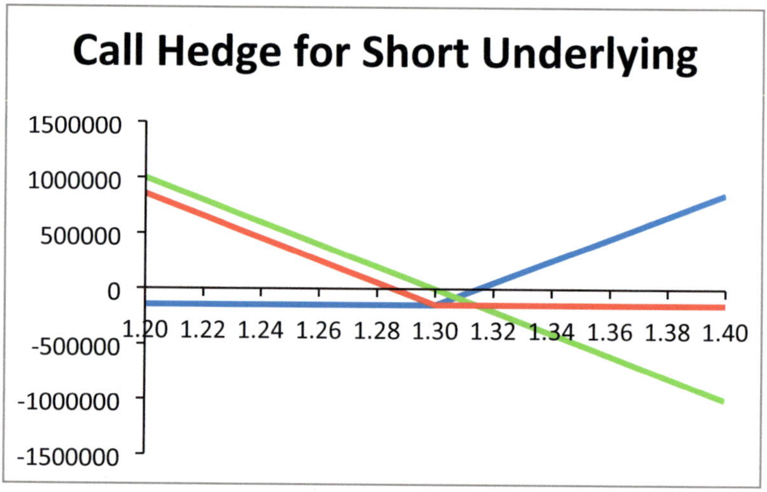

Figure #1: Profit and Loss diagram of a long call option used to hedge a short exposure with limited risk and unlimited potential profits. The green line represents the underlying short exposure, the blue line the call option hedge and the red line the resulting combined exposure.

Purchasing a call option to hedge an underlying short foreign exchange exposure has been a prudent risk management strategy used by many multinational businesses and financial institutions for decades.

For example, a typical foreign exchange hedging transaction would involve a corporate client buying a Euro call/U.S. Dollar put option if they have a short exposure in the EUR/USD exchange rate expected in two months' time.

A Euro call option purchase would be especially appropriate if the corporation's underlying short currency exposure was uncertain in its amount or was in some way contingent upon another event occurring. Furthermore, a Euro call option purchase might also make sense for the hedger if the corporate risk manager expected the underlying currency pair to decline favorably for their known short underlying exposure, but they needed protection or insurance against foreign exchange losses just in case the rate did not fall, but rose instead.

If the EUR/USD spot rate were currently at 1.3000, the hedger could purchase a two month 1.3000 Euro call/U.S. Dollar put option for the same amount as the anticipated short exposure. This would let them lock in the current spot rate as the strike price of the option contract. The cost of the Euro call option purchase would depend on the implied volatility quoted on the option by the market maker used to determine its price, and on the principal amount of the option transaction.

The breakeven exchange rate of the combined long Euro call option hedge and the underlying short EUR/USD exposure at the hedge's expiration would be the option's strike price minus the price of the option expressed in U.S. Dollar pips. Profits would begin to accrue on the combined position once the market fell below that breakeven point.

Put Option Buying to Hedge an Underlying Long Exposure

As illustrated in Figure #2 below, a long put hedge for an underlying long exposure has a limited risk equal to the premium paid for it, while the its profit potential is unlimited in the direction of rising exchange rates once the option's breakeven point has been attained. The kink in the curve is at the long put option's strike price.

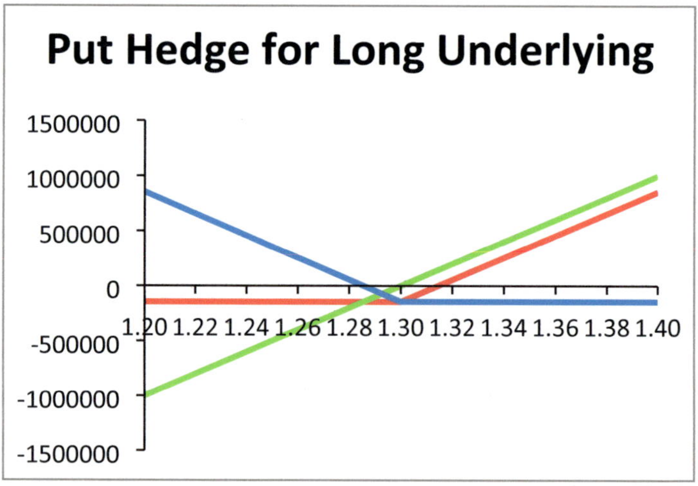

Figure #2: Profit and Loss diagram of a long put option used to hedge a long exposure in the underlying with limited risk and unlimited potential profits. The green line represents the underlying

long exposure, the blue line the put option hedge and the red line the resulting combined exposure.

Purchasing a put option to hedge an underlying long foreign exchange exposure has been a prudent risk management strategy used by many multinational businesses and financial institutions for decades.

For example, a typical foreign exchange hedging transaction would involve a corporate client buying a Euro put/U.S. Dollar call option if they have a long exposure in the EUR/USD currency pair expected to materialize in two months' time.

A Euro put option purchase would be especially appropriate if the corporation's underlying long currency exposure was uncertain in its amount or was in some way contingent upon another event occurring. Furthermore, a Euro put option purchase might also make sense for the hedger if the corporate risk manager expected the underlying currency pair to rise favorably for their known long underlying exposure, but they needed protection or insurance against foreign exchange losses just in case the rate did not rise, but fell instead.

If the EUR/USD spot rate were currently at 1.3000, the hedger could purchase a two month 1.3000 Euro put/U.S. Dollar call option for the same amount as the anticipated long EUR/USD currency exposure. This would let them lock in the current spot rate as the strike price of the option contract. The cost of the Euro put option purchase would depend on the implied volatility quoted on the option by the market maker used to determine its price, and on the principal amount of the option transaction.

The breakeven exchange rate of the combined long Euro put option hedge and the underlying long exposure at the hedge's expiration would be the option's strike price plus the price of the option expressed in U.S. Dollar pips. Profits would begin to accrue on the combined position once that breakeven point was exceeded.

In the case of an option purchase for hedging a long or short exposure to the underlying exchange rate, the hedger can take a number of follow up strategies. For example, if a protective call buyer's short currency position has appreciated in value with a decline in the market, the position lends itself to a possible sale of a put at a lower strike price to give up their profit potential beyond its strike price. This could even be combined with rolling down the protective call's strike price to improve their hedge rate. A better cap rate for the currency purchase can then be locked in at the lower call strike price, which is at least partially financed by taking in an option premium from the put sale.

If the exchange rate ends up above the sold put strike price at expiration, but below the purchased call strike, then neither option is exercised, and the currency is purchased at the market. If the sold put is in the money at expiration, then it will be exercised so that the required currency is purchased at the strike price of the put. If the purchased call is in the money at expiration, then the hedger will exercise it to buy their currency at the call strike price.

Follow up strategies for a put option purchased as a hedge for a long currency exposure would work in much the same way as the purchased call hedge for a short exposure, just in the opposite direction. If the market moves in a favorable direction, the hedger could lock in their upside profit by selling a covered call on the underlying exchange rate position with the same expiration and a higher strike price. They could also roll up the strike price of the protective put to give them a better floor rate.

At expiration, if the exchange rate is under the call's strike price, the call expires worthless. If the rate is higher than the call strike, the call position is exercised at the strike, thereby capping their profits on the long underlying exposure. If the exchange rate is between the put and the call strikes, neither option is exercised, and the hedger can just sell their long currency in the market. If the exchange rate is below the put strike, then the put is exercised to provide a worst case sale level for their currency.

Selling Upside Potential

A somewhat more controversial currency option hedging strategy involves selling a covered option to provide some extra funds to buffer an underlying currency exposure against adverse exchange rate moves.

Commonly known as a covered write, such a strategy involves selling the underlying exposure's upside potential in exchange for receiving an up front premium. The strategy involves selling an option with a strike price set at an acceptable level beyond which the hedger is comfortable forgoing any profits on the underlying exposure.

The following sections will cover the various types of short option strategies used to buffer underlying currency exposures from losses.

Call Option Selling to Buffer Losses on an Underlying Long Exposure

As illustrated in Figure #3 below, a covered short call hedge for an underlying long exposure has a limited reward equal to the premium received for it that also helps buffer against losses on the underlying long exposure, although its upside potential is limited above the option's strike price. Nevertheless, the position's loss potential is unlimited in the direction of falling exchange rates once the option's breakeven point has been reached. The kink in the curve is at the short call option's strike price.

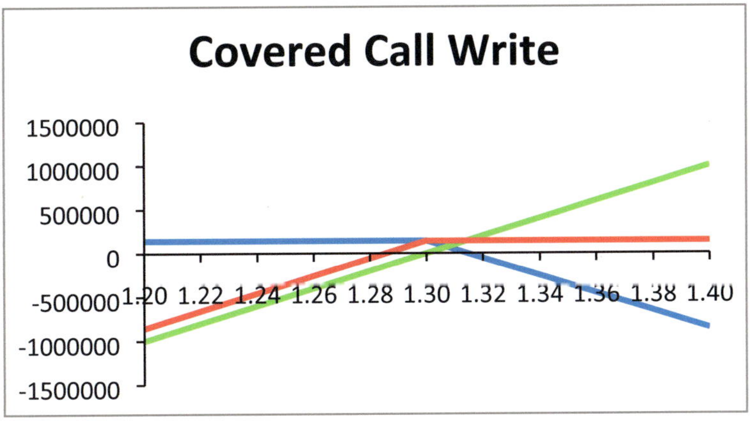

Figure #3: Profit and Loss diagram of a covered short call option hedge used to help buffer losses on a long exposure, while leaving the downside unprotected and giving up upside potential beyond the option's strike price. The green line represents the long underlying exposure, the blue line the sold covered call option and the red line the resulting combined exposure.

Put Option Selling to Buffer Losses on an Underlying Short Exposure

As illustrated in Figure #4 below, a covered short put hedge for an underlying short exposure has a limited reward equal to the premium received for it that also helps buffer against losses on the underlying short exposure. Nevertheless, its loss potential is unlimited in the direction of rising exchange rates once the option's breakeven point has been reached. The kink in the curve is at the short put option's strike price.

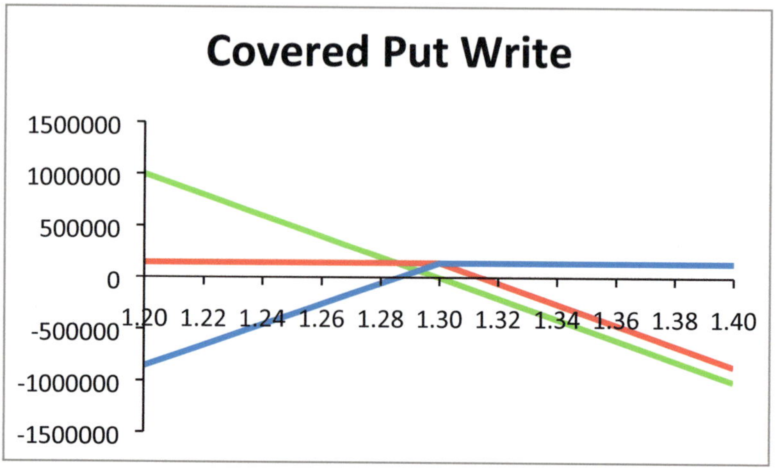

Figure #4: Profit and Loss diagram of a covered short put option hedge used to help buffer losses on a short exposure, while leaving the downside unprotected and giving up upside potential beyond the option's strike price. The green line represents the short underlying exposure, the blue line the sold covered put option and the red line the resulting combined exposure.

A number of follow up strategies can be used for a covered call or put write on an underlying foreign exchange position. The simplest involves rolling the option position into a different strike price as the option nears expiration. In the case of an existing short call position, if the sold call is in the money as its expiration approaches, a higher strike call could be sold for a longer expiration while using the proceeds to finance covering the short call position.

The main disadvantage of using a covered write strategy to buffer against losses on an underlying currency position is the unlimited risk on either the upside, in the case of a put write, or on the downside in the case of a written call. Although the premium received to sell the covered option helps to offset a limited amount of losses in case of an adverse move, the downside still remains unlimited once losses exceed the premium initially received.

Also, the best exchange rate when using this type of covered write strategy is going to be the strike price improved by the price received for the option in pips. The covered write strategy might be especially appropriate in the case when a flat or ranging market is anticipated over the lifetime of the option.

Collars or Range Forwards

A Collar is a common type of option hedging strategy in use among corporations that involves protecting against downside risk on an underlying exposure by purchasing an option and at the same time giving up their upside potential on the same underlying exposure by selling a covered option.

Collars are also sometimes called Range Forwards due to the fact that a range of participation in foreign exchange rate risk remains unhedged between the two option strike prices that can result in either a limited gain or a limited loss for the hedger on their underlying currency exposure. When the Collar hedge profit and loss profile is plotted together with the profile of the underlying exposure, the combined position resembles a long call spread for a long underlying exposure and a long put spread for a short underlying exposure.

Collars are typically structured economically so as to result in zero net cost to the hedger. This means that no funds change hands when the hedge is initiated since the sale of one option pays for the purchase of the other option. Zero cost collars generally have their upper and lower strike prices roughly equally displaced around the prevailing forward rate for the option's delivery date.

Both upper and lower Collar strike prices usually have a similar Delta. This Collar structure also helps neutralize the strategy with respect to changes in implied volatility because a rise in implied volatility will benefit the long option position by a similar amount that it will hurt the value of the short option position.

Nevertheless, the Collar strategy's value is somewhat sensitive to the implied volatility skew that might widen in favor of the puts or in favor of the calls, thereby causing movements in the Collar's mark to market value. Typically, a consistently falling market will cause the lower strike out of the money puts to rise in implied volatility levels relative to similarly out of the money higher strike calls as supply and demand effects skew the option market.

In practice, this volatility skew can go considerably beyond what the theoretically equal and balanced probabilities of a rise or fall in the underlying market would suggest option prices would be as option market makers react to pronounced trends in the underlying combined with client transactions reflecting the reality of this directional bias.

For example, in a downwards trend clients might seek to buy out of the money puts and/or sell of the money calls. Conversely, in an upwards trending market, they might look for opportunities to buy out of the money calls and/or to sell out of the money puts. These transactions are typically done in the anticipation of the prevailing directional trend continuing over the lifetime of the option positions.

In the foreign exchange option market, risk reversals and collars are often directly quoted among professionals in terms of the option's implied volatility. Collars sold to corporate clients by professional market makers are often offset with other market makers by transacting risk reversals via Interbank option brokers or option exchanges. The risk reversal position consists of a short out of the money put and a long out of the money call with the same expiration date.

Furthermore, the Deltas of the out of the money options that comprise a risk reversal or Collar are additive. For example, a long 25 Delta call has a positive or long spot equivalent position equal to 25 percent of the option's notional face value. A short 25 Delta put also has a long spot equivalent position equal to 25 percent of the option's notional face value. Hence, a 25 Delta risk reversal will have a combined 50 Delta equivalent spot position required to hedge it with respect to changes in the exchange rate of the underlying currency pair. A

30 Delta risk reversal would have a combined 60 Delta equivalent spot position, and so on.

Outside of its flat range between its two strike prices, the risk reversal mimics an outright long or outright short position in the underlying exchange rate. A reversal involves being long a call and short a put at the same strike price that results in an equivalent position to being long the underlying exchange rate. The main way to hedge the reversal position is to take an opposite forward position by shorting the underlying currency pair.

Although a risk reversal involves taking unlimited upside and downside risk when used as a trading strategy, its profit and loss profile changes to a limited risk and limited reward profit when used as a hedging tool often known as a Collar. Nevertheless, the Collar hedge strategy still involves taking underlying market risk between the two strike prices when combined with an underlying exposure.

Collars are popular corporate hedge strategies because being long a put and short a call effectively makes one short the underlying rate, which is a suitable hedge for a long currency exposure. Similarly, being long a call and short a put results in a long exposure to the underlying exchange that suitably hedges a short currency exposure.

Since Collars involve the sale of options, they should only be used to hedge certain, rather than contingent, currency exposures. Exposures that involve uncertainly in their existence, their amount and/or their timing are typically better hedged with long options that do not obligate the holder to actually deliver the underlying currency pair. Basically, if a contingent exposure fails to materialize as anticipated, then the sold option involved in using a Collar hedge strategy can expose the hedger to unlimited loss potential if the short option is exercised but no underlying exposure exists to help offset losses.

Using a Range Forward to Hedge a Long Exposure

The appropriate Range Forward or Collar strategy used by corporations to hedge a long exposure to a currency pair involves the purchase of a protective base currency put to provide a worst case floor rate at which the currency can be sold, and the simultaneous covered sale of a base currency call to give up the upside potential on the exposure beyond its strike price.

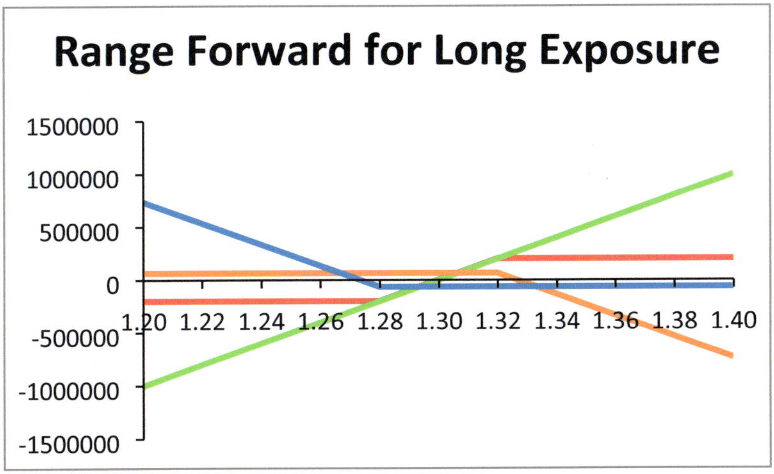

Figure #5: Profit and Loss diagram of a zero cost Collar or Range Forward hedge consisting of a long put option used to protect against losses on a long exposure and a short call option used to give up upside potential beyond its strike price. The green line represents the long underlying exposure, the blue line the purchased put option, the orange line the sold call option, and the red line the resulting combined exposure.

As the diagram above shows, when combined with the underlying long exposure, this sort of Collar resembles the profit and loss profile of a long base currency call spread. The profile shows limited risk of loss below the purchased put strike and limited profit potential above the sold call strike price.

Using a Range Forward to Hedge a Short Exposure

The Range Forward or Collar strategy used to hedge a long exposure to a currency pair involves the purchase of a protective base currency call to provide a worst case cap rate at which the currency can be purchased, combined with the covered sale of a base currency put to give up the profit potential on the short exposure below its strike price. When combined with the underlying exposure, this sort of Collar resembles a long base currency put spread in terms of its profit and loss profile.

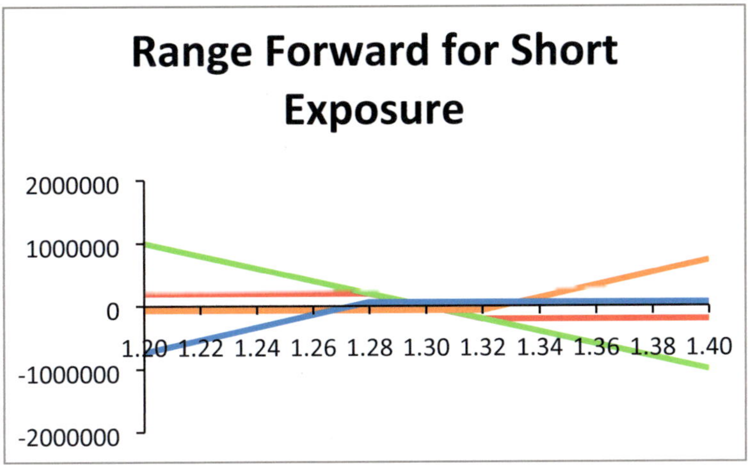

Figure #6: Profit and Loss diagram of a zero cost Range Forward or Collar hedge consisting of a long call option used to protect against losses on a short exposure and a short put option used to give up profit potential below its strike price. The green line represents the short underlying exposure, the orange line the purchased call option, the blue line the sold put option, and the red line the resulting combined exposure.

The diagram above illustrates that, when combined with the underlying long exposure, this sort of Collar resembles the profit and loss profile of a long base currency put spread. The profile shows limited risk of loss above the purchased call strike and limited profit potential below the sold put strike price.

Participating Forwards

Like the Range Forward, a Participating Forward is another quite popular option hedging strategy that remains in regular use among corporations that have international foreign exchange exposures.

The Participating Forward hedge strategy generally involves protecting against downside risk on an underlying exposure by purchasing an out of the money option to protect a particular floor exchange rate and at the same time giving up a percentage of their upside potential on the same underlying exposure by selling a covered option for a portion of the total exposure amount to be hedged.

Participating Forwards are usually economically structured by most corporate hedgers to have a zero net premium cost, although they can also involve a net premium or credit by adjusting the strike price. Like with the zero cost Collar, no funds change hands initially when a zero cost Participating Forward is transacted because the purchase of the out of the money option is completely compensated for by the sale of a lesser amount of the in the money option.

Furthermore, a zero cost Participating Forward will generally have its strike price situated at a less attractive rate than the prevailing forward rate for the option's delivery date so that some degree of participation in favorable exchange rate movements can be experienced. In general, the more out of the money the Participating Forward's strike price is set, the more participation the hedger receives in such favorable moves.

Since both of the options that comprise a Participating Forward hedge have the same strike price, they generally have Deltas that add up to 100 percent. In a zero cost Participating Forward, the larger principal amount option used for fully protecting the underlying exposure will usually have a Delta less than 50 percent since its strike price will need to be out of the money to make the structure cost free. The lesser principal amount option that is sold against the underlying exposure will usually have a Delta greater than 50 percent, and roughly equal to 100 percent minus the Delta of the purchased out of the money option.

Although using a Participating Forward hedge strategy has some mark to market exposure with respect to changes in implied volatility, a natural partial offset to this risk exists to the long option portion that is equal to the lesser amount of the sold option. Nevertheless, a Participating Forward always results in a long Vega exposure that benefits the position if implied volatility rises, since a larger amount of the long option hedge is purchased than is sold of the short covered option.

For example, in a downwards trending market, a hedger might use a Participating Forward strategy to protect a short position in a currency pair by buying an out of the money base currency call and selling half that amount of an in the money base currency put of the same strike price as the call. This Participating Forward strategy would allow the hedger to set a worst-case maximum budgeted rate for the exchange of their foreign currency exposure into their base currency at the strike price of the options. At the same time, the Participating Forward hedge would allow them to participate in

50 percent of any exchange rate decline seen below the strike price of the options by their expiration date.

A similar hedging choice to use a Participating Forward might be made by a corporation looking to protect a long position in a currency pair in an upwards-trending market. In this case, they might look for opportunities to buy a protective out of the money base currency put and sell a percentage of that amount of an in the money base currency call with the same strike price. Note that both types of Participating Forward transactions provide complete downside protection and are typically done in the anticipation of the prevailing directional trend continuing over the lifetime of the option positions.

In the foreign exchange option market, Participating Forwards typically involve no volatility spread between the two options, due to the conversion relationship between puts and calls of the same strike price. Nevertheless, they are usually priced at the offer side of the implied volatility market for options of that Delta, strike price and expiration date since the strategy involves a net sale of options to the client. Since a participating forward generally involves currency options that are away from the money by a significant amount, the implied volatilities at which they are priced will usually be higher than those for the corresponding at the money options of the same expiration date.

As with Range Forwards, the Deltas of the out of the money and the in the money options that comprise a Participating Forward are additive, and they will together always add up to roughly 100 percent. For example, a long 25 Delta call in 10 million Euros has a positive or long spot equivalent position equal to 25 percent of the option's notional face value or 2.5 million Euros. A short 75 Delta put in 5 million Euros also has a long spot equivalent position equal to 75 percent of the option's notional face value or 3.75 million Euros. Hence, a 50 percent Participating Forward at that strike price will have a combined Delta equivalent spot position of 2.5 million Euros plus 3.75 million Euros or 6.25 million Euros that need to be sold to hedge it initially with respect to changes in the exchange rate of the underlying currency pair. In percentage terms, this combined Delta would be a 62.5 percent amount of the original 10 million Euro amount of the purchased call option.

When combined with the underlying exposure it is intended to hedge, the Participating Forwards mimics a call in the case of a long exposure or a put in the case of a short exposure at the strike price of the options multiplied by the percentage of the original position's upside potential not sold.

Participating Forwards are also popular corporate hedge strategies for partially contingent exposures because they provide full downside protection for the full potential amount of the exposure, but they only commit the hedger to the partial amount of the short option sold. Since Participating Forwards involve the sale of options, they should only be used to hedge certain, rather than contingent, currency exposures for the amount of the option sold.

Exposures that are completely uncertain in terms of their existence, amount and/or their timing are typically better hedged with long options that do not obligate the holder to actually deliver the underlying currency pair. Basically, if a contingent exposure fails to materialize as anticipated, then the sold option involved in using a Participating Forward hedge strategy can expose the hedger to unlimited loss potential if the short option is exercised but no underlying exposure exists to help offset losses.

Using a Participating Forward to Hedge a Long Exposure

The appropriate Participating Forward strategy used by corporations to hedge a long exposure to a currency pair involves the purchase of a protective base currency put to provide a worst case floor rate at which the currency can be sold, and the simultaneous covered sale of a base currency call to give up the upside potential on the exposure beyond its strike price. Both options have the same strike price.

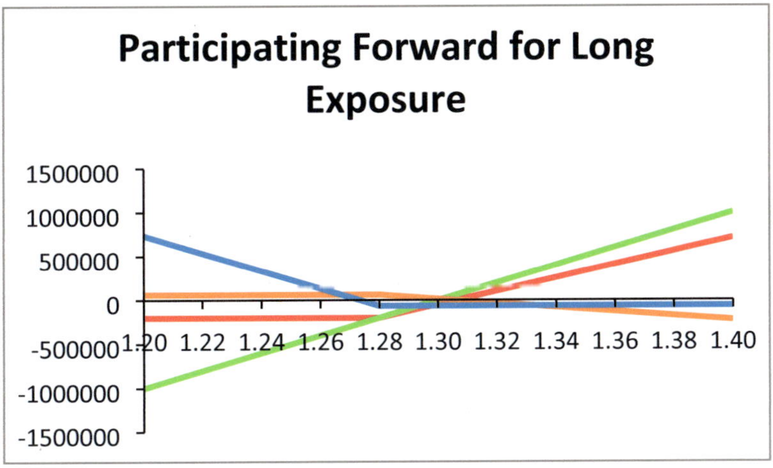

Figure #5: Profit and Loss diagram of a zero cost Participating Forward hedge consisting of a long put option used to protect against losses on a long exposure and a short call option in a reduced amount used to give up upside potential beyond its strike price. Note that both strike prices are the same. The green line represents the long underlying exposure, the blue line the purchased put option, the orange line the sold call option in a lesser amount but with the same strike price, and the red line the resulting combined exposure.

As the diagram above shows, when combined with the underlying long exposure, this sort of Participating Forward resembles the profit and loss profile of a long base currency call in a reduced principal amount, so that the upside has a softer slope.

The profile shows limited risk of loss below the purchased put strike and unlimited profit potential above the sold call strike price, but to a lesser degree due to the hedger having sold part of their upside potential in order to finance the zero cost strategy.

Using a Participating Forward to Hedge a Short Exposure

The Participating Forward strategy used to hedge a long exposure to a currency pair involves the purchase of a protective base currency call to provide a worst case cap rate at which the currency can be purchased, combined with the covered sale of a base currency put in a lesser amount in order to give up a portion of the profit potential on the short exposure below its strike price. Both options have the same strike price.

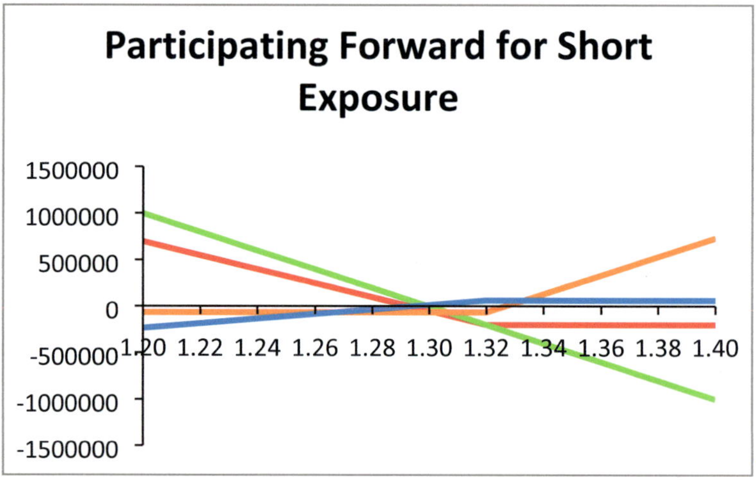

Figure #6: Profit and Loss diagram of a zero cost Participating Forward hedge consisting of a long call option used to protect against losses on a short exposure and a short put option in a reduced amount used to give up upside potential beyond its strike price. Note that both strike prices are the

same. The green line represents the short underlying exposure; the blue line the purchased call option, the orange line the sold put option in a lesser amount but with the same strike price, and the red line the resulting combined exposure.

The diagram above illustrates that, when combined with the underlying long exposure, this sort of Participating Forward resembles the profit and loss profile of a long base currency put, but in a lesser amount.

The profile shows limited risk of loss above the purchased call strike and limited profit potential below the sold put strike price, but to a lesser degree due to the hedger having sold part of their upside potential in order to finance the zero cost strategy.

Chapter 8: Hedging Currency Exposures with Exotic Forex Options

Introduction to Hedging With Exotic Options

Fluctuations in foreign exchange rates can be advantageous for those with currency exposures, as any profitable forex trader can attest. Furthermore, exotic options can offer a perfect hedging vehicle for numerous outright long or short foreign exchange positions, and they offer a plethora of ways to offset direct foreign exchange exposures strategically.

Corporations, fund managers and individuals looking to hedge a forex exposure may find that their underlying risk or market view may lend itself well to using an exotic option hedging strategy. Exotic options can not only provide those hedgers with a different and possibly more attractive risk profile from plain Vanilla options and forward contracts, but they are also sometimes simply the best and most cost effective hedge for the currency risks involved.

Exotic option hedges start to become more attractive than forwards or Vanilla options when some risk element specifically covered by their unique characteristics is involved in the hedging process. For example, the budget rate may be subject to an averaging process, thereby making an Average Strike option an appropriate hedge. Alternatively, perhaps the exposure to be hedged may be contingent upon the signing of a contract, making a Compound Option a better hedge.

In case such as these, choosing the appropriate purchased exotic forex option hedges for the risk involved can serve to protect the currency exposures far more accurately than by using Vanilla options or a forward contract.

Using exotic forex options as a hedge can also be very beneficial when a hedger believes that the underlying currency pair may move in a favorable direction for their exposure or when the market has known support and resistance levels that can be used to place Knock out or Knock in barriers strategically.

For example, if they have a long exposure in the base currency and think it is likely to appreciate considerably in the future if the market rises above a key resistance point, then hedging by selling a forward contract would eliminate any potential for future gain on their exposure. By purchasing a protective base currency Knock out put instead, with a trigger set just above the resistance level, the hedger can leave their long exposure's profit potential unlimited if the base currency rises as expected, while still having covered their downside risk as long as the market stays below the resistance level protecting their option Knock out trigger.

One of the main downsides to using exotic options as hedges is their relative illiquidity in comparison to Vanilla options. Competitive prices for Vanilla forex options can be found on major exchanges such as the Chicago IMM and the Philadelphia Stock Exchange, which contributes to their considerable liquidity and the transparency of their pricing, even in the Over the Counter market.

In contrast, the market for most exotic options is quite illiquid, and they are largely only available in the Over the Counter market. Thus, the risk exists that the pricing a hedger obtains from a market maker or customer dealer at a bank or other financial institution for an exotic option hedge may not be in line with its fair value. The widespread tendency of bank customer dealers to mark up prices to their clients significantly can contribute to this problem, which can make the exotic option hedge seem less attractive as a result.

A hedger can help minimize this significant exotic option pricing risk by having access to a suitable pricing model to enable them to compute or approximate an exotic option's fair value. The hedger can also obtain quotes from several banks based on a given spot rate for easy comparison purposes. Those banks that show the best quotes based on a given spot rate can then be asked to provide a live dealing price at the same time so that the hedger can deal the exotic option on the best price.

The following sections will discuss how each of the most common types of exotic options can be applied to hedging foreign currency exposures.

Buying Knockout Options for Contingent Downside Protection

A typical currency option hedging strategy involves purchasing an option to protect an underlying currency exposure from adverse exchange rate moves. Knockout options are also useful for this purpose, although using them as a hedge typically requires a follow up strategy to be executed if the purchased Knockout option is ever triggered out of existence. This cancellation possibility makes protective purchased Knock Out options contingent hedges, since their ability to protect an exposure again adverse exchange rate moves is contingent upon the option's continued existence.

The main advantage of buying a protective Knock Out option is that they generally cost less than an otherwise equivalent Vanilla option. Nevertheless, if the Knock Out option's trigger level is hit, then the protective option is cancelled, and the hedger's underlying exposure again has unlimited profit and loss potential.

Also, the purchased option's trigger level can be set strategically where the likelihood of the option being knocked out prior to expiration is relatively low given the hedger's view on the market. This would indicate the hedger would be buying the Knock out option with a trigger level set safely beyond a significant technical support or resistance point, or at a level where the hedger would be comfortable locking in an exchange rate with a forward contract.

The possibility of the knock out trigger being hit should be planned for if the hedger desires additional protection at that point. In this case, hedging with a forward contract, by buying an additional Knock out option or a Vanilla option, or by putting on a Vanilla Range Forward hedge, which could all be possible follow up strategies.

For example, consider the case of a U.S. based corporate hedger who expects their company to be receiving 10 million Euros in one month's time. Their market view is that the Euro may appreciate considerably over the coming month from its present 1.3000 level. Nevertheless, they feel that if the market gets to the 1.3200 level, then they would be interested in locking in that rate with a forward contract to sell Euros and buy U.S. Dollars. They would also like to reduce the cost they pay for this hedge, just in case their view is incorrect and the Euro falls this month, instead of rising as expected.

Purchasing a knockout Euro Put/U.S. Dollar option with a 1.3000 strike price and a 1.3200 knockout trigger level expiring in one month's time in a notional amount of 10,000,000 Euros could be quite suitable for this particular hedger. Assuming an implied volatility of 10 percent, this knockout option might cost the hedger 121 U.S. Dollar pips or 0.0121 points, which would be $121,000.

If the spot rate were to decline without ever reaching the option's 1.3200 knockout trigger level, then they would be able to sell their Euro receivables at 1.3000 and their breakeven would be that 1.3000 strike price minus the amount paid for the option in U.S. Dollar points, or 0.0121, yielding a result of 1.2879.

If the spot rate ends up at the option's expiration date between 1.3000 and 1.3200, without ever having touched 1.3200 prior to expiry, then the hedger will let their 1.3000 Euro Put expire worthless and can sell their Euros in the spot market instead. Their breakeven would be this sale rate less the 0.0121 price paid for the Knockout option.

Alternatively, if the spot rate trades up to 1.3200 within the coming month, the hedger can have preemptively placed an order to sell 10,000,000 Euros in the spot market at that trigger level when their protective option hedge will be cancelled. If executed, this sale of Euros can then be rolled out to the forward date when their Euro receivables are expected as a forward hedge. Their breakeven rate on this forward hedge would be 1.3200 minus the amount paid for the Knockout option in U.S. Dollar pips, or 1.3079.

Selling Covered Knockout Options to Buffer Losses

Shorting a covered Knock Out Call or Put option acts as a buffer against losses on an existing long or short currency exposure, but it limits a hedger's upside potential on their underlying exposure to the strike price if the option is not cancelled prior to its expiration. Furthermore, this strategy only provides a limited degree of protection in the form of the premium received, which is typically less than that received from the sale of an otherwise equivalent Vanilla option. In addition, a sold Knock Out option's premium yield drops significantly as its trigger price is moved closer to the prevailing spot rate.

The main advantage of selling a covered Knock Out option is that the option's trigger level can be set strategically where the likelihood of the option being knocked out prior to expiration is relatively high given the hedger's view on the market. This would indicate the hedger would be writing the Knock out option with a trigger level set fairly close to the current underlying exchange rate or at an attainable level given a prevailing trend in the underlying. If the Knock Out option's trigger level is hit, then the covered option is cancelled, and the hedger's underlying exposure again has unlimited profit (and loss) potential.

The primary risk with selling covered Knock out options, as with sold covered Vanilla options, is that the protection afforded by the sold knock out option's premium might not be sufficient to protect the hedger's exposure in the event of a sharp adverse move in the underlying exchange rate. Knock out options generally yield a lower premium from their sale than Vanilla options with the same strike price, due to the chance that they might be cancelled prior to expiration.

This fact reduces the short covered option's ability to provide a buffer for any losses that might accrue on the underlying exchange rate position. As a result, while the covered Knock Out option might end up being cancelled if the hedger's market view is correct, its ability to buffer potential losses on the underlying exposure is somewhat reduced compared to a Vanilla option in the case of an adverse move.

Also, if a hedger is writing knockout options against an underlying exchange rate exposure, and their sold knock out option ends up getting triggered and hence cancelled, a subsequent hedging strategy might be appropriate. This possibility should be planned for if the hedger desires additional protection at that point. In this case, selling an additional covered Knock out option could be a possible follow up strategy.

As an example, consider the case of a U.S. based corporate hedger who expects their company to be receiving 10 million Euros in one month's time. Their market view is that the Euro should remain relatively stable over the coming month and will end up near its present 1.3000 level. Nevertheless, they think the market may initially dip down to the 1.2800 level within that time frame. Selling a covered Knock Out Euro Call/U.S. Dollar Put option with a 1.3000 strike price and a 1.2800 knockout trigger level expiring in one month's time in a notional amount of 10,000,000 Euros could be quite suitable for this particular covered writer.

Assuming an implied volatility of 10 percent, selling this Knock Out Euro Call option might yield 123 U.S. Dollar pips or 0.0123 U.S. Dollar points, which would be $123,000 on a principal amount of

10,000,000 Euros for the hedger to use to buffer against any adverse exchange rate movements should the Euro decline.

If the EUR/USD spot rate were to decline to the 1.2800 Knock Out trigger level, then the sold option would be cancelled and would immediately expire worthless. They could then employ another option hedging strategy or sell another covered option against their exposure as a follow up strategy.

Alternatively, if the EUR/USD exchange rate were to rise over the coming month without ever reaching the sold option's 1.2800 knockout trigger level, then they would be obligated to sell their Euro receivables at the 1.3000 strike price, so their breakeven would be that 1.3000 strike price plus the amount received for the option in U.S. Dollar points, or 0.0123, yielding a result of 1.3123.

Furthermore, if the spot rate ends up at the option's expiration date below the option's 1.3000 strike price, then the sold 1.3000 Knock Out Euro Call will expire worthless, and the hedger can sell their Euros in the spot market instead. Their breakeven would be this sale rate plus the 123 pips the covered seller received for the sold Knock Out Call option.

Buying Knock in Options for Contingent Downside Protection

A Knock in option is similar to a Vanilla option, but it does not exist until a pre-set trigger level trades prior to its expiration. For this reason, Knock In options are considerably cheaper than Vanilla options, so purchasing a Knock In option to hedge an existing currency exposure offers the hedger a relatively inexpensive alternative to a Vanilla put or call purchase.

Thus, the primary advantage of purchasing a knock in option to potentially protect against losses on an existing exchange rate exposure is its relative cheapness compared with an otherwise equivalent Vanilla option. If the option gets knocked into existence by having its trigger level trade prior to expiration, then the hedger has obtained cheap insurance for their exposure.

Nevertheless, the main additional risk in using a Knock In option as a hedge is that if the exotic option's trigger level does not trade prior to expiration, the hedger's exposure may be left uncovered with the potential risk of unlimited losses. This makes a Knock In option a contingent hedge, since it has no actual utility as a hedge until it is knocked in by having its trigger level trade in the underlying spot market.

A hedger with an existing currency position to protect, and who is willing to take the risk that their option hedge may never come into existence, could place the strike price and the trigger at levels where the option, if triggered, will help cover losses the trader would incur at that exchange rate on their existing currency position. A contingent hedge of this type could be constructed from either an Up and In or a Down and In type of Knock In option, depending on the hedger's market view and desired risk profile.

When purchasing a Knock In option, a hedger will generally decide on the strike price, the Knock In exchange rate or trigger level, the expiration date and the notional amount, while the market maker selling the option determines the appropriate implied volatility level, as well as spot and forward exchange rates, in order to compute the option's fair value and show a price to their client.

As an example, consider the case of a U.S. based corporate hedger who expects their company to be receiving 10 million Euros in one month's time. Their market view is that the Euro may appreciate considerably over the coming month from its present 1.3000 level where they have set their budget level for the transaction. Furthermore, while they would like to put on some type of option hedge now, they feel that the market might very well trade quickly up to the 1.3200 level first. They would like to reduce the cost they pay for this hedge, just in case their view is incorrect and the Euro falls later this month, instead of rising as expected.

Purchasing an Up and In type Knock In Euro Put/U.S. Dollar option with a 1.3000 strike price and a 1.3200 Knock In trigger level expiring in one month's time in a notional amount of 10,000,000 Euros could be quite suitable for this particular hedger, as long as they are willing to take evasive action to protect their long Euro exposure if the EUR/USD market declines significantly.

Assuming an implied volatility of 10 percent, this Knock In option might only cost the hedger 27 U.S. Dollar pips or 0.0027 points, which would be $27,000.

If the spot rate were to end up below the option's 1.3200 Knock In trigger level without ever having reached it, then the hedger would have to sell their Euro receivables at the market spot exchange rate. Thus their breakeven would be that spot exchange rate minus the amount paid for the option in U.S. Dollar points, or 0.0027. This could result in potentially unlimited losses since the hedger's long Euro exposure would not be protected against a decline in the Euro.

If the spot rate trades up above the option's 1.3200 Knock In trigger level then the option comes into existence. In this situation, the hedger would have locked in a worse case price to sell their Euro receivables at the option's 1.3000 strike price level minus the amount paid for the option in U.S. Dollar points, or 0.0027 for a worse case rate of 1.2973.

If the spot rate then ends up at the Knock In option's expiration date above 1.3000 after the option has been knocked in, then the hedger will let their 1.3000 Euro Put expire worthless. They can then sell their Euros in the spot market instead, and their breakeven would be this sale rate less the 0.0027 price paid for the Knock In option.

Selling Covered Knock in Options

A hedger could use the premium received from selling a Knock In option to buffer against losses on an adverse movement affecting an underlying currency exposure.

While the strategy makes sense if the knock in level was set to benefit the seller, generally the option buyer has a say in the general terms of the contract, with the exception of the option's premium. In order for the strategy to provide a sufficient hedge for the seller, the option premium, trigger and strike price levels would have to fit their underlying position.

The hedger would also have to work or have access to a forex trading desk specializing in exotic options to be able to sell a knock in option appropriate to their underlying exchange rate exposure. Besides the difficulty in arranging for the sale of the option, knock ins generally carry a lower premium than regular vanilla options, giving the hedger a lower buffer level for any potential losses on their underlying exposure.

As an example, consider the case of a U.S. based corporate hedger who expects their company to be receiving 10 million Euros in one month's time. Their market view is that the Euro should remain relatively stable over the coming month and will end up near its present 1.3000 level. Furthermore, they see good technical support just above the 1.2800 level in EUR/USD so they think the market will probably not trade there. Selling a covered Down and In Knock In Euro Call/U.S. Dollar Put option with a 1.3000 strike price and a 1.2800 knock in trigger level expiring in one month's time in a notional amount of 10,000,000 Euros could be quite suitable for this particular covered writer.

Assuming an implied volatility of 10 percent, this Knock In option might yield 27 U.S. Dollar pips or 0.0027 points, which would be $27,000 for the hedger to use to buffer against any adverse exchange rate movements should the Euro decline.

If the EUR/USD spot rate were to decline to the 1.2800 Knock In trigger level, then the sold option would come into existence and would effectively cap gains on their underlying long Euro exposure at the 1.3000 level. In addition, their long Euro exposure could be subject to further losses if the Euro declines.

On the other hand, if the EUR/USD exchange rate were to stabilize as expected or rise over the coming month without ever reaching the sold option's 1.2800 knock in trigger level, then they would be able to to sell their Euro receivables at the market spot price. In this case, their breakeven would be that spot price received plus the amount received for the option in U.S. Dollar points, or 0.0027.

Combining Vanilla and Trigger Options in Hedge Strategies

Exotic options that feature triggers — such as knock out, knock in and one touch binary options — can be readily combined with Vanilla forex options to create a plethora of unique hedge strategies. Such combinations can help a hedger to better reflect their market view with a hedging strategy, and they can also often incorporate specific contractual or budgetary requirements into their currency protection program.

A relatively popular example of this sort of exotic/vanilla option combination hedge is sometimes called a Cable Car strategy. For a hedger looking to protect a long currency exposure, this combination hedge strategy might involve buying a protective Vanilla Put on that currency to establish a floor rate for the sale of their currency. They would also simultaneously sell a covered Reverse Knock In or Up and In Call option with the same strike price and a trigger price set considerably above the prevailing spot rate.

Depending on the strike and knock in trigger price chosen, this combination hedge strategy has a significantly reduced cost over buying a Vanilla put option, and it can sometimes even often be structured for a zero or low overall premium cost.

The main advantage this combination offers revolves around the fact that until the sold Reverse Knock in Call option's trigger price trades, that option does not actually exist, so upside potential exists on the position until that trigger level is touched.

If the combination option hedge expires before that Knock in trigger is reached, then the hedger's worse case rate is limited to the purchase Vanilla

Put's strike price, while their best case rate is limited to the Knock in trigger level.

Nevertheless, once that Knock in trigger level is touched, the combination transaction basically becomes a synthetic forward hedge with an exchange rate set at the identical strike price of the purchase Put and the now-triggered sold Knock in Call.

As a more concrete example, consider the case of a U.S. based corporate hedger looking to protect an expected long exposure of 10,000,000 Euros due in one month's time. They have a budget rate of 1.2800 and think that the EUR/USD exchange rate is probably going to rise further over the coming month, but not above strong resistance seen on the charts at the 1.3200 level.

With the EUR/USD spot rate currently at 1.3000 and one month implied volatility at 10 percent, they could enter into a Cable Car strategy. They might do this by buying 10,000,000 Euros of a protective 1.2800 Vanilla Euro Put/U.S. Dollar Call expiring in one month's time for 267 pips, and selling the same amount of a covered 1.2800 Reverse or Up and In Knock in Euro Call/U.S. Dollar Put with a trigger at the 1.3200 level and the same expiration date for 246 pips or 0.0246 points. The net price of the strategy would be 21 pips for a total premium of $21,000.

In this situation, losses on the underlying long Euro exposure would be limited to the 1.2800 strike price of the purchase Euro Put, less the initial 21 pips in premium paid. In addition, gains on the underlying long Euro exposure would accrue up to the 1.3200 Reverse Knock in trigger level. Nevertheless, once the market trades above that trigger level, the sold 1.2800 Euro Call comes into existence, so the hedger has effectively locked in a 1.2800 rate for their Euro receivables with a synthetic forward hedge, less the 21 pips premium paid, for an all in hedge rate of 1.2779.

Buying Average Rate Options for Downside Protection

Average Rate forex options are cash settled exotic derivatives that have a given strike price and an intrinsic value computed by comparing the strike to the average of a series of exchange rate observations or fixings. Averages can be computed arithmetically or geometrically, and the fixing dates for Average Rate options traded in the Over the Counter market do not usually need to be spaced evenly. Also, the first observation date can start significantly later than when the option was initially purchased.

While Vanilla forex options are often used to hedge specific transaction risks and contingent exposures, Average Rate options can be used to hedge budgets, regular cash flows, projected profits and other related foreign exchange exposures that have some form of intrinsic averaging process involved.

One common application of Average Rate options is as a hedge purchased by international corporations with a series of periodic recurring exposures to fluctuating exchange rates. Like other purchased options, the risk on the purchase of an Average Rate option is limited to the amount of money invested in the hedge, although the hedger might run some additional risk on the underlying exposure if the option's strike price is not set at the money.

A purchased Average Rate option can also be compared to a series of purchased Vanilla options with expirations matching the fixing dates. While this series also represents a suitable hedge for a series of currency exposures, the Average Rate option will generally have a lower premium than the series of plain Vanilla options, and so it may be a more cost effective hedge.

When purchasing an Average Rate option, a hedger typically establishes the option's expiration date, the notional base or counter currency amount, and strike price. In addition, they will set agree upon the fixing source, frequency of observations and averaging type for computing the average underlying exchange rate. Generally, the more fixing dates to be observed during the life of the Average Rate option, the lower the exotic option's premium will be.

For example, consider the situation of a U.S. based corporate hedger who expects their company to be receiving 1,000,000 Euros at the end of each month over the coming year for a total of

12,000,000 Euros. Their market view is that the Euro might appreciate over the coming year, but they want their long Euro exposure to be covered at their 1.2800 budget level just in case the average exchange rate received for their Euros declines instead. Since they are willing to pay an up front option premium for this protection, buying a protective Average Rate Euro Put/U.S. Dollar Call option with a 1.2800 strike price expiring in one year's time with twelve month end fixings at noon New York Time to be arithmetically averaged in a notional amount of 12,000,000 Euros could be quite suitable for this particular hedger.

Assuming a spot EUR/USD exchange rate of 1.3000 and a flat implied volatility over the year of 10 percent, this Average Rate option might cost 166 U.S. Dollar pips or 0.0166 points, which would be $199,200 for the hedger to purchase to protect their total 12,000,000 Euro exposure against any adverse declines in the average EUR/USD exchange rate below the 1.2800 level over the coming year.

If the month end average of the EUR/USD spot rate were to decline below the 1.2800 strike price by expiration, then the purchased Average Rate Euro Put/U.S. Dollar Call option would end up in the money. In this case, the hedger would receive a cash settlement amount in U.S. Dollars from the option writer that would be computed by subtracting the arithmetic average of the fixings from the 1.2800 strike price and multiplying the result by the 12,000,000 Euro total notional amount. If the computed average were 1.2550, for example, then the cash settlement the Average Rate option buyer receives would be $300,000. This payment would help offset any losses they might experience on their series of twelve underlying Euro sales each month, although their breakeven rate would also be reduced by the initial premium of 0.0166 paid up front for the option.

The hedger would also need to take action each month to sell their Euro receivables on each of the month end fixing dates around the noon New York fixing time. This makes sure that the average exchange rate they receive for their Euros is comparable to the average rate used to compute the intrinsic value of their Average Rate option hedge.

Of course, if the average rate at the Average Rate option's expiration date ends up above its 1.2800 strike price, then the Average Rate Euro Put/U.S. Dollar Call option expires worthless. In this case, the hedger is compensated by having received the better average rate that they sold their series of 1,000,000 Euro receivables at each month end fixing date over the preceding twelve months, less the premium of 0.0166 they initially paid for the option.

Buying Average Strike Options for Downside Protection

Average Strike options, which are also sometimes called Average Strike Rate options or ASROs, have some utility as a hedging vehicle. They can be cash settled or settled by delivering currencies, and their intrinsic value at expiration is computed by comparing the spot rate at expiration to their strike price, which is computed by averaging a series of observed fixings and so it not known until the last fixing is observed.

Buying Average Strike options offers hedgers a specific type of protection against adverse exchange rate fluctuations. Over longer time periods involving more observations, purchasing an Average Strike option as a hedge will also cost considerably less than what a Vanilla option would cost, which may not even hedge the exposure properly. To further customize the strategy, the fixing dates on the Average Strike option can be assigned weightings, and they can be unevenly spaced.

Average Strike options are especially suitable for companies that routinely set a budgetary or contractual exchange rate for an expected cash flow based on an average exchange rate observed over an extended period of time on fixing dates.

When purchasing an Average Strike option, a hedger typically establishes the option's expiration date, its notional currency amount and the moneyness of its strike price relative to the spot rate, as well as the fixing source, frequency of observations and averaging type for computing the average strike price. Generally, the more fixing dates observed during the life of the Average Strike option, the lower the exotic option's premium will be.

For example, consider the situation of a U.S. based corporate hedger who expects their company to be paying out 10 million Euros at the end of the coming month. Their market view is that the Euro might depreciate over that period, but in case it rises instead, they want to be covered at their budget rate, which will be set at the average exchange rate observed at daily EUR/USD exchange rate fixings made at noon New York time each trading day during the coming month.

They are willing to pay an up front option premium for this protection, so it could be quite suitable for this hedger to purchase a protective Average Strike Euro Call/U.S. Dollar Put option in a 10,000,000 Euro notional amount with an at the money spot strike price to be determined by taking an arithmetic average of daily EUR/USD spot fixings at noon New York Time.

Assuming a spot EUR/USD exchange rate of 1.3000 and a flat implied volatility over the one month period year of 10 percent, this Average Strike option might cost roughly 84 U.S. Dollar pips or 0.0084 points, which would be $84,000 for the hedger to purchase to protect against any adverse rises in the actual EUR/USD exchange rate at expiration above the option's computed averaged strike price sampled over the coming month.

If EUR/USD closes the month above the computed average strike of the option, then the purchased Average Strike Euro Call/U.S. Dollar Put option would end up in the money. In this case, the hedger could receive either a cash settlement amount in U.S. Dollars or would exchange currencies at the averaged strike price. If cash settled, the value of the settlement would be computed by subtracting strike price determined by an arithmetic average of the fixings from the final spot rate observed at the option's expiration and multiplying the result by the 10,000,000 Euro notional amount. Thus, if the computed average strike was 1.2500, for example, and the spot rate was 1.3000 at expiration, then the cash settlement for the Average Strike option that its buyer receives would be 1.3000 minus 1.2500 times 10,000,000 Euros or a cash amount of $500,000. This payment would help offset any losses the hedger might experience on purchasing the Euros they require for that month at the 1.3000 spot rate relative to their budgeted rate of 1.2500 that is computed by taking an average of the same fixings as the strike price.

Of course, if the spot rate ends up below the computed average strike price of the Average Strike Euro Call/U.S. Dollar Put, then this option will expire worthless. In this case, the hedger is able to purchase their 10,000,000 Euros at the prevailing spot rate at the option's expiration, which will be better than their budgeted average rate.

Buying Basket Options for Currency Portfolio Protection

Forex Basket options are a class of exotic derivatives that group several different currencies into a basket or portfolio quoted against a common base currency. The base currency of a Basket option is typically a major currency like the U.S. Dollar, Euro, Pound Sterling, Japanese Yen, but it can be any one of a number of other currencies, depending on the hedging requirements of the corporation, individual or fund manager using the product.

Basket options can be a perfect fit for a multinational corporation doing business in multiple countries and hence having receivables or payables in various currencies that need to be converted into their home currency. Basket options can also be suitable hedges for international investment funds that have money invested in a portfolio of assets denominated in various currencies other than their base currency.

Basically, if a hedger needs to protect against various currency exposures on an ongoing basis relative to their base currency, then a basket option might be a suitable hedge. A primary advantage of using Basket options is that they have a lower overall cost than a hedge portfolio consisting of a series of plain Vanilla options, which is an upper limit on the Basket option's value. This reduced price is due to the cross correlations involved among different national currencies. Nevertheless, basket options still base their pricing on a plain Vanilla pricing model. The model uses a log normal process for each individual basket component and incorporates the interest rates of each currency and correlates each individual component.

In practice, foreign exchange Basket options can be obtained for as little as a portfolio of only two currencies quoted against one base or denominating currency or for as many currencies as might be needed by the hedger quoted against the base currency. The fact that the portfolio of counter currencies is traded as a group or basket significantly reduces the inherent volatility of the basket of currencies' value due to cross correlations.

As a result, Basket option premiums are generally lower than the series of plain Vanilla options that would be required to hedge each individual currency component of the Basket into its base currency. Basket options are also generally easier to manage for a hedger than a portfolio of individual options, since one single Basket option can take the place of numerous Vanilla options that would otherwise be required to hedge the component counter currencies.

Typically, a hedger seeking to purchase a Basket option will establish the option's expiration date, the notional currency amount or weighting of each component of the basket, the base or denominating currency, and its strike price. The Over the Counter market maker providing a price on a Basket option will take implied volatilities for all involved base and cross currency pairs into account, as well as other market parameters that determine the current value of the basket like the spot and forward rates of each component in order to compute a fair value price to show to their client.

As an example, consider the case of a U.S. based hedger who is looking to protect a series of long U.S. Dollar/short currency exposures in varying counter currency amounts over a one month time frame. For illustration purposes, the counter currency portfolio might contain 1,000,000 Pound Sterling, 1,000,000 Euros, 100,000,000 Japanese Yen, 1,000,000 Swiss Francs, 1,000,000 Australian Dollars, 1,000,000 Canadian Dollars and 1,000,000 New Zealand Dollars.

In terms of their market view and risk tolerance, the U.S. hedger thinks the U.S. Dollar will appreciate considerably against the basket of other counter currencies over the coming month, but they wish to protect against adverse moves by buying a Basket option hedge. They could purchase a Basket Call/U.S. Dollar Put option with an at the money spot strike price expiring in one month's time. Each counter currency component of the basket would need to be specified in advance, and the corresponding spot, forward and implied volatilities obtained, in order for its fair value price to be computed.

At expiration, the Basket Call option's strike price will be compared to the prevailing price of the basket computed from the spot rate of each counter currency quoted relative to its base currency, which is U.S. Dollars. If the Basket Call's strike price is lower than the basket's current spot rate, then the Basket Call option is either exercised or cash settled, and any gains will help to offset losses on the hedger's underlying counter currency exposures. If the basket's strike price is higher than the basket's current spot rate at expiration, then the Basket Call option expires worthless, and the hedger will have accrued profits on their basket of underlying short counter currency exposures versus their U.S. Dollar base currency.

In either situation, the U.S. hedger's breakeven rate to sell U.S. Dollars against the basket of counter currencies will be decreased by the amount of the premium they initially paid for the protective Basket option hedge.

Buying Compound Options for Contingent Downside Protection

Compound options are options on options. They are typically cheaper than purchasing an option outright, and their primary application in hedging is that they allow a hedger to pay a reduced premium for downside protection on an underlying currency exposure, which is especially appropriate if the exposure is somehow contingent upon another event occurring.

In general, a hedger looking to purchase a Compound option will establish the Compound option's expiration date, the underlying option's expiration date, the option's notional base or counter currency amount, the type of the Compound option and that of its underlying option (i.e. European or American style and whether the options are Puts or a Calls), and the strike price. In order to compute a fair value Compound option price to show to their client, an Over the Counter market maker will determine the implied volatility for the relevant currency pair, in addition to other market parameters that determine the current value of the Compound option like the prevailing spot and forward rates,

As an example, consider the case of a U.S. based hedger who is not sure whether a foreign currency exposure may or may not materialize in the coming month since their company is bidding competitively on a contract denominated in Euros based on a 1.3000 exchange rate for EUR/USD that will be paid in full at the end of a one year period, if their bid is accepted. If their bid is not accepted, they will have no associated Euro exposure or gains from the contract, and so they wish to minimize the initial premium paid. If they do win the contract, they will have more funds available to purchase a protective Euro Put/U.S. Dollar Call option as a hedge.

In terms of their market view and risk tolerance, the U.S. hedger thinks the Euro might appreciate considerably against the U.S. Dollar over the coming month, but they wish to protect against adverse foreign exchange moves in the EUR/USD rate by buying a Compound option hedge. They could purchase a European style Compound Call option with an at the money strike price and expiring in one month's time on a European style 1.3000 Euro Put/U.S. Dollar Call option expiring in one year's time from the Compound option's expiration date. The corresponding spot, forward and implied volatilities would need to be obtained by the over the counter market maker in order for them to compute the Compound option's fair value price and make a quote to their client.

At expiration, the Compound Call option's strike price will be compared to the prevailing price of its underlying European style Euro Put/U.S. Dollar Call option with a strike price of 1.3000 expiring in one year. If the Compound Call's strike price is lower than the market value of the underlying option, then the hedger will exercise their Compound Call option to obtain their desired one year 1.3000 Euro Put option hedge. If they won the contract, they can retain this option as a suitable hedge, but if their bid was unsuccessful, they can sell it back.

If the Compound Call's strike price is higher than the market value of the underlying option at its expiration, then it will expire worthless, and the hedger will have be able to either purchase an option hedge at a better price if they won the contract or do nothing if they did not win the contract.

In any case, the U.S. hedger will pay a reduced premium for the one month Compound option than they would have paid to purchase the underlying one year option. Nevertheless, if they do end up buying the longer term Euro Put/U.S. Dollar Call option, then they would end up paying more than if they had just purchased that option initially.

Buying Contingent Premium Options for Contingent Downside Protection

Contingent Premium options differ from Vanilla options in that they typically incorporate a feature that their premium payment is only due upon expiration of the option if a pre-specified condition is met, such as the option being in the money. If the condition is not met, then the buyer pays nothing for the option.

If the premium payment condition is met, Contingent Premium options typically cost more than plain Vanilla options. This is due to the fact that they basically consist of a purchased Vanilla option and a purchased at expiration binary option that has the option's premium amount as its payout. Since both component options cost money, the Contingent Premium option's cost will always be greater than that of a plain Vanilla option alone.

A Contingent Premium option's primary application in hedging is when a hedger does not want to pay a premium for a protective option if they do not end up needing that option because of a movement in the underlying exchange rate that favors their exposure. If they do end up needing the option's protection due to an adverse exchange rate movement, then they are willing to pay more for it than they would otherwise have paid. This is especially suitable for a hedger who thinks the exchange rate will move strongly in their underlying exposure's favor, but they prudently do not wish to remain unhedged, just in case their view turns out to be incorrect.

For example, consider the case of a U.S. based hedger who wishes to protect a long exposure in Euros against a drop in the EUR/USD exchange rate over a one month time frame. They think EUR/USD will very probably rise over the coming month, but they want to have purchased a protective EUR Put/U.S. Dollar Call option just in case the exchange rate falls instead. They would feel considerably more justified in paying for such an option's premium if they actually needed to use it.

This hedger could purchase a European style Contingent Premium EUR Put/U.S. Dollar Call with an at the money spot strike price and expiring in one month's time. They want to pay no up front premium for this option, but they will pay a specified premium for it, if it ends up in the money at expiration. The corresponding spot, forward and implied volatility would need to be obtained by the over the counter market maker in order for them to compute the Contingent Premium option's fair value price and make a quote to their client.

If the Contingent Premium option is in the money at expiration due to a decline in the EUR/USD exchange rate, the hedger will need to pay the agreed upon premium for this hedge, which they will also exercise to help offset losses on their underlying exposure.

On the other hand, if the Contingent Premium option is not in the money at expiration, the hedger pays nothing for it, and their underlying long Euro exposure will have benefited from a favorable upward moment in the underlying EUR/USD exchange rate.

Chapter 9: Forex Option Portfolio Risk Management

Currency Options Portfolios

Trading a large number of options in a portfolio can become extremely intricate with the different strategies, hedges and other risk offsets that an options trader has available to them using the various option products and strategies. Therefore, having an understanding of the underlying variables involved in options pricing and risk management is essential for the option portfolio trader's long term success.

Managing such portfolios has been made considerably easier by the use of portfolio additive risk management parameters that allow a trader to grasp the general nature of their overall portfolio's risk in terms of its sensitivity to the underlying exchange rate, implied volatility, domestic and foreign interest rates, the passage of time, as well as how such sensitivities can change with movements in the spot exchange rate of the underlying currency pair. Each of these key risk management measures have been given a Greek or pseudo-Greek letter to refer to them by, and they are together collectively known as the option risk management Greeks.

That these key risk management parameters are portfolio additive means that that the individual risk management parameters corresponding to each option can be weighted by their respective principal amounts and then summed up to determine the overall risk to the option portfolio with respect to one or more chosen market factors, such as spot, time passage and implied volatility.

In managing a substantial currency options portfolio, a trader can always use transactions in the underlying currency pair to adjust the portfolio's overall spot equivalent position that determines its exposure to exchange rate shifts. This sort of rebalancing is often preferable to using option hedges for a similar purpose once the position is established. The main reason for this is that the forex option market's liquidity is far less than the spot foreign exchange market's liquidity, so using the spot market to hedge is considerably more efficient. Also, depending on the established option position, forwards and futures contracts can also be used to adjust the overall option portfolio's Delta, which is the key risk management parameter that measures its sensitivity to exchange rate movements.

Seasoned option risk managers generally have developed a complete familiarity with the Greeks, which are quantities represented by Greek or pseudo-Greek letters that measure the sensitivity of options to changes in various market parameters. Although not a necessary study for trading basic option strategies, the Greeks are essential to understanding the risks involved in managing complex forex option portfolios that go well beyond the basic trading and hedging strategies described in the above sections. Other terms sometimes used for the Greeks are “option hedge parameters” and “option risk measures”.

Perhaps the most familiar Greek parameter for most option traders will be the Delta of an option, which measures the option’s sensitivity to movements in the underlying asset’s market price or exchange rate. The Delta is very commonly used in forex option trading, since most over the counter currency options are immediately Delta hedged to neutralize their spot risk once they are transacted. This is a useful practical example of how a Greek risk management parameter is used in the forex option market, and it will be discussed in detail in the following section.

Delta

The Greek option risk management parameter with the most influence on an option’s price is known as the Delta. For forex options, this parameter is the first derivative of an option’s price with respect to the underlying exchange rate.

In practice, Delta measures the spot equivalent risk of a currency option position and is expressed in terms of the change in the option’s price for a one percentage move in the underlying exchange rate. Another interesting way of looking at and interpreting the Delta is that it represents the odds or percentage chance that the market is giving that particular option to end up in the money at expiration.

For example, if the underlying exchange rate of a currency pair rises by 100 pips, and an at the money base currency call option's price only moves by 50 pips, then that option is said to have a positive 0.50 or 50 percent Delta. The corresponding at the money base currency put option would have a negative 50 percent Delta. Furthermore, these 50 percent Delta indicate that the forex option market is currently giving those particular at the money options a 50-50 chance of ending up in the money at expiration.

The mathematical formulas for the put and call Delta derived from the Garman Kohlhagen currency option pricing model are as follows:

$$\text{delta} = e^{-qt}\Phi(d_1)$$

Call Option Delta formula.

$$\text{delta} = e^{-qt}[\Phi(d_1)-1]$$

Put Option Delta formula.

In the two above equations, d_1 is computed according to the following formula:

$$d_1 = \frac{log(s/x)+(r-q+\sigma^2/2)t}{\sigma\sqrt{t}}$$

In the above equations, each of the terms used are defined as follows:

s = the current exchange rate (domestic currency per unit of foreign currency)

x = the strike price expressed as an exchange rate

r = the continuously compounded domestic risk free interest rate

q = the continuously compounded foreign risk free interest rate

t = the time in years until the expiration of the option

σ = the market determined implied volatility for the currency pair's exchange rate corresponding to the option's expiration date.

Φ = the standard normal cumulative distribution function.

Log(x) = the natural logarithm of variable x.

Furthermore, using a standard currency option-pricing model, the Delta of an option can be readily computed by measuring the change in the option's price for a one percent move in the underlying exchange rate.

A vanilla option's Delta increases as the underlying exchange rate approaches and exceeds the option's strike price until the option's Delta reaches 1.00 or 100 percent, which is its maximum value. Such a high Delta implies that the deep in the money option is very likely to end up in the money at expiration, and that its price will move just as much as any moves seen in the underlying exchange rate.

Conversely, if the underlying exchange rate moves away from the strike price and the option moves further out of the money, the Delta of the option decreases until the option's Delta reaches 0.00 or 0 percent. A very low Delta like that will imply that the option is very likely to end up out of the money at expiration, and that its price is relatively insensitive to movements in the underlying spot rate.

For example, an at the money option with a Delta of 0.50 or 50 percent has a 50 percent chance of ending up in the money at expiration. A long position in a 0.50 Delta base currency call option or a short position in a 0.50 Delta base currency put option could be quickly hedged with respect to movements in the underlying currency pair's exchange rate by selling 50 percent of the option's face value in the spot market. A long position in a 0.50 Delta base currency put option or a short position in a 0.50 Delta base currency call option could be hedged by buying 50 percent of the option's face value in the spot market.

An out of the money base currency call option with a higher strike price would have a lower Delta and a lower probability of closing in the money at expiration. For example, a 0.30 Delta base currency call option would have a 30 percent chance of ending up in the money at expiration. A long position in such an option could be quickly hedged with respect to movements in the underlying currency pair's exchange rate by selling 30 percent of the option's base currency face value in the spot market.

In contrast, an in the money base currency call option with a strike price below the current spot rate would have a higher Delta and a higher probability of closing in the money at expiration. For example, a 0.70 Delta base currency call option would have a 70 percent chance of ending up in the money at expiration. A long position in such an option could be hedged with respect to movements in the underlying currency pair's exchange rate by selling 70 percent of the option's base currency face value in the spot market.

The absolute value of vanilla base currency call and put Deltas of the same strike price and expiration date will almost invariably add up to roughly 1.00 or 100 percent. For example, an out of the money base currency call may have a Delta of 0.35 and the corresponding base currency put of the same strike price will then have a Delta of roughly -0.65. An at the money 0.50 Delta call will correspond to a 0.50 Delta base currency put. An in the money base currency call may have a Delta of 0.65 and the corresponding base currency put of the same strike price will then have a Delta of roughly -0.35.

Note that in each case illustrated above, the sum of the absolute values of these call and put Deltas is 1.00, or 100 percent. This makes sense intuitively because there is a 100 percent chance that one of these two options will end up in the money at expiration.

Delta hedging to neutralize an option position with respect to movements in the underlying exchange rate is commonly done by currency option market makers as soon as they execute a forex option trade with a client. Delta hedges are also generally exchanged between professional forex option trading counterparties at a mutually acceptable spot rate used to price the option or options being transacted. The primary exception occurs when a combination of options makes the overall transaction Delta neutral, with a common example of this being an at the money forward straddle that involves buying or selling both a call and a put with the same strike price equal to the prevailing forward rate. Since the call Delta is the same but opposite in direction to the put Delta, the resulting combination has no net Delta equivalent spot position.

The Delta is therefore a key element of option trading and is the first parameter one considers when determining an overall option position's bearish or bullish bias with respect to the underlying currency pair's exchange rate. More positive Deltas versus negative Deltas in a portfolio result in a bullish bias for a portfolio and an effective long underlying currency pair position, while the reverse is true for a bearish position stacked with negative Deltas that is effectively short the underlying currency pair.

In hedging an option portfolio, the sum total of all option Deltas, both positive and negative are calculated to arrive at a net portfolio Delta position for a particular currency pair or other underlying asset, such as a basket of currencies. The net Deltas for a portfolio determine whether it has an effective long or short position in the underlying exchange rate's market. Excess positive Deltas indicate a long position, with the opposite being the case if the position has a net negative Delta, which would indicate an overall short position in the underlying currency pair.

It is important to note that the overall Delta position can change in an option portfolio as the underlying exchange rate fluctuates, especially if the trader has a significant amount of long or short at the money options. This shift in the portfolio Delta as spot moves happens irrespective of whether the trader is long options or short options, or has calls or puts in their portfolio. Such Delta shifts tend to be favorable to rebalance if the trader is long options, but unfavorable to rebalance if the trader is short options, although calendar spreads can complicate this relationship somewhat. Nevertheless, the risk of loss from this shifting Delta phenomenon can often be avoided by being net long options.

For example, consider the case of an option trader being short three units of an out of the money 33 Delta base currency call against one unit of an underlying long spot position being held as a hedge. The overall position is initially roughly Delta neutral, and so gains on the options will offset losses on the spot position — and vice versa — within a modest exchange rate range and time frame.

Nevertheless, if the spot rate moves up to the strike price of the three sold call options, they would then become at the money, and so would have roughly 50 Deltas. At that point, the trader would need to have a long total spot position of 150 percent or 1.5 units (50 percent x 3 options = 150 percent or 1.5 units) to have a balanced portfolio with respect to spot market changes. If they had not already done so as the market moved higher, they would then need to purchase 0.5 of a unit or 50 percent in the spot market in the underlying currency pair to rebalance their portfolio to maintain a Delta neutral position.

The same is true for a short put position held against a short exchange rate unit. If the trader is short out of the money puts and the exchange rate declined, their overall Delta position would get longer as the short put Deltas increased as the puts approach being in the money. Unless they were able to anticipate this decline in advance and position their portfolio's Delta accordingly, the trader would need to sell out some of this longer Delta equivalent potion at a less favorable spot rate, thereby causing a likely rebalancing loss.

These Delta hedging examples illustrate the fact that the short option trader gets shorter as the underlying exchange rate increases and longer as the exchange rate drops. In the case of the short call option example, this is because the options' short Delta would decrease as the exchange rate dropped making an additional sale necessary at lower rates. The options' short Delta would also increase as the spot rate rises, making an additional purchase necessary at higher rates.

Overall, this phenomenon makes rebalancing a short option position's Delta typically unprofitable, although such losses can be offset by gains due to the short options' time decay. Nevertheless, the opposite is true of a long option trader's Delta position, which gets shorter as the market declines, and longer as the market rises. Rebalancing the Delta of a long option portfolio is therefore typically profitable, although such profits are often at least partially offset by the time decay on a long options position.

In addition, the Delta of vanilla out of the money options generally falls as they approach expiration, while the Delta of in the money options rises, with all other market factors remaining the same. This makes sense because the market is less likely to move sufficiently to make an out of the money option go in the money as its expiration approaches, and the market is similarly less likely to move sufficiently to make an in the money option go out of the money as time passes.

From a strategic trading perspective, options can be traded dynamically in order to adjust the Delta position, reduce exposure and take additional risk as the underlying exchange rate fluctuates. For example, this sort of dynamic strategy might have an experienced swing trader covering risk by buying back options as they move further out of the money. They might also incur additional risk by selling at the money or modestly out of the money options when they anticipate a retracement that will give them an opportunity to buy these new shorts back more cheaply. If the right directional option strategies are implemented at the right times, option positions with extremely favorable risk reward profiles can be established, often locking in a profit or yielding a wide range of profitability.

Nevertheless, if the trader's objective mainly revolves around maintaining Delta neutrality for the portfolio they are managing, then it is usually preferable to adjust the portfolio's position in the underlying currency pair, rather than with options. This procedure helps minimize transaction costs since the spread in the spot market is generally considerably narrower than the option price spread, not to mention the fact that commissions may apply to exchange traded option transactions.

Gamma

In general terms, Gamma is the Greek option risk management parameter that represents the change in the Delta, or the underlying asset price sensitivity, of an option for a one percent movement in the underlying asset's price. The cumulative measure of Gamma in an option position is the chief measure of option premium a trader is long or short, which represents an invaluable tool for option traders and market makers.

The mathematical formula for Gamma derived from the Garman Kohlhagen currency option-pricing model is as follows:

$$\text{gamma} = \frac{\phi(d_1)e^{-qt}}{s\sigma\sqrt{t}}$$

Call Option Gamma formula.

$$\text{gamma} = \frac{\phi(d_1)e^{-qt}}{s\sigma\sqrt{t}}$$

Put Option Gamma formula.

In the two above equations for the put and call Gammas, d_1 is computed according to the following formula:

$$d_1 = \frac{log(s/x) + (r - q + \sigma^2/2)t}{\sigma\sqrt{t}}$$

In the above equations, each of the terms used are defined as follows:

s = the current exchange rate (domestic currency per unit of foreign currency)

x = the strike price expressed as an exchange rate

r = the continuously compounded domestic risk free interest rate

q = the continuously compounded foreign risk free interest rate

t = the time in years until the expiration of the option

σ = the market determined implied volatility for the currency pair's exchange rate corresponding to the option's expiration date.

Φ = the standard normal cumulative distribution function.

Log(x) = the natural logarithm of variable x.

As the first derivative of the Delta and the second derivative of the value function in relation to the underlying exchange rate, the Gamma is basically the Delta of the Delta, or the rate of change of the rate of change of an option's price with respect to changes in the underlying asset. The overall Gamma of an option position is very important both to professional options traders and option portfolio risk managers.

For example, a high positive Gamma, but Delta neutral, portfolio of options will give a trader plenty of opportunities to rebalance their portfolio profitably to a Delta neutral position if the underlying spot market is actively moving up and down. This is because the portfolio's Delta gets more positive as the spot market rises so the trader needs to sell to rebalance their portfolio, and more negative as it falls so the trader then needs to buy. Nevertheless, such a long Gamma portfolio generally has significant undesirable time decay if the long options expire in the near term, thereby potentially losing the trader money if the market remains relatively stable until they expire.

Interestingly, Gamma has a more complex relationship to implied volatility when considered over a range of strike prices. The Gamma of at the money options will typically decrease as implied volatility rises, but the Gamma of deep in the money or deep out of the money options will generally increase with a rise in implied volatility.

In general, positive Gamma in an option portfolio is generated by being long options — especially short dated at the money options that have the highest Gamma — while negative Gamma is accumulated by being short options. Also, positive Gamma will increase the net Delta position of an options portfolio in a rising or falling exchange rate environment, effectively making the trader respectively longer in a rising market or shorter in a falling market — an advantageous situation when it comes to rebalancing the portfolio.

While the Delta equivalent spot position is typically modest initially in a Delta-neutral managed option portfolio, it varies due to Gamma as the exchange rate of the underlying currency pair moves. Thus, the long Gamma portfolio becomes longer as the underlying exchange rate rises and shorter as the underlying asset declines in price. Also, when an option portfolio has positive Gamma, rebalancing its Delta hedge is generally a profitable exercise, so the option trader desires as much movement as possible in the underlying currency pair.

The opposite is true of a portfolio with negative Gamma, since as the exchange rate increases, the position gets shorter, while in a declining market, the negative Gamma portfolio results in its Delta position getting longer. Thus, rebalancing the Delta of a short Gamma portfolio as the exchange rate fluctuates is typically a unprofitable endeavor, with the short Gamma option trader having to buy into rising markets and sell into declining markets to maintain a Delta neutral position.

Basically, negative Gamma acts on an option portfolio in an inverse way to positive Gamma. Negative Gamma is inversely proportional to the amount of time decay the short premium position is paying the trader per day in that the more negative Gamma the trader accumulates on a position, the more positive time decay they receive with the passage of each day. Negative Gamma in an option position indicates the trader is expecting the underlying exchange rate to trade within a limited range during the life of the constituent options, allowing the trader to collect juicy time decay each day as the options approach their expiration date.

With time working in the trader's favor, if the underlying exchange rate trades in a range and fails to fluctuate sufficiently over a period of time, volatility tends to decrease making the short options worth even less. Conversely, if the underlying exchange rate begins to fluctuate more actively, historical and probably implied volatility goes up and causes the short Gamma position to go against the trader by increasing the value of the short options.

In a negative Gamma option position, adjusting the Delta position could be counterproductive, especially if the exchange rate is trading actively but inside a limited range. While the net Delta position shifts with the underlying exchange rate's fluctuations, making the trader shorter as the rate increases and longer as the rate decreases, over adjusting the Delta position could have the trader lose money in the long run by locking in substantial spot trading losses despite the offsetting premium decay of the short options. In this situation, it would probably be best if the trader adjusted their portfolio's spot balance as little as possible, despite short term volatility in the underlying exchange rate.

Depending on an option portfolio trader's perception of the future volatility in the underlying exchange rate, a Gamma positive or negative position can be established by respectively buying or selling close to the money options with a relatively short time to expiration. If the trader is expecting significant, fluctuating moves in the underlying exchange rate, then a positive Gamma position would probably be optimal. Conversely, if the expectation is that the exchange rate will be moving gradually, or stabilize and trade calmly within a range during the life of the option, then a negative Gamma position would probably be established.

Gamma remains one of the most important parameters watched by option traders. Not only does Gamma tell an option risk manager how much Delta rebalancing a portfolio containing options might require, but it is directly proportional to the rate of time decay of the component option positions. Understanding and assessing the Gamma of a portfolio is therefore one of the most important risk management elements for any option portfolio trader.

Theta

Theta is the Greek option risk management parameter that measures time decay in the value of an option over time, and which is typically expressed as the loss in an option's premium or price for a one day movement forward in time. Theta is negative for long options and positive for short options.

The mathematical formula for Theta derived from the Garman Kohlhagen currency option pricing model is as follows:

$$\text{theta} = -\frac{se^{-qt}\phi(d_1)\sigma}{2\sqrt{t}} + qse^{-qt}\Phi(d_1) - rxe^{-rt}\Phi(d_2)$$

Theta formula for a put or call option.

In the two above equations for the put and call Theta, d_1 is computed according to the following formula:

$$d_1 = \frac{log(s/x) + (r - q + \sigma^2/2)t}{\sigma\sqrt{t}}$$

In the above equations, each of the terms used are defined as follows:

s = the current exchange rate (domestic currency per unit of foreign currency)

x = the strike price expressed as an exchange rate

r = the continuously compounded domestic risk free interest rate

q = the continuously compounded foreign risk free interest rate

t = the time in years until the expiration of the option

σ = the market determined implied volatility for the currency pair's exchange rate corresponding to the option's expiration date.

Φ = the standard normal cumulative distribution function.

Log(x) = the natural logarithm of variable x.

A positive Gamma option position also has negative Theta, so in other words, a portfolio of options that is long Gamma will be simultaneously negative in Theta or time decay, resulting in a daily cost to continue to hold the position unless notable market fluctuations are seen to justify rebalancing the portfolio's Delta. Conversely, a short Gamma option position will have positive Theta or time decay, which will yield a daily cash flow to benefit the portfolio as long as the market remains relatively stable so that the portfolio does not require much Delta rebalancing.

Basically, the Theta parameter is a measure that quantifies the daily rate of deterioration of the time value portion of an option. With the exchange rate at levels which make the option out of the money, as the option approaches expiration, the negative Theta value of the option accelerates due to the decreasing likelihood the option will have intrinsic value at expiration.

For example, a three month USD call/JPY put currency option with a strike price of 100.00 and an implied volatility of 11 percent has a Theta of -0.012% of the U.S. Dollar amount and a price of 2.22% of the U.S. Dollar amount when spot is at 100.00. This Theta value means that the option's value will decline by -0.012% of the U.S. Dollar amount by the following day to 2.208%, with all other parameters remaining equal. This amount of time decay will accelerate its decline as the option approaches its expiration date, until the option has no further time value at all at its moment of expiration, and only its intrinsic value remains.

Theta is a useful parameter for managing an option position or portfolio because it gives a trader a daily indication of the cost of holding a net long premium position and/or the amount of income a net short premium position will generate. Nevertheless, the portfolio Theta simply gives a daily monetary calculation that is an estimate of the premium amount to be taken in or paid out for the coming day. Of course, the actual daily mark to market profit and loss can vary depending on movements in implied volatility and the need to rebalance a portfolio's Delta due to Gamma, making Theta of secondary importance in option risk management.

Vega

Vega is the Greek option risk management parameter that represents the change in the price of an option for a one percent move in the implied volatility of the underlying asset. Only option positions can have a non-zero Vega.

The mathematical formula for Vega derived from the Garman Kohlhagen currency option pricing model is as follows:

$$\text{vega} = se^{-q\tau}\phi(d_1)\sqrt{t}$$

Call Option Vega Formula

$$\text{vega} = se^{-q\tau}\phi(d_1)\sqrt{t}$$

Put Option Vega Formula

In the two above equations for the put and call Vegas, d_1 is computed according to the following formula:

$$d_1 = \frac{log(s/x) + (r - q + \sigma^2/2)t}{\sigma\sqrt{t}}$$

In the above equations, each of the terms used are defined as follows:

s = the current exchange rate (domestic currency per unit of foreign currency)

x = the strike price expressed as an exchange rate

r = the continuously compounded domestic risk free interest rate

q = the continuously compounded foreign risk free interest rate

t = the time in years until the expiration of the option

σ = the market determined implied volatility for the currency pair's exchange rate corresponding to the option's expiration date.

Φ = the standard normal cumulative distribution function.

Log(x) = the natural logarithm of variable x.

Vega takes on a special importance for option traders because the implied volatility is one of the most influential elements in the pricing of an option contract. Implied volatility is a market determined quantity affected by supply and demand factors for options that is quoted by a market maker for a particular currency pair, expiration date and strike price. As an illustration of this phenomenon, professional market makers operating in the over the counter forex options market often quote options of a particular Delta and expiration date in terms of their implied volatility, and the actual strike price is then agreed upon later.

Unlike the other option risk management "Greeks", Vega is not actually a Greek letter, but the symbol used to represent Vega, the Greek letter nu (ν), looks like an English "v" and is traditionally used to represent implied volatility. According to some researchers, coining the pseudo Greek term Vega for an option's implied volatility sensitivity was an analogy of the pronunciation of theta, beta and eta in the English language. Others speculate the name was taken from author Joseph De La Vega, writer of a book on complex trading operations entitled *"Confusion of Confusions"*. The Greek letter Tau (τ) has also been used for the Vega parameter by well-known option trading educators O'Connell and Piper Associates and by the Union Bank of Switzerland. In other financial texts, the Greek letter Lambda (λ) has been used as an alternative for Vega. Thanks in part to the standardization provided by market dominant off-the-shelf forex option risk management and pricing systems, the currency options market now traditionally uses Vega to refer to this risk management parameter, and so that is what will be used here despite its status as a pseudo "Greek".

The Vega option risk management parameter for a long option position is usually expressed in terms of the percentage amount the position's value will increase given a one-percentage point move in the implied volatility. Vega can be an invaluable risk measure to an experienced option trader with a large portfolio of options to manage. This is especially true in the case of a position with a large Vega exposure, in which an upward spike in implied volatility could cost a short option trader or make a long option trader a significant amount of money on paper. Of course, these gains are only on paper until the positions are closed out because implied volatility — and hence Vega — only affects an option's mark to market time value prior to expiration, but it has no effect on any intrinsic value the option position may have. The Vega of an option goes to zero, along with the option's time value, at the moment of the option's expiration. At that point, all that is left over is the option's intrinsic value.

Furthermore, no matter whether a trader is long or short options, the Vega of the overall position is an excellent indicator of the position's exposure to changes in implied volatility, which in turn reflects the risk perceived by the market of holding a position in the underlying currency pair. Also, when options begin getting pumped up in value or drained of time premium as implied volatility rises and falls, the Vega is the risk management parameter to watch since it indicates how much the option portfolio's resulting value fluctuation might be, as implied volatility shifts.

In general, longer dated at the money options will have a higher Vega than shorter dated at the money options. In addition, a high Vega for an option would indicate that the option's price would increase significantly with a one percent move in the implied volatility for the underlying currency pair and the option's expiration date. Conversely, a lower Vega would indicate the option's price would not change as much due to a one percent move in the underlying exchange rate's volatility. When a high-implied volatility is reflected in the rich pricing of a forex option, this means that the market is expecting the underlying exchange rate to fluctuate dramatically within the time frame covered by the option's lifetime, which could drastically affect the option's value at expiration.

For example, if the USD/JPY currency pair is trading for spot value at 100.00 with an implied volatility of 11 percent for options of a 103.00 strike price expiring in three months' time, then the three month 103.00 strike USD call/JPY put would have a theoretical value of 1.06% of the U.S. Dollar principal amount. If USD/JPY's three month implied volatility then increased to 12 percent, the fair value for that same 103.00 USD call would rise to 1.24% of the U.S. Dollar amount, with all other factors remaining equal. Simply calculated, the Vega of this option would therefore be 1.24% - 1.06% or 0.18% of the U.S. Dollar face amount.

Rho and Phi

Rho is the Greek option risk management parameter that measures the change in the theoretical price of a forex option for a one percentage point move in the prevailing base or domestic currency interest rate. Phi is analogous to Rho, and is sometimes called the foreign Rho, but it pertains to an option's sensitivity to changes in the prevailing counter currency or foreign interest rate.

The mathematical formula for Rho and Phi derived from the Garman Kohlhagen currency option-pricing model are as follows:

$$\text{domestic rho} = xte^{-rt}\Phi(d_2)$$

$$\text{foreign rho} = -ste^{-qt}\Phi(d_1)$$

The Rho and Phi (foreign Rho) Formulas

In the two above equations for an option's Rho and Phi, the d_1 term is computed according to the following formula:

$$d_1 = \frac{log(s/x) + (r - q + \sigma^2/2)t}{\sigma\sqrt{t}}$$

In the above equations, each of the terms used are defined as follows:

s = the current exchange rate (domestic currency per unit of foreign currency)

x = the strike price expressed as an exchange rate

r = the continuously compounded domestic risk free interest rate

q = the continuously compounded foreign risk free interest rate

t = the time in years until the expiration of the option

σ = the market determined implied volatility for the currency pair's exchange rate corresponding to the option's expiration date.

Φ = the standard normal cumulative distribution function.

Log(x) = the natural logarithm of variable x.

For example, if a currency option has a Rho of 5 pips and Euros are its base currency, then a one percent increase in Euro interest rates would make the value of that option increase by 5 pips. Rho is greater for options that are in the money relative to options that are out of the money.

Phi, also sometimes known as the foreign Rho, is the change in the price of a forex option for a one percentage point move in the foreign or counter currency's prevailing interest rate. The option's Phi is related to the counter currency's interest rate like the option's Rho is related to the base currency's interest rate.

For example, if a currency option has a Phi of 5 pips, and its counter currency is Euros, then a one percent increase in Euro interest rates would make the value of that option increase by 5 pips. Phi is greater for options that are in the money relative to options that are out of the money.

The importance of Rho and Phi when trading currency options revolves around the fact that a European style currency option's price is based on the forward rate for the underlying currency pair, which is computed based on the principle of interest rate parity. A change in either of the foreign or domestic interest rates will therefore directly affect the value of a forex option because it has a discernible impact on the forward rate for the underlying currency pair.

Furthermore, to a currency option trader, the direction of interest rates can be an indicator of option pricing. For example, if the forex market is expecting higher interest rates for the base currency than the counter currency in future, the counter currency forward rate would trade at a discount to the spot rate, thereby making the options relatively cheaper in counter currency terms. In the case of market expectations of a higher interest rate in the counter currency, then the forward rate for the counter currency would trade at a premium to the spot rate, thereby making the options relatively more expensive in counter currency terms.

The effect of Rho and Phi in a currency option portfolio does not typically have as significant an impact on an option position as the other Greek parameters, so they are generally considered secondary in importance compared to Delta,

Gamma and Vega. Furthermore, interest rates are closely managed by central banks and so have remained relatively stable throughout the international financial arena in the past few years. Nevertheless, the effect of Rho and Phi on currency option prices could increase notably if the global interest rate market were to become considerably more volatile in future.

Chapter 10: Transacting Forex Options

Computing Forex Option Fair Values

Knowing how to compute the fair value of an option and how a series of forex options are priced using implied volatility is essential for trading and managing an option portfolio successfully.

For vanilla forex options, the key to this is having an accurate currency option pricing computer program based on the Garman Kohlhagen model's currency option pricing formulae. This model should be properly coded into a thoroughly tested computer program, and the trader should be familiar with how to obtain all of the relevant market parameters and how to enter them correctly into the program.

The fair value of an option has several determining variables that must be input into the model to determine a fair theoretical option price. The calculation of vanilla currency option fair values typically involves using the Garman Kohlhagen model. This forex option-pricing model typically requires the following input variables to compute an option's fair value:

- The Domestic or Base Currency
- The Foreign or Counter Currency
- Whether the option is a Call or Put on the Base currency
- Whether the option is a Call or Put on the Counter currency
- Exercise Type, i.e. American or European style
- Trade Date of the option
- Spot Value Date for delivery of the option premium
- Expiration Date of the Option
- Delivery Date of the Option if exercised

- The Spot Foreign Exchange Rate
- The Forward Exchange Rate or Forward Points
- The Option's Strike Price
- The Domestic or Base Currency Interest Rate in percent
- The Foreign or Counter Currency Interest Rate in percent
- The Implied Volatility in percent

Most of the variables listed above are standard requirements when pricing just about any option contract. Note that foreign exchange options are somewhat different from other options in that they require two currencies; two interest rates and the forward rate to compute a fair value price.

If a trader does not have the budget to purchase a professional quality option pricing model nor the expertise to program one, a number of online foreign exchange option calculators can be found on the Internet. These calculators are relatively easy to use, and they typically have the user input the required variables into the model to obtain a theoretical option valuation using the Garman Kohlhagen pricing model.

Implied volatility, as with other option contracts, is one of the option pricing variables with the most influence on a forex option's pricing. For this reason, Over the Counter forex options for a particular expiration date are generally quoted between professionals in terms of their implied volatility and Delta not the option strike price or actual price.

An option's Delta is also used by an Over the Counter forex option market maker to quote an appropriate implied volatility for the option. Due to the volatility smile effect, out of the money options with lower Deltas are typically offered at higher implied volatilities than at the money options that have a roughly 50 Delta. Lower Delta options may also be bid slightly higher than the at the money options in implied volatility terms, but this smile effect is less pronounced. Sometimes the implied volatility curve is skewed by supply and demand effects in a highly directional market. For example, in the case of a falling market for the underlying currency pair, a market maker might offer 25 Delta base currency calls of a higher strike price than the spot rate at a lower implied volatility than the 25 Delta base currency puts struck below the spot rate.

Options listed on the Philadelphia Options Exchange and the International Monetary Market or IMM of the Chicago Mercantile Exchange are all traded in currency principal amounts and their prices are quoted in U.S. Dollar pips. The premium for transactions in such exchange traded forex options is computed by taking the number of option lots transacted, multiplying it by the amount of currency per lot, and then multiplying the total currency amount by the price in U.S. Dollar pips after converting the price in pips to decimal terms. For USD/JPY, one pip is 0.01 in decimal terms, while for just about all other currencies like EUR/USD for example; one pip is 0.0001 in decimal terms. Settlement on such contracts is in futures contracts in the case of those currency options traded on the Chicago IMM exchange, and with the delivery of the net U.S. Dollar amount owed or due for the Philadelphia Stock Exchange forex option contracts.

Option Pricing Factors

Perhaps the most volatile — and hence risky — market component involved in computing a currency option's price is the spot rate of the underlying currency pair. Forex option traders need to be aware that some currency pairs are quoted with the U.S. Dollar as the base currency, such as USD/JPY, USD/CHF, USD/CAD and most minor currencies, while other major currency pairs have the U.S. Dollar quoted as the counter currency like in the EUR/USD, GBP/USD, AUD/USD and NZD/USD currency pairs.

Next most important is the implied volatility used to price options. Implied volatility is often compared to historical volatility to determine how rich or cheap such options are relative to recent history. For comparison purposes, the historical volatility of the underlying exchange rate — which would be the most suitable for comparing to an option's current implied volatility and its resulting fair value — is calculated for an equal amount of time as the option's duration. Thus, if the option is expiring in thirty days' time, for example, then the annualized historical standard deviation of the underlying exchange rate observed over the previous thirty day period will give an approximate historical volatility reading for the exchange rate. This can then be compared to the implied volatility for the future 30 day period that reflects the market's expectations for future exchange rate fluctuations over a 30 day period and which is implied by the observed market prices for options expiring in 30 days.

After the spot rate and implied volatility, the forward rate would be the next important variable that is determined by the interest rate differential between the two currencies involved in the pricing of a currency option. In practice, the forward rate is usually computed by entering in the forward points obtained from professional forex forward traders and the prevailing spot rate for the currency pair obtained from a spot trader. Unless the forward rate was significantly lower or higher than the spot rate because of the expectation of an interest rate hike or cut, the forward rate would not be as influential in the option's pricing as the implied volatility and sot variables.

The next variable used in currency options which would influence the option price is the domestic and foreign interest rates. Short-term rates influence the price of options because one currency position will be receiving interest, while the other currency position will be paying it out. On a longer-term option, the amount of the differential will have a greater bearing on the option's price because of the interest income or deficit of the underlying exchange rate interest differential. The interest rate relevant to the currency in which option's premium will be paid up front also has a minor impact due on the option's price to the cost of carry on that amount.

Option Pricing Risks

A number of potentially costly errors can occur when pricing currency options that can result in significant option mispricing risks. This option pricing risk is more relevant to the over the counter market since the relative openness of the exchange traded option markets on the PHLX and the Chicago IMM exchanges helps prevent such option pricing errors from occurring.

Nevertheless, the risk of mispricing an option quoted in the over the counter market is significant since there are no other market makers to check quoted prices since each option contract is uniquely tailored to a client's request for its strike price, expiration date and currency pair. Due to the fact that an over the counter forex option transaction between a bank and its client is a rather private matter, no price checks typically occur to make sure that the option's value has been computed correctly. This situation makes it even more important to accurately price and to even re-check the price of an over the counter forex option before making the quote and confirming the transaction.

.

Basically, a cautious OTC option trader making a price for a client will need to correctly obtain all of the necessary market and option parameters, and then enter them carefully into their option pricing model. Not only should they then re-check their price, but they should also routinely re-confirm all option details with their clients before agreeing that an over the counter option transaction is completed.

For example, some common forex option pricing errors an OTC option trader would want to avoid might include:

(1) Pricing a base currency put instead of a base currency call.

(2) Quoting the incorrect option price requested, such as a price in pips when a price in percent of the base currency amount was needed.

(3) Entering a market parameter incorrectly, such as the spot rate or forward points.

(4) Entering an option parameter incorrectly, such as the strike price or expiration date.

(5) Pricing a European style option when an American style option requested or vice versa.

Since exchange traded options have several market makers quoting and checking option prices, an option pricing error is less likely to occur. Even so, exchange traded option fair values can be computed by a trader to compare them with observed market prices being traded on the exchange to help them assess the relative richness and cheapness of specific exchange traded forex options. Exchange traded options are generally only available for standardized strike prices and expiration dates, which may not be suitable for the specific needs of a particular option trader or hedger.

Obtaining a Forex Option Quote

Getting a quote for an exchange-traded forex option listed with a major exchange is typically simply a matter of calling a broker that has access to that exchange. An appropriate account type — either for commodity futures or securities — that is typically funded with U.S. Dollars is necessary for obtaining an exchange traded forex option quote from a broker or from an online trading platform that offers forex options.

For example, forex options listed on the Chicago Mercantile Exchange's IMM are quoted in U.S. Dollars pips for a specific amount of currency and deliver into the underlying futures contracts. These options are regulated by the Commodities Futures Trading Commission or CFTC. For a quote from the IMM, a CFTC regulated commodity futures account is required in order to trade forex options. The IMM forex options are traded on the floor of the Mercantile Exchange by open outcry, and a quote can be obtained either from a broker or through the IMM's official website. The IMM forex options are typically American Style options on currency futures contracts.

Forex options listed on the Philadelphia Stock Exchange are regulated by the Securities and Exchange Commission or SEC, and they are also quoted in U.S. Dollar pips for a specified amount of currency. Such PHLX forex options are typically cash settled in U.S. Dollars instead of going to delivery. A quote for a forex option from the Philadelphia exchange would require an SEC regulated account, and it could be obtained either through a broker or online through an account with access to the Philadelphia Exchange's trading platform. The PHLX forex options are typically European Style options with quarterly expirations corresponding to standardized expiration dates in March, June, September and December.

All of the forex option quotes obtained from the exchange traded sources mentioned above are quoted in U.S. Dollar pips, instead of by implied volatility as in the Interbank over the counter forex options market. For standardization purpose, exchange traded forex options are generally quoted in a series that has a set of fixed expiration dates and a set of strike prices struck either at forex quotation big figures or halfway between big figures.

For example, exchange traded strike prices for Euro calls/U.S. Dollar puts in the EUR/USD currency pair might be set at 1.3000, 1.3250, and 1.3500. If a trader wanted a specific EUR/USD strike price set at, say, 1.3303, then they would have to go to the over the counter forex option market to obtain a quote on such an option.

Over the counter forex clients of a major international bank will typically contact the forex-trading desk at their bank to obtain a forex options quotation from a customer dealer. Such transactions are typically made on the basis of credit lines and do not require a margin deposit, but the client needs to have previously obtained approval from the bank's credit department for a transaction of that type and amount.

Although clients typically obtain live option price quotes from bank dealers, options traded on the OTC forex market between professionals are quoted by implied volatility. All OTC options can have custom strike prices and expiration dates. Obtaining a quote on these options requires access to an account with a bank or financial institution with a foreign exchange department or trading desk. Calling the trading desk and asking for a quote on an option requires the client have all the pertinent information for the option they desire to get a quote on. Once the information is given to the trading desk, a volatility figure is determined by the trading desk and a quote is given to the client.

Retail traders may also be able to access an online forex option trading platform, such as that provided by Saxo Bank, which allows them to participate in the over the counter forex option market using a margin trading account. For Saxo Bank, an account with the bank with a minimum deposit of $100,000 is currently required for trading forex options on their online trading platform. The Saxo Bank options trading platform gives quotes on a number of forex options with the bank making markets and acting as counterparty to trades made on the platform. Saxo bank uses a combination of a Delta margin and a Vega margin for traders holding positions in their account.

All of the above methods of obtaining a forex option quote require a trader to have opened an appropriate trading account or credit line with the exchange or banking counterparty they are going to be dealing with.

Executing a Forex Option Trade

Once a quote has been obtained for the desired forex option, the trade can be executed by placing an order with a broker if the option is exchange traded. If a market maker is willing to trade at the price specified in the order, then the order will be filled and the option transaction confirmed as completed.

If the option is quoted through a bank operating in the Over the Counter market, then the execution of a transaction with a client is done via the bank's customer dealing desk. Such dealing desks typically act as a profit center within their banks, and so they often show a worse price to their clients than is presently available in the Interbank market. Since they have no open outcry competition like is seen on the option exchanges because the forex option transaction is privately negotiated, it therefore makes sense to be aware of the approximate current fair value of a currency option whenever dealing with a bank's customer desk. Banking clients can also shop around to check forex option prices with several banks at the same time, just to make sure they are receiving a fair price for their option transaction.

If the transaction is done between professionals, or via an OTC currency option broker, then the financial institutions deal directly with each other based on credit lines. The back offices of each financial institution will then confirm the forex option transaction between themselves.

When the option is executed through a U.S. exchange such as the Chicago IMM or PHLX, a broker is generally contacted to place the order on the exchange for execution by market makers and other floor traders. A number of brokers that execute trades on the Chicago IMM or PHLX offer their clients access to an online trading platform where their trades can be automatically executed.

In the situation where a trade is executed on an option-trading platform, the trade can be entered and executed directly from a computer terminal. The transaction should then show up in the trader's position.

Glossary of Forex Options Related Term Definitions

Actual Volatility: A measure of the actual degree of movement observed in an underlying asset's price. Actual current volatility is the volatility of a financial instrument or asset observed over a specific period of time, while actual future volatility, which is the volatility of an instrument or asset measuring from the present time until a future date (such as an option's expiration date, for example).

American Style: A type of vanilla option which allows the holder to exercise their option at any time until the expiration date and cutoff time of the option. American Style options give the holder more flexibility and hedging opportunities during the life of the option, although it is not always advantageous to exercise options early if they have a significant amount of time value.

Assign: To exercise an option against its writer. When a European style over the counter option is nearing its expiration cut off time, the option's holder will typically compare its strike price to the underlying market. If it is advantageous for the holder to exercise their option, they will contact the option's seller to assign the option.

At the Money (ATM): Describes an option's strike price that is either equal or relatively equal to the price of the underlying asset.

At the Money Forward (ATMF): Describes a foreign exchange option having the same exercise price as the prevailing forward rate for the ultimate settlement date of the option after its expiration.

At the Money Spot (ATMS): Describes a foreign exchange option having the same strike price as the prevailing spot rate.

Average Rate Option: An exotic derivative contract that has its value at expiration computed by comparing a fixed strike price with the average value of the underlying asset observed at specific fixing dates during the life of the option. Average rate options or AROs generally pay out either a cash settlement or nothing to the holder at expiration depending on whether they expire in the money or out. The ARO is considered in the money at expiration if the currency pair's exchange rate at expiration is above the average of the observed fixings for a call option or below the average of the observed fixings for a put option.

Average Strike Option: An exotic derivative contract that, in the forex option market, confers to the holder the right to exchange a fixed amount of one currency for another at an exchange rate computed using a pre-specified type of averaging process over a given period of time. Also called ASROs, the strike price of an Average Strike Option is often determined by a specific degree of money-ness relative to a specific currency pair-fixing rate. Thus an ASRO might be struck at the money spot or two percent out of the money spot. An ASRO option is considered in the money at expiration if the prevailing exchange rate for the currency pair is less advantageous to exchange the currencies at than the computed average.

Base Currency: The accounting monetary unit in which another monetary unit is valued that appears as the first currency in a currency pair, for example: USD/JPY, the U.S Dollar is the Base Currency. Also known as the primary currency.

Basket Option: An exotic derivative contract that, in the forex option market, confers to the holder the right to buy (if a call) or sell (if a put) a portfolio consisting of a selection of various underlying currencies at a particular total value. A basket option cannot simply be split into its individual currency pair components because the volatility of a basket of currencies is generally lower than the weighted average of its components due to the existence of cross correlations.

Beta: A number describing the volatility of an asset compared to the overall market or benchmark in which the asset trades. For example, the Beta of a currency portfolio could have a beta of 0.36 as expressed in U.S. Dollars, which would indicate that the currency portfolio correlates the movement of the U.S. Dollar by a factor of 36 percent.

Binary Option: An exotic derivative contract that pays the holder a fixed amount of money, known as the payout, in the event that its strike price is in the money relative to the price of the underlying asset or a lesser amount (typically nothing) if the contract expires out of the money. Binary options are usually subject to automatic exercise at their expiration, and the holder generally does not have the right to purchase or sell the underlying asset, but only receives the payout, if any. Binaries can either have their payout determined at expiration, which are often called "at expiration" binaries, or their payout can be triggered prior to expiration if their strike price is touched, which are often called "one touch" binaries.

Breakeven: The point at which an investment or trade can be liquidated for the same amount for which the position was originally established. For options, the breakeven is computed by adding the price in points or pips to the strike price for a call, or subtracting the price in points or pips for a put.

Butterfly: An option strategy consisting of a low strike and a high strike option spread against two options with the same middle strike price, usually either consisting of all calls or all puts, or obtained by spreading a strangle against a straddle. The Butterfly spread is a neutral view strategy, and a trader might sell the Butterfly if they expect little movement of the underlying asset, or they might buy it if they expected considerable movement, each with limited risk and a limited return.

The long Butterfly spread's maximum profit is seen if the underlying asset settles at or beyond the strike prices of either short option, while the short Butterfly has its maximum profit if the underlying settles exactly at the middle options' strike price. For a long Butterfly, the trader's risk is limited to the amount paid for the position, while a short Butterfly's maximum risk is the difference between the middle strike price and the widest side strike price less any premium initially received.

Calendar Spread: An option strategy in which the trader establishes a long position in one expiration month, and simultaneously sells another option in another expiration month. Calendar spreads are often used when the options trader needs to roll their current position into the next month, or when the trader feels that a currency pair might depreciate in the month they went short, and subsequently gain in the expiration month the trader took a long position in.

Call: An option that confers the right to buy the underlying asset upon its holder. Traders buying a call option usually have a bullish view on the underlying asset.

Condor: An option spread strategy consisting of two call or two put spreads with the same expiration date but over four strikes, which is effectively the same as a near the money strangle spread against a further out of the money strangle. For example, a long Condor spread could consist of a purchased near the money put and call, spread against a sold further out of the money put and call.

Conversion: A type of option arbitrage position in which the trader takes a long position in the underlying asset and simultaneously sells a call and buys a put, hopefully for a sufficient credit to offset expenses and make a profit. The formula for a Conversion arbitrage is Call Price + Strike Price – Underlying Price + Put Price. Essentially, the short call added to the strike price is the short artificial underlying asset, while the real underlying asset with the put represents the actual long underlying position. If the difference comes out to a credit, then an arbitrage exists as long as the carrying cost of the position is lower than the credit.

Counter Currency: The monetary unit that is valued in terms of another monetary unit, and which appears as the second currency in a currency pair. In the USD/JPY currency pair the Japanese Yen (JPY) is the counter currency.

Currency Pair: Two national monetary units consisting of a base currency and a counter currency. The exchange rate of a currency pair in the foreign exchange market is the quotation of one currency's value expressed in terms of another currency's value.

Delivery or Settlement Date: The calendar day on which the counterparties of a financial contract are required to meet their obligation. In the foreign exchange market, the Delivery or Settlement Date is when one currency is exchanged for the other by the counterparties.

Delta Hedging: An option strategy in which an option position is offset by the risk equivalent amount of the underlying asset or other options to neutralize the overall position's sensitivity to movements in the price of the underlying asset. To Delta hedge refers to the act of neutralizing the underlying asset movement risk of an option, while a Delta hedge refers to the underlying asset transaction typically used for that purpose when an option trade is executed. For example, Delta hedging a long at the money USD call/JPY put currency option with a Delta of 0.50 or 50%, would take either the sale of a USD/JPY spot position in 50% of the option's face amount or the sale of, for example, two 25% Delta USD Call/JPY Put options with the same face amount as the original option to be hedged.

Delta: An option risk management parameter that measures the spot risk in an option, and which is expressed as the change in the price of an option for a one percent change in the price of the underlying asset. The Delta is generally expressed as a percent of a one unit move in the underlying asset. For example, the delta of an at the money currency option tends to be 0.50, meaning that for a one figure move in the underlying currency, the option will move 50 percent.

Derivative: A financial product that obtains its value based upon the value of an underlying asset. A forex option involving a particular currency pair is a derivative with its value determined by the prevailing exchange rate for that currency pair.

Downside: The potential amount of money or percentage at risk on a market, asset, investment or trade. In options trading, the downside can be limited or hedged at a certain price level by buying an option struck at that price level.

Early Exercise: When the holder of an American Style option elects to assign the option writer at any time before the option expiration date. Early exercise of American style options is often not more advantageous than selling the option back due to the time value lost when exercising the option.

European Style: A type of vanilla option in which the exercise of the option is only possible on the expiration date up to the cutoff time. Most over the counter currency options are European style options.

Exchange Traded Market: A central location where dealers, traders and market-makers meet to transact business. Exchange Traded Markets include the world's best known stock and commodity exchanges, such as the New York Stock Exchange and the Chicago Board of Trade. Currency options trade actively on the CME Group's International Monetary Market or IMM and the NASDAQ's Philadelphia Stock Exchange or PHLX.

Exercise: The action taken by an option holder of either buying the underlying asset — in the case of a call — or selling the underlying asset — in the case of a put to the option writer. American style options can be exercised at any time until expiry, while European Style options can only be exercised on the Expiration Date.

Exotic Option: A derivative contract to buy or sell a particular underlying asset within a specified period of time that is not a plain vanilla European or American style option. Exotic options include binary options, knock out and knock in options, average rate and average strike options, and basket options.

Expiration Date: The day that options contracts either expire worthless or are exercised by the holder if they are in the money.

Fair Value: The estimated value of a security or asset in the open market, taking into account all the pertinent variables that would influence the price of the asset. In options trading, the Fair Value of an option would be its theoretical price calculated with a mathematical pricing model using a number of pricing variables including: the underlying asset's price, time until expiration, strike price, interest rates and implied volatility.

Fat Tails: A statistical probabilistic distribution phenomena akin to the "bell curve" that has a bell shape. The fat tails curve is graphically similar to the bell curve, except that the standard bell is stretched out, making the events in the tails on either side more probable. Some forex option market makers believe that movements in the foreign exchange market follow more of a fat tails curve than the bell curve used in the traditional theoretical options pricing models, and they correct for this by raising the implied volatility — and hence the price — of out of the money options.

Foreign Exchange Rate: The value of one currency, known as the base currency, expressed in terms of another, known as the counter currency. The foreign exchange rate to exchange U.S. Dollars into Japanese Yen is known as USD/JPY, where the U.S. Dollar is the base currency and the Japanese Yen is the counter currency. If the USD/JPY exchange rate is trading at 100.00, then that means 100 Japanese Yen equals one U.S. Dollar.

Forward Contract: An agreement to make a transaction at some future date. In the foreign exchange market, a forward contract involves the promise to exchange one currency for another at a certain price on a specified date beyond the normal spot settlement date.

Forward Rate: The exchange rate for a currency pair for delivery at a future date different from the current spot settlement date. The Forward Rate is based on the current price of an asset plus any forward points determined according to the cost of carry computed from the prevailing money market interest rates for the time frame of the forward contract. In the foreign exchange market, the Forward Rate is based on the spot exchange rate and contracts are priced according to the maturity of the contract and the interest rate differential between the two currencies.

Futures Contract: An exchange traded standardized contract giving a buyer the obligation to buy from the seller the asset for delivery at a fixed price in the future. The most popular assets that have futures contracts include commodities, currencies, indexes, bonds and stocks. In the futures market, the obligation to receive delivery is typically placed upon the buyer of the futures contract, while the seller is not obligated to deliver and the majority of all futures contracts are offset in the market before settlement date.

Gamma: An option risk management parameter for the change in the Delta, or asset price sensitivity, of an option for a one percent movement in the underlying asset. As the first derivative of the Delta, Gamma is basically the Delta of the Delta, or the rate of change of the rate of change of an option's price with respect to changes in the underlying asset, and is very important to professional options traders and option portfolio managers. For example, a high positive Gamma, but Delta neutral position will generally have significant undesirable time decay if the long options expire in the near term, thereby potentially losing the trader money if the market remains stable.

While the Delta is typically neutral initially in a managed option portfolio, this varies due to Gamma as the underlying asset fluctuates, so the long Gamma portfolio becomes longer as the underlying asset rises in price and shorter as the underlying asset declines in price. Thus, when an option portfolio has positive Gamma, rebalancing its Delta hedge is generally a profitable exercise, so the option trader desires movement in the underlying. The opposite is true of a portfolio with negative Gamma.

Garman Kohlhagen: A mathematical option pricing model for European Style currency options developed specifically for the foreign exchange market that was first published in 1976 by Mark Garman and Steven Kohlhagen and has become the standard pricing model in the forex options market. The Garman Kohlhagen model enhanced the traditional Black-Scholes option-pricing model to include continuous returns and separate interest rates for each currency in a currency pair.

Historical Volatility: A measure of the past degree of movement observed in an underlying asset's price. Historical volatility is usually computed by determining the average or standard deviation from the average price observed over a given time frame.

Holder: The buyer of an option contract. The option holder has the right to exercise their option against the seller until the option expires.

Implied Volatility: The market determined expected degree of momentum in an underlying asset that is implicit in an option's price. Implied volatility is a key input into an option-pricing model to calculate an option's theoretical price.

In the Money (ITM): Describes an option's strike price that is more attractive than the prevailing market for the underlying asset. A call option is in the money when its strike price is below the market, while a put option is in the money when its strike price is above the market.

Intrinsic Value: The part of an option's premium that reflects the amount the option is in the money relative to its strike price. Generally this measure is calculated by subtracting the strike price from the price of the underlying asset in the case of a call option, and subtracting the value of the asset from the strike price in the case of a put option. If the option is out of the money, it will have no intrinsic value.

Knock In Option: An exotic derivative contract that becomes activated only when a certain price level, sometimes called a barrier or trigger point, in the underlying asset is touched. If the barrier is hit, the option becomes a European style vanilla option and pays out accordingly, if the trigger is never hit by the time the knock in option expires, it then has no payout.

Knock Out Option: An exotic derivative contract that is only active as long as a certain price level, sometimes called a barrier or trigger, in the underlying asset is not touched. As long as the barrier remains untouched by expiration, the option becomes a European style vanilla option and pays out accordingly. In the event the barrier is hit prior to expiration, the option immediately ceases to exist and has no payout.

Leg: A component of a multiple position option strategy. For example, in a call spread in which the option holder buys one option and simultaneously sells another option, the two positions, if separated would constitute two “legs”. A trader will say they are “taking a leg” when they intend to execute a multiple options position, one option at a time.

Naked Write: The selling or writing of an option contract without having or establishing an offsetting position in either the underlying asset or another option. For example, a trader might want to naked write an option that is so sufficiently out of the money that is has very little risk of ending up in the money at expiration given their market view on the underlying asset. Naked writing an option is considered quite risky since it has unlimited downside potential but limited upside potential, and the strategy generally requires a considerable amount of margin for a trader to establish and hold such a short option position without any form of offsetting hedge.

Option Portfolio Management: The process of developing and implementing a strategy to take, control and assess the market risk in a portfolio of options. Currency option portfolios can also be made up of foreign exchange positions, options positions, forward positions or currency futures positions, or any combination thereof. Managing such an option portfolio professionally typically involves minimizing the various risk management parameters — especially the portfolio's volatility and spot sensitivities known respectively as the Vega and Delta — unless a certain type of risk is considered desirable for maximizing the portfolio's returns.

Option: A contract that confers a right, but not an obligation, on its buyer. The option buyer can either buy (for a call option) or sell (for a put option) the underlying asset at an agreed upon price known as the strike price for a particular time frame. In contrast, the option writer or seller has the obligation to deliver the underlying asset to the buyer at the strike price if they exercise their option.

Out of the Money (OTM): Describes an option's strike price that is less attractive than the prevailing market for the underlying asset. A call option is out of the money when its strike price is above the market, while a put option is out of the money when its strike price is below the market.

Over the Counter (OTC) Market: An informal network made up of dealers, traders and market-makers working at banks and other financial institutions transacting business via telephones, brokers and decentralized electronic dealing systems. The foreign exchange market is largely an over the counter market.

Phi: The change in the price of a forex option for a one percentage point move in the foreign or counter currency's prevailing interest rate. For example, if a currency option has a Phi of 0.50 percent, and its counter currency is U.S. Dollars, then a one percent increase in U.S. interest rates would make the value of that option increase by 0.50 percent. Phi is greater for options that are in the money relative to options that are out of the money. Also sometimes called the foreign Rho.

Pip: The lowest possible unit of price fluctuation in a currency pair. The term is actually an abbreviation for "Percentage in Point", and is traditionally the fourth decimal place or 0.0001 in the quotation of a currency pair. A notable exception is made for the Japanese Yen, in which pips are quoted to the second decimal point or 0.01.

Premium: The cost or amount of money paid by the holder for the right conferred by an option contract, which is the same as the amount of money the writer receives for its sale. Also, traders often use the term "premium" to refer to a portfolio's overall Gamma, since a short premium position refers to a short Gamma position, while a long premium position refers to one that is long Gamma.

Price: The effective amount per standardized unit that an option buyer pays to the option seller. For example, if a USD/JPY forex option has a price of 1.00% of the U.S. Dollar amount for an option with a $10,000,000 principal amount, then the premium cost of the option will be $100,000.

Pricing Model: A mathematical formula for determining the fair price of an option taking into account the variables of the underlying asset.

Profit and Loss Profile: In the option market, this refers to a visual graph of an option position showing areas of potential financial gain and deficit on the vertical axis plotted versus the price of the underlying asset on the horizontal axis. This graph can be generated either before or at expiration by taking into account the particulars of all option and underlying positions in the portfolio under consideration.

Put: An option that confers the right to sell the underlying asset upon its holder. Traders buying a put option usually have a bearish view on the underlying asset.

Ratio Spread: A combination option strategy in which a trader buys options and sells options other than on a one for one basis for a specified net price. For example, a trader that is bullish on a particular currency pair might establish a ratio spread by buying three out of the money calls and selling one at the money call. If the exchange rate rises by expiration, the trader will wind up being long three units of the underlying at a worse price than the rate they sold one unit at. If the exchange rate stays unchanged or declines by expiration, the trader will only have either gained or lost the initial net price of the transaction, depending on whether it was originally established for a net debit or credit.

Reversal: A type of option arbitrage position in which the trader takes a short position in the underlying asset and simultaneously buys a call and sells a put, preferably for a credit or for an amount small enough that the interest on the position held until expiration will offset the initial cost of the position. Basically, the short put, short underlying is the actual short position, while the long call plus strike represents the artificial long underlying asset. The formula for a Reversal arbitrage is Call Price + Strike Price – Underlying Price + Put Price. An arbitrage exists if the interest proceeds from the position are greater than the cost. If the difference comes out to a credit, then an arbitrage exists in addition to the interest return on the position.

Rho: The change in the theoretical price of a forex option for a one percentage point move in the prevailing base or domestic currency interest rate. For example, if a currency option has a Rho of 0.50 percent and U.S. Dollars are its base currency, then a one percent increase in U.S. interest rates would make the value of that option increase by 0.50 percent. Rho is greater for options that are in the money relative to options that are out of the money.

Risk Event: A possible detrimental eventuality which could adversely affect a project, investment or trading position, Risk Events can be recurring, scaled, discrete or one time only events.

Risk Management: The process of identifying and taking action on the areas of vulnerability and strength in a portfolio, trading or other managed financial account. In options, foreign exchange and other trading, Risk Management often involves the assessment of risk parameters known as Delta, Gamma, Vega, Rho and Phi, as well as determining the overall expected return per trade and the monetary loss the trader is willing to forego if the trade sours. Having good Risk Management can make the difference between success and failure, especially when dealing in the forex and options markets.

Risk Reversal: An option position that involves spreading a call against a put of a similar degree of moneyness, or Delta, in the same amounts and for the same expiration date. For example, in a bullish long Risk Reversal strategy, a trader would typically buy an out of the money call and sell an out of the money put with the same maturity. In contrast, a bearish short Risk Reversal would involve the opposite transactions of buying an out of the money put and selling an out of the money call with the same expiration date.

Spot Contract: A foreign exchange contract to exchange one currency for another at a certain price on the normal spot settlement date for a pair of currencies. Spot settlement is two business days from the transaction date for almost all currency pairs, other than USD/CAD, which is only one business day.

Spread: In the forex market, the Spread refers to the difference between the bid and offer for a currency pair. In options terminology, a spread is generally the consecutive buying and selling of two or more options positions for a specified price differential. Spreads can also be executed with a combination of the underlying security using both puts and calls. For example, in a horizontal or time spread, a trader would purchase an option in one month and simultaneously sell another option in a different month.

Straddle: An options strategy consisting of a long or short position in both a call and a put of the same strike price and expiration date. Straddles are generally purchased when a big move in the underlying asset is anticipated with no knowledge or preference for the direction of the underlying asset's price. A short Straddle position is generally established when the trader expects the underlying asset to remain at roughly the same level until expiration. The trader would then collect a large portion of the premium if the short straddle position is held until the expiration date.

Strangle: An option strategy consisting of a position in both a call and a put in the same expiration month, but with different strike prices. A strangle is often used instead of a straddle by a trader expecting a big move either way in the underlying asset. This is because the Strangle has a lower cost due to its separated strike prices, so one or both options will always be out of the money, thereby making the strangle more affordable than a straddle, which often has the most premium and the greatest rate of time decay. A short strangle follows the same reasoning as the short straddle, the trader expects the underlying asset to move between the strikes and the options to expire worthless.

Strike or Exercise Price: The value or exchange rate at which the underlying asset can be obtained for (in the case of a call) or sold for (in the case of a put) if the option is ultimately exercised by its holder.

Theta: An option risk management parameter that measures time decay in the value of an option over time, and which is typically expressed as the loss in an option's premium or price for a one day movement forward in time. Theta is negative for long options and positive for short options. For example, a three month USD call/JPY put currency option with a strike price of 100.00 and an implied volatility of 11 percent has a theta of -0.012% and a price of 2.22% of the USD amount when spot is at 100.00. This theta value means that the option's value will decline by -0.0121% of the USD amount by the following day to 2.208%, with all other parameters remaining equal.

Time Decay: The depreciation of an options' value over time. Time decay affects only the time value portion of an option's premium value, and it generally accelerates notably as the option approaches the expiration date. If the option remains out of the money approaching expiration, its time value is reduced with each passing day due to time decay since the possibility of the underlying asset reaching the strike price diminishes the closer in time the option is to its expiration date.

Time Value: The part of an option's premium that does not represent the intrinsic value of the option. For example, if the underlying asset's price is below the strike price of a call option, the entire premium consists of time value since the option has no intrinsic value. Similarly, if the strike price of a put option is below the underlying asset price, then the option's premium consists of only time value. For in the money options, their Time Value is equal to the market price of the option minus its intrinsic value.

Underlying: The asset upon which a derivative's value is based. The underlying asset for currency options is a currency pair, such as U.S. Dollar/Japanese Yen or USD/JPY.

Upside: The potential amount of money or percentage return on a market, asset, investment or trade. In options trading, the upside can be limited or given up at a certain price level by writing an option struck at that price level.

Vanilla Option: A derivative contract to buy or sell a certain amount of a particular underlying asset within a specified period of time at a particular price known as the strike price. Vanilla options can be American or European style calls or puts.

Vega: The change in the price of an option for a one percent move in the implied volatility of the underlying asset. For example, let's say that the USD/JPY currency pair is trading for spot value at 100.00 with an implied volatility of 11 percent for a three month period, so the three month 103.00 strike USD call/JPY put would have a theoretical value of 1.06% of the USD amount with a Vega of 0.18. If USD/JPY's three month volatility then increased to 12 percent, the fair value for that same 103.00 USD call would rise to 1.24% of the USD amount, all other factors remaining equal. The Vega of this option would therefore be 1.24% - 1.06% or 0.18%.

Volatility Curve: The level of implied volatility plotted versus time to expiration for a particular delta option as a two dimensional curve.

Volatility Skew: An implied volatility curve where options struck away from the at the money strike price have higher implied volatilities on one side of the at the money strike price than on the other side of the at the money strike price. The Volatility Skew is basically an asymmetrical Volatility Smile that typically reflects supply and demand factors. Such skews often arise in a highly directional underlying market, such as a bull market where out of the money put options struck below the prevailing market tend to trade at lower implied volatilities to the out of the money call options struck above the market.

Volatility Smile: An implied volatility curve where options struck away from the at the money strike price have higher implied volatilities than those struck at the money. The Volatility Smile tends to reflect greater client demand for cheaper out of the money options, as well as a tendency of professional option market makers to correct out of the money option prices upward for their relative theoretical cheapness even though they can end up having substantial value after a large market movement.

Volatility Surface: The level of implied volatility plotted versus time to expiration on the first horizontal axis and versus delta on the second horizontal axis as a three dimensional surface.

Volatility: Variation in the price of an asset or exchange rate over a period of time. Volatility is often expressed as a regular or normalized standard deviation, and the term Historical Volatility refers to the price variations actually observed in the past, while Implied Volatility refers to the volatility that the market expects in the future as implied by the prices of options. Implied volatility is an actively traded market determined observable that is one of the most important variables in the pricing of options.

Writer: The seller of an option contract. The option writer is obliged to deliver in the case of a call or accept in the case of a put the underlying asset from the holder of the option until the option expires.

Index

A

B

C

D

E

F

G

H

I

K

L

M

N

O

P

R

S

T

U

V

W

Z

Made in the USA
Las Vegas, NV
03 November 2026

57421649R00209